MY 30 YEARS OF SPEED

SIR MALCOLM CAMPBELL

Daredevil Books

My Thirty Years of Speed was originally published by Hutchinson & Co. London. This edition follows the text of the original editions with minor emendations and a revised selection of photographs.
Sir Malcolm Campbell's obituary reproduced courtesy of *Motor Sport* magazine.

Hardback ISBN   978-1-7391597-5-7
Paperback ISBN   978 -1-7391597-6-4

This edition published in 2023 by Daredevil Books

With thanks to Jane Hartwell for her tireless and perceptive proofreading and Jill Sawyer for the stylish typesetting of this new edition.

Daredevil Books is the home of classic accounts of derring-do from the last century. We create illustrated edition of often hard to find iconic books that explore the feats of the brave and daring on land, ice, sea and in the air. For more information about our current books and plans for the future, please visit us at www.daredevilbooks.co.uk.

www.daredevilbooks.co.uk
"Dangerously Good Reads"

11 March 1885–31 December 1948

The news that Sir Malcolm Campbell passed away in his sleep on December 31st at the age of 63 comes as a great shock, not only to the motoring world but to the entire sporting fraternity. His health and sight had been failing of recent years, but Sir Malcolm made valiant attempts to stave off the depression that had begun to assail him and, indeed, he hoped to attempt to raise his own water speed record with a jet-propelled boat when he was taken from us.

Malcolm Campbell was interested in speed from his schooldays and before the 1914–18 war was a regular competitor at Brooklands, at first with motor-cycles, then with his 'Blue Bird' Gregoire, Sunbeam, Charron and Darracq cars. In one of the latter he had a remarkable escape when both wheels on one side of the car collapsed as it was running up the Finishing straight at full speed. After the war, in which he served with the infantry and then in the R.F.C., Campbell resumed his Brooklands work with an astonishing variety of cars — Lorraine-Dietrich, Talbot, Peugeot, Austro-Daimler, Ballot, Itala, Sunbeam, Star, Ansaldo, La Pearl, Chrysler, Bugatti, Mercédès-Benz and Delage. Campbell moved to a house near Brooklands and took the premises at the track now occupied by the Brooklands Engineering Co., Ltd. His successes were many. In the first year of Mountain racing he set the lap record for the new course, with his 1½-litre straight-eight Grand Prix Delage, and in 1934, in the rebuilt 4-litre V12 Sunbeam, he set a Class C Mountain lap record of 76.31 mph, which was never beaten.

It was in the field of record-breaking Campbell really left his mark. He broke the absolute car speed record no fewer than nine times, commencing in 1924 with the V12 350-h.p. Sunbeam, at 146.16 mph, and making his last record in 1935, at 301.13 mph, in his huge Rolls-Royce-Campbell, being the first man to exceed 300 mph in a car. His run at Daytona at 276.82 mph in 1935 is the highest speed ever achieved over a sand course. Not long before this, in 1931, Campbell received a knighthood for his work for Britain in the land speed record sphere, his speed that year being 246.09 mph in the Napier-Campbell.

Sir Malcolm Campbell was just as successful, just as painstaking over the motor-boat speed record, which he raised to 124.86 mph in 1937, to 130.86 mph in 1938, and which he leaves at the magnificent figure of 141.7 mph, a speed attained in 1939.

Campbell even contrived to do dispatch work on a motorcycle during the last war and gave a very detailed lecture to the N.L.E.C.C. only last winter. He appeared to have many years before him, but possibly his easy withdrawal from a world he must have found increasingly oppressive, was a merciful stroke of fate. Looking back it is hard to recall all this purposeful little man did for his country – he searched for treasure, flew vast distances in light aeroplanes, and broke the land and water speed records with equal facility. He was responsible for the Brooklands road circuit and, less to his credit, the sale of Brooklands.

That the world is poorer by far for the loss of such individuals as Sir Malcolm Campbell is undeniable.

Reproduced courtesy of *Motor Sport* magazine.

Campbell pictured in the cockpit of 'Blue Bird' after one of his record-breaking runs on the Utah Salt Flats in 1935 – Chroma Collection: Alamy Stock Photo.

THE FIRST CHAPTER

§1

MY GREAT-GRANDFATHER WALKED SIX HUNDRED miles to join the Duke of Wellington's army and fight in the battle of Waterloo. He came down to London from Tain, by the Dornoch Firth, and the tale of his great walk always impressed me as a boy. I remembered him when I found myself near the old battlefield, in 1915, almost exactly a century later as part of a force that was fighting with France against Germany; this was exactly opposite from that which my great-grandfather had done.

He was descended from the Campbells who bore arms for Bonnie Prince Charlie at Culloden Moor. They escaped in the rout which followed 'Bloody' Cumberland's victory, all their property was confiscated and a reward was offered for their capture, but they retained their liberty and finally settled down in Tain.

I have a sword which was used at Culloden. It was fashioned by Andrea Ferrara, the famous sword-maker of Belluno, Italy, and its steel is so finely tempered that it is possible to bend the tip of the blade almost round to the haft. The guard, however, is so small that it is hardly large enough when the fist is closed about the hilt, which seems to suggest that these Campbells were not big men. Neither am I, for that matter, but I believe that I have inherited something of their good health, and something of the quickness which helped them to avoid their enemies. Every man's traits and tendencies are moulded for him by his ancestors, and that is why I am trying to indicate something of my background and of the Scottish stock from which my family has come.

My great-grandfather was a direct descendant of those hardy old Campbells who now lie in the little churchyard at Tain. He was probably a good soldier, and he was certainly a fine business man. After the victory of Waterloo he founded a firm of diamond merchants, with offices in Cheapside. He became comparatively wealthy, and first his son, then my own father, continued the business, and it was on March 11th, 1885, that I was born in Chislehurst, Kent.

Whatever debt I may owe to my ancestors, my debt to my father is still greater. His outlook was Victorian, and his views concerning the upbringing of a son were very definite. My early days were subject to rigorous discipline, he was exceedingly strict, and there was not a little corporal punishment at various times. Yet I grew up with a very deep regard for him, because he always did what he believed to be best for myself, following his own unswerving views.

§2

I was brought up with horses at Chislehurst, and could ride when I was three years of age. As I grew older, I often worked with a curry comb and dandy brush, helping the grooms. I liked horses, but railways and engines had a much greater attraction for me. That is not exceptional, where small boys are concerned, although my interest was not entirely superficial; I think it lay in the fascination of watching men control powerful engines, rather than in the spectacle which trains provided.

I can now appreciate that this interest has developed and, looking back, I can discover many small things which foreshadowed the future. When I was eleven or twelve years old I read *King Solomon's Mines*, and the story fired my imagination to an extraordinary degree. I read all Rider Haggard's other stories, but it was this particular book which left me with a real longing for adventure.

That wish has always been with me, and my experience is that most men retain their boyhood desire to travel in strange places, particularly if there is a promise of hidden treasure at the end of the journey. This is directly responsible for the expeditions and enterprises which I attempted in later years.

I was at a preparatory school when I read Rider Haggard's books, and from this I was sent to Uppingham School, Rutland. In those days, Uppingham was very different. It was a rough public school, where a boy had to learn to hold his own.

On arriving, in company with other new boys, I was told that we had to learn the names of all the masters, of the football fifteen, the shooting team, and the nicknames of all the school servants. A 'fags exam' would follow at the end of our first week, and anyone who was 'ploughed' would have cause to regret it. We found it very difficult to discover the necessary names, because those boys already at the school would disclose no information; they had been through the initiation, and newcomers had to do the same.

I failed badly and received two dozen strokes from the cane of a prefect – or 'preposter', as they are known at Uppingham. The examination was repeated seven days later, when I failed again and learned how much the flat back of a hairbrush can sting. These weekly ordeals continued for more than halfway through my first term, by which time the series of vigorous hidings had made me so hardened that I took them as a matter of course. The old custom continues at the school but, now, a boy who fails merely receives a lecture from a 'preposter' and is told to try again.

All boys at Uppingham had either to play rugger or cover a run of at least two miles every weekday afternoon. I grew very keen on cross-country running and, eventually, thought nothing of eight or ten miles in an afternoon. I also became adept at the school pastime of riding rams, to which most Sunday afternoons were devoted.

Dressed in our best clothes, we were supposed to stroll decorously in the open air until tea-time; it was then that the rams in the fields outside the town suffered. We used to select a ram and run it down; at first it could keep well ahead, but when the animal tired it was possible to mount and ride triumphantly across the field. This rough work took its toll of Sunday garments, which were not improved by contact with the oily wool of the ram during the ride.

Discipline at Uppingham was necessarily severe, but it could not always control the high spirits of boys, who frequently attempted foolhardy pranks. One morning, after prayers, the school was informed that a boy had walked through the railway tunnel at Glaston, that he had been flogged for doing it, and that anyone else who attempted it would be expelled.

Glaston tunnel formed part of the old Kettering and Manton line, some four miles from the school, and was rather more than a mile and a half long. The threat of expulsion was like a challenge and, on the spot, I resolved to accept it.

After prayers, I talked it over with another boy who was of the same mind as myself, and we agreed to make an attempt to go through the tunnel that afternoon. We put on running kit and started across the fields, past Bisbrooke, making for the railway junction formed by lines to Uppingham, Manton, Stamford and Peterborough.

These crossings were near the tunnel, and shunting operations were under way when we arrived. We talked to one of the engine drivers, and managed to persuade him to take us up and down a siding on the footplate of his old engine, spending half an hour with him before we went on up the line.

The tunnel started from a cutting, and a curve in the middle made it impossible to see daylight at the far end. We walked into complete blackness, and stumbled on over the sleepers, travelling without mishap until we were near the centre, when we heard the roar of a train, its vibration transmitted by the rails. Unknown to us, an express was due and, since we could not tell over which lines it was travelling, we stopped and waited for it to appear.

It was fully five minutes before we actually saw it, when we dashed for the opposite track and pressed against the wall. The train shook the ground as it passed, and we were half-choked by the smoke which was left behind. We walked on when it had gone, finally emerging safely into daylight and returning to the school.

We had accomplished the forbidden feat, and we told no one of it, while possession of the secret gave us a good deal of private satisfaction. Possibly other boys also walked through the tunnel but, in that case, they kept it to themselves.

A few terms later, my schooldays ended. My father believed that a boy should see something of the world, and he took me to Egypt for four months. Almost immediately after my return, he sent me to Germany for the double purpose of learning the language and studying at an engineering works –not, however, with the object of making engineering my profession. The study was merely to keep me occupied.

§3

I went to Neu Brandenburg. This old-world town had about twelve thousand inhabitants, only two of whom could speak English. The works at which I was to study built agricultural machinery and steam engines, but I did not attend very often. For the first time I found myself completely free, no longer under direct parental control, while everything was as complete a change as possible after the discipline and comparatively hard living at Uppingham.

I stayed in a little country hotel some five miles outside the town. Woods came right down from the hills to the back of the building, and at the front was Lake Tollense – ten miles long, five miles wide, and fifty-five feet deep in the middle – I remember the dimensions well. I spent a great deal of time boating and fishing with Freido Geertz, a boy who lived near the hotel and whom I called 'Fritz'. We became great friends, and were soon inseparable.

I needed a friend just then, because it was at the time of the Boer War, and the sympathies of the Germans were all against the British. This tended to make matters a little difficult for myself, and I soon lost the Union Jack which I hoisted to the top of a small sailing boat that I had acquired. I knew that it had been torn down and, as the only Englishman in the town, I felt that I had to keep my end up. I hoisted a new flag and kept watch, catching the man when he was halfway up the mast after the second flag. In the struggle which followed he fell into the lake, but I was not so triumphant next time I found myself against the local pro-Boer feeling.

It occurred in a little beer garden to which Fritz and I went sometimes in the evening. Men at the next table, knowing that I was English, exchanged pointed and insulting remarks which reached a climax with one involving Queen Victoria. I suggested that the man who had made it should come outside and repeat the remark.

He did, and a fight began. I eventually walked straight into a punch to the jaw and another to the eye which ended the matter. Although I had the worst of the fight, there were no more insults of that sort.

I imagine that I must have been more than a little foolhardy in those days, although it was not this alone which made me take risks on Lake Tollense. The name means 'mad lake', given because of sudden and dangerous storms which frequently spring up. I liked to ride out a storm with my boat, enjoying the sense of control which it gave me. It was dangerous, but Fritz, like myself, had the same appreciation for anything which held a tang of adventure.

We built a hut in the woods, and defied all authority by poaching and shooting over the preserves around. We had a keg of gunpowder, and used this to make cartridges for our guns, employing the weapons in an unusual way one afternoon.

I was curious concerning the feelings of soldiers who found themselves under fire in the Boer War, while Fritz also wanted to know how they felt. We lay down in a field, some distance apart, and fired at one another. By the time we had satisfied ourselves, we both knew exactly what bullets sound like when they pass just a few inches above one's head.

It was our hut which brought about a series of incidents, any one of which might have ended fatally for myself. The hut caught fire one night, and we salvaged what we could. The place was then well alight, with the roof on the point of collapse, when I suddenly remembered the keg of gunpowder, which had been left on the table. I ran in through the burning doorway, saw the keg and picked it up, tucking it under my coat before I bolted out again, safely rejoining Fritz. The gunpowder had not been easy to acquire, and we did not want to lose it.

We watched the hut burn to the ground, and the fire robbed us of our retreat in the woods. We had both enjoyed the possession of a more or less secret rendezvous, and I suggested that we should now find a cave; this, since it was winter time, would be cosy, while there would be no risk of another fire. When our search for a suitable cave proved unsuccessful, we began to dig one where the hillside was so steep that it formed what was almost a cliff.

We worked hard, often until very late at night, devoting ourselves entirely to the excavation of this cave. As there was danger from footpads and poachers, I was always armed with a revolver, which often became very dirty while we were digging, so that I had to clean it on my return home. We had been working until past midnight on one occasion, and I was about to turn in, when I noticed that the weapon was smothered with earth. Although very tired, I felt obliged to clean it, removing the cartridges and setting to work. It did not take very long, and when the sand had been wiped off and the mechanism oiled I pointed the weapon towards myself, clicking the trigger and watching the chambers as they spun round.

Everything worked smoothly. I reloaded the revolver and set it on the table, then noticed that I had neither cleaned nor oiled the trigger. I did this, then lifted the gun as I had done before and, forgetting that it was loaded, pressed the trigger.

I was deafened by the resultant explosion. The bullet actually grazed my hair, while I dropped the gun and sat motionless, recovering from the shock. I remained there for what seemed a long time, sitting quite still and thinking about the narrowness of my escape, when I became aware that something was burning. The shot had set alight the handkerchief in my breast pocket, and the cloth of my coat was smouldering. I had extinguished it by the time that people in the little hotel knocked on the door, insisting upon explanations. I have since thought that, if the shot had should have been a couple of inches out of its direction, been the subject of what must have appeared a perfect case of suicide.

By this time, Fritz and I had hollowed out a good-sized room. We were anxious to complete it, because the country was in the grip of winter and the cave promised to worked there be very snug. It was because of this that alone one night, Fritz being unable to accompany me, but promising to come up later on. I dug until two o'clock in the morning, by which time I was tired out; Fritz had not come, and I decided to go back to the hotel.

I turned in, and at half-past six in the morning the door of my room was burst open by Fritz. He was pale and startled, and I could see that something was wrong. He appeared most relieved to find me there, and he soon explained why. He had been into the town the night before and had only just returned, making his way straight to the cave, expecting to find me there. He had been horrified to discover that part of the hillside had collapsed, undermined by our excavation. The cave had been crushed under hundreds of tons of earth and trees.

A thaw had set in during the early hours of the morning, and this had loosened the frost-bound earth above where we had been digging. It was a very fortunate escape for myself, and it is extraordinary that, on the same morning, I received a letter from my mother. I had told her what Fritz and I were doing, and in her letter she implored me to give up the whole plan. She actually asked if I realized what was likely to happen when a thaw came.

The latter part of my stay in Germany was marked by letters from my father, asking if I had decided upon my future and if I was ready to come home. I was very reluctant to return, and managed to stave this off on one pretext or another. Before he finally ordered me home, I had my initial experience of racing.

I had brought out a cycle fitted with a free wheel. This was the first ever seen in that part of Germany, and it was regarded as so unusual by the inhabitants of Neu Branden that they used to stand and stare when I coasted down hills. It was natural that I should want to show the machine off, and I was always ready to race anything that I met on the road. This culminated in my entering against professionals on a bicycle track in the town. I borrowed a racing machine, and secured third place. That was the first race I ever rode on wheels.

My father's letters became more insistent and, finally, I said *auf wiedersehen* to Fritz. Our ways parted from that day; he went to America. It was thirty years before I heard his voice again.

§4

On my arrival home, I was unable to tell my father that I had come to any definite decision concerning my future. I could not express any particular leaning towards agricultural machinery or steam engines, although the new 'horseless' carriages held some interest for me. My father, however, did not think very much of motor cars, and sent me to Caen, with instructions to learn French and come home, after six months or so, with my mind made up.

I had to lodge with a French Protestant clergyman and his family. The house had a high wall around the garden, and the huge iron gate which guarded the grounds from the outer world was locked punctually at ten o'clock every night. My companion was destined for the Indian Civil Service, and we contrived to make the best of things, using bicycles which we had brought out, and occasionally doing some shooting. But I found it very different from Germany.

I have always like guns, admiring the precision of their mechanism, and this put me in a difficult situation towards the end of my stay. I was never allowed very much pocket money, and when my father sent my fare home for the Christmas holidays I saw a chance to acquire a gun that I had wanted for a long time. I sold my overcoat and some other things, abstracted additional money from the fare, and bought the gun. This left me with just enough to travel from Caen to Havre, book a steerage passage to Southampton and pay the third-class fare up to London.

I left Caen at six-thirty in the morning, after the ordinary French breakfast of coffee and rolls. On arrival at Havre, I booked my passage, buying a ticket which would carry me right through to London, and this left me with an English threepenny piece. The coin was useless in Havre, and I had to walk hungrily around the town for the rest of the day, waiting to go aboard the boat.

When the time came, I discovered that steerage passengers were expected to sleep in bunks which were set in rows; to reach his bunk, a man had to climb over other sleepers. I found, also, that my companions consisted mainly of Breton onion sellers, all of whom smelled strongly of garlic. In addition, the crossing was exceedingly rough, and most of the steerage passengers were ill; I judged it best to spend the night on deck, and remained there until we docked at Southampton.

In landing, I lost even the threepenny piece. It slipped out of my pocket as I produced my landing ticket, so that I was penniless when I caught the train which was due to reach Waterloo at midday. During the journey, I began to wonder how I should get home from the terminus, burdened with luggage; it was hardly possible to walk all the way to Chislehurst, and I dared not let my father know that I had put my fare money to other uses.

In addition, it was a day and a half since I had eaten anything. Fortunately for me, my mother came to meet the train, and her presence resolved all my difficulties.

It was not long after this that my father insisted upon a decision concerning my future activities. I repeated that I had nothing in mind, except an inclination towards the motor business. He would not even listen to my suggestions about this, and I discovered that he had already virtually settled the matter for me.

He told me that some of his friends, faced with problems similar to that which I presented, had put their sons into Lloyds. As they had done very well, it seemed possible that I might do the same. Accordingly, and as a preliminary step, I was apprenticed to Messrs Tyser and Company, a well-known firm. It was not long before I found myself working at an office in the city and living at home, with an allowance of fifteen shillings a week for pocket money and lunches.

§5

Up to this time I had experienced a well-disciplined boyhood, followed by a youthful period of freedom. I was healthy and very fit and knew how to take care of myself, but I still had a good deal to learn.

Sitting beside me at the long office desk in Tyser's was a clerk who developed an amazing ability for selecting horses that would win races. Morning after morning, he came into the office and named his selection; invariably, the evening papers reported that the horse had won. He picked out the winners by himself and his luck was almost incredible.

This continued for some time, but I had never made a bet on a horse and I did not avail myself of the opportunity until, early in one week, I found myself with almost nothing left of the fifteen shillings which I was allowed. I had spent recklessly the evening before, and it seemed an excellent idea to recoup myself by backing my companion's selection for the day. This was a horse named Ambush the Third, and I believe it was running in the Grand National. I made my bet, and his luck changed. Ambush the Third lost, but it was a natural thing to try and retrieve my money by betting the next day. After that, just as regularly as my companion had once named winners, he now selected horses which were never even placed. I lost what money I had in the bank, which represented sums received as gifts on birthdays and at Christmas; in the desperate hope of recovering it, I began to sell such things of value as I possessed, finally parting with a gold watch which my father had given me. All the money went into the hands of a bookmaker's tout in Leadenhall Market; none of it ever came back, while I grew more and more afraid that my father would discover not only that I had sold the watch, but the reason why it had gone.

In time, I reached the stage when I had nothing on which I could raise more money, and it was then that my companion gave me a tip which he assured me was a certainty. The horse was named Robert le Diable, an outsider about which odds of thirty to one were offered. If I could back it, and if it won, the money would straighten out my affairs.

I decided to plunge, and managed to scrape up a stake which was sufficiently large to bring me forty pounds, if the horse won. Robert le Diable did win, but the bookmaker never paid out.

I did not bet again. Gradually, I managed to put myself right financially, and since the day that bookmaker welshed, I have never seriously placed money on a horse. I have never been lucky in gambling.

I remained with Tysers until I had learned enough to persuade my father to enter me in partnership with an underwriter at Lloyds. It was during the closing months of the Russo-Japanese war, when fabulous sums had been made from insurance premiums on ships running the Japanese blockade to Vladivostok. The Japanese navy was engaged in the siege of Port Arthur, and I went to Lloyds just after the siege was raised, when the port was captured from Russia.

Some underwriters overlooked the fact that the end of the siege would release Japanese naval vessels, which could then give attention to ships bound for Vladivostok. As a result, large sums of money were lost where, a little time before, fortunes had been made. Business became bad at Lloyds, and continued depressed for some time afterwards.

Matters were not going well for my partner and myself, when a motor rally at Dieppe brought a complete change in my business affairs, and was the direct cause of my starting an entirely new type of business which, in the course of time brought me a great deal of money. A writer sent a report of the Dieppe meeting to an English newspaper and, in order to create the accepted atmosphere of a Continental resort, he drew on his imagination. He invented a fictitious character, portraying an Englishman on holiday in Dieppe and whose activities were suggested as more than a little disreputable.

Unfortunately for the writer, a man of this name actually existed, and he brought an action against the paper. It was admitted that neither the writer nor the editor knew the gentleman, but he proved that many of his friends had read the article and thought its defamatory remarks referred to himself. Judgment was delivered against the newspaper for £1,750 damages, and although an appeal was carried to the House of Lords, the original judgment was upheld. The case created a good deal of attention at the time, because it meant that any newspaper might suddenly find itself sued for damages under similar circumstances.

The initial action in the case had just been concluded when I paid a visit to an uncle who manufactured printing inks. He asked how I found business at Lloyds, and I was obliged to tell him that I was not doing very well.

He suggested that I should try to institute some novel kind of insurance, and mentioned this libel case.

It had astonished the newspaper world, and people were bring-ing actions on all sorts of pretexts. There was a labourer who had been injured in blasting operations at a granite quarry. A newspa-per published an account of this and the labourer sued them on the grounds that their report suggested that he was an inefficient workman. He lost his action, but my uncle pointed out that every newspaper ought to be insured against this kind of claim. No one had ever instituted a libel insurance policy and there was no reason why I should not be the first to do so; if it could be done, there should be scope for new business.

The possibilities were easy to appreciate, but I did not know whether the Lloyds underwriters could be persuaded to issue such a policy. However, my uncle offered me all the introduc-tions to newspaper proprietors that I could possibly want, and I began work at once. My greatest difficulty was to formulate the necessary insurance policy, and it was quite six months before I achieved this. I then spent a great deal of time climbing stairs in Fleet Street, urging newspapers to take up my new insur-ance. I secured the interest of the firm, which was then known as Odhams, Southward and Company; they accepted the policy and, after that, success was only a question of time.

I was soon making an income which rendered me independent of my father, and I went to live at a private hydro in Sundridge Park. Here began my first real experience of motor vehicles. I had been drawn to them for a long time, and now I bought a sec-ond-hand Rex motorcycle which had been built in 1902. It cost me fifteen pounds and, in order to acquire it, I took out nearly all the money that I had in the bank.

§6

I was very interested in this old Rex, and was always eager to get back from the City and ride it. The hydro was a mile and a half from the railway station, and I used to run this distance every evening.

Often I would miss dinner altogether, and take the machine out immediately; hardly an evening passed without its breaking down, so that I was obliged to push the Rex home again. It brought me many adventures, one of which indicates the limited knowledge that I had of the machine. I was caught in a thunderstorm, and suddenly discovered wild flashes coming from the sparking plug. I switched off the engine and pushed the machine back to the hydro; it was quite a long time before I discovered that it would have been quite safe to ride the motorcycle home, because the flashes had been caused only by rain playing on the plug terminal.

Once I crashed the machine, breaking both front forks; I lashed them up with string and rode on, but my next smash with the Rex was a little more serious. I was riding through Bromley when the machine skidded badly, sliding across the pavement and hitting a low brick wall. I was catapulted over this, landing partly on my head in a flowerbed. I was almost knocked out, and came round to find that I was sitting in the flower bed with the owner of the nearby house confronting me. He had rushed straight from his dinner table, and a serviette hung down from under his collar. He was in a towering rage because of the damage that I had done to his flowers, but I forgot him when I was able to climb back over the wall and look at my machine. It was very badly knocked about, smothered with water from the acetylene lamp, and it was obvious that it would take some time, and cost much money, to repair.

This meant a great deal to me, because I used to deny myself everything in order to find money with which to maintain the Rex. I went without new clothes, and I never visited theatres; I cut out midday lunches at times, and rarely indulged in the ordinary luxuries which a young man normally enjoys. I gave up everything to this one interest, and that period of spartan living had its reflection in later years. Even when my business at Lloyds prospered, I would not spend anything on theatres or similar pleasures. I was ready to spend any amount that was necessary on cars, but things outside this seemed unessential.

I followed the Rex with a 3½ h.p. Quadrant motorcycle, which cost forty-five pounds when it was new, and I ran this through the London-Land's End trial in 1906, winning a gold medal. That medal was the first trophy which I had ever secured with a motor vehicle, and I was naturally proud of it. Friends regarded my success as an accident and, to prove that it was not a fluke, I rode a motorcycle in the 1907 trial and again in 1908, managing to secure a 'gold' each time.

Once I was away from the City, I thought about very little other than motorcycles, and I became eager to extend my knowledge to cars, while I was very anxious to drive one. There were not many about, and my chance to drive came in an unusual way. Staying at the hydro was an old gentleman named Fraser; his wife and daughter were with him, and all showed some interest in the Quadrant. I asked Mr Fraser why he did not buy a car and, to my surprise, he said that he would, if someone would teach him to drive. I immediately offered to give him the necessary instruction, in spite of the fact that I had never sat in a car when it was moving.

Mr Fraser placed himself entirely in my hands, offering to buy any second-hand model that I suggested, provided that it did not cost more than three hundred pounds. I saw in this an opportunity to learn to drive, and consulted a mechanic with whom I had become friendly, and who had helped me with the Rex and the Quadrant. I made a bargain with him to teach me to drive, before handing the car over to Mr Fraser.

Eventually he produced a 15–18 h.p. Germain, fitted with a Phoenix engine which had originally been provided with tube ignition. The purchase price was two hundred and fifty pounds. Mr Fraser inspected the car and approved it, after which the mechanic drove it over to the hydro. All this time, I hovered in the background, aching to try and drive the machine but not daring to let Mr Fraser discover how little I knew about it.

Presently, I suggested that I should take it out with the mechanic and get used to handling the car. Mr Fraser agreed and, in all, the mechanic gave me five minutes' tuition on the road. We then turned the car round, I drove back to the hydro and put the Germain away in a shed.

The machine had two change-speed levers, one for first and second gears, and the other for third and top speeds, while the side brake was so designed that it threw out the clutch. The controls were simple enough if one could remember them, and I made careful mental notes of everything which I saw the mechanic do. I had everything fairly clear in my mind when, that evening, Mr Fraser asked me to take him over to Sevenoaks the following day and, on the way, teach him to drive.

This quite natural request came as something of a shock, and I had a nightmare after I went to sleep. I dreamed that I took the car out and smashed down the fence which bordered the drive from the hydro to the road, and this had something to do with my early appearance the following morning. Before anyone was about, I slipped down to the shed and looked over the car, reviewing everything that I knew about it.

I decided that a little practice would be advisable and made everything ready, then swung the engine. It started up at once and I climbed in, shifted into bottom gear, raced up the engine and let in the clutch, but the car refused to move. I sat there for almost ten minutes, wondering what was wrong, repeating my efforts to make the machine go until, when I was growing nervous and desperate, I remembered the side brake. I had left it on, and this was holding the clutch out. I released it and the old Germain rolled steadily into the yard.

I drove round and round to get used to the machine, then put it away again, and I was full of confidence when Mr Fraser and his family came out to begin the journey. We started off, and a perfect run followed to Sevenoaks. The car behaved magnificently and, on the way, Mr Fraser had his first driving lesson. Later on, when Mr Fraser left, I drove the car all the way to Appleby, in Westmorland, again with a trouble-free run.

It was after he had gone that another guest at the hydro approached me concerning a car. His name was Wrigley, and he was a wealthy bachelor; he offered to buy and maintain a machine, if I would drive it for him. We found a 1906 Panhard, with a twin-cylinder 7–11 h.p. engine, and I drove the machine many hundreds of miles. I learned a good deal about motors from that car and, in the end, I bought it from him. I ran it for a little while, then sold it and bought another car. From that time onwards I was hardly ever without a machine.

My business in the City was virtually doubling itself each successive year, and I could now command more money than I had ever had before. Looking ahead, I thought that my future was outlined clearly enough, but I suddenly found myself plunged into an interest entirely different from motor cars.

I went to the old Egyptian Hall, in Piccadilly, and saw one of the early cinematograph films, showing Wilbur Wright's aeroplane in full flight. The picture impressed me strongly, and I came to the conclusion that flying was the thing of the future. Its definitely adventurous side made a great appeal to me and, although I knew nothing at all about aviation, I decided that I would build an aeroplane and get into the air.

It was this decision which brought me to what I regard as the greatest disappointment of my life and, directly as a result of this, I entered the world of motor-racing.

THE SECOND CHAPTER

§ 1

DURING THE PIONEER PERIOD OF flying, every aviator had to experiment for himself and, inspired byby that old film of Wilbur Wright, I began the wholehearted study of aviation. I secured what information I could from photographs of existing machines, then began building models and learning all that I could about the theory of flight. What I discovered only strengthened my feeling that aviation was the thing of the future.

At that time, Louis Bleriot and Hubert Latham were awaiting favourable weather for an attempt to fly the Channel. Latham tried first, but his Antoinette fell into the sea, bearing out the opinion of those who believed that the Channel would never be crossed. I felt certain that Bleriot would do it, because Latham had got nearly halfway across during very indifferent weather, and I arranged insurance at Lloyds against the 'risk'. On July 25th, 1909, he crossed the Channel and landed at Dover, and my insurance plan brought in seven hundred and fifty pounds, which I afterwards employed to meet the cost of experimental work when I began to construct a plane for myself.

Up to this time, I had never actually seen an aeroplane, but my opportunity came when Bleriot's machine was put on exhibition in an Oxford Street store. I spent an entire day there, making notes and studying the frail monoplane, then went away to absorb what I had discovered, and to build more models.

Shortly afterwards, I heard that an aviation meeting, the first of its kind, was to be held at Reims, and I decided to go there; it was due to open one Sunday, about a month after Bleriot had flown the Channel. I found a companion and we left Dover on the Saturday night in a French packet boat. The weather was foggy, and we narrowly escaped a collision in mid-Channel, while the boat ran aground a mile from Calais harbour. The captain made frantic efforts to get the vessel afloat again, but the tide was receding and, when dawn came, it appeared as though my hopes of being at the opening of the meeting were doomed. I was leaning over the rail, looking gloomily down at the water, when I heard a shout from below; a man had waded out from the shore, coming over the sandbank on which the ship was stranded. The shallowness of the water showed that the steamer could not possibly be refloated for many hours, and I was wondering whether I should wade ashore when I saw a number of small boats coming out. They were willing to take people off, and we chanced jumping down into one of them, accompanied by other passengers who were as anxious as ourselves to get ashore.

My companion and I arrived at Reims in time for the opening ceremony, both determined to obtain as close a view as possible of the machines. We discovered that an ex-President of the French Republic, Emile Loubet, was making a tour of inspection, and we slipped in amongst the dignitaries who were with him. No one questioned us, and we enjoyed a perfect view of everything that was to be seen, so that I returned to England with my knowledge of early aeronautical practice considerably enhanced.

At that time, various prizes were being offered as an incentive to pioneer airmen. In flying the Channel, Bleriot had won £1,000, and a similar sum was put up for a circular mile flight on an all-British machine. This prize formed an objective, and it was in an attempt to win it that I now began work.

I had a friend who was as enthusiastic as myself, and we engaged a carpenter, then rented a barn on the edge of a strawberry field near Orpington; I had moved from Sundridge Park and was living at Bromley. We began work, learning a good deal as we went along, and my interest was even greater than it had been when I had run my first motorcycles. I thought of nothing but planes and flying. The moment that I could leave the City, I hurried home, ate hastily and made at once for the barn, working there until two or three o'clock in the morning.

Gradually, the machine began to take shape, and I often remained all night, returning home sleepless, with just enough time to wash and catch a train for the City.

That continued for months on end and, looking back on those days, I wonder how I managed to stand the strain and why my health did not fail.

Our only visitors during those nights in the barn were occasional policemen who came to warm themselves by our brazier, and to comment on the slow construction of the plane. I encouraged their visits, because I knew that we should need their help when we actually began to fly. In those days, would-be aviators roused as much hostility and ridicule amongst the public as the first motorists had done ten years earlier, and friendly police would be useful to keep the crowd in hand.

The machine very soon absorbed the money I had made at Lloyds over Bleriot's flight, and I sold my car to secure further finance. Everything was very costly, although we worked as economically as possible, even making our own propellers. I have one of them still; it is made up from laminated wood, now much worn-looking and with its edges badly chipped, but it forms a souvenir which I should not care to lose.

We fitted the machine with a twin-cylinder J.A.P. engine from a motorcycle. The undercarriage had two bicycle wheels, and a third took the place of a tail skid. The wings were fitted with ailerons, and the plane actually demonstrated one or two other ideas which we worked out for ourselves and which eventually found a place in later aeronautical practice.

News of what we were doing soon spread in the locality. People used to gather near the barn on the chance of seeing something, long before we were ready to attempt our first flight. Their interest was derisive, and this attitude became intensified as time went on. I began to see that, when we did push the plane out, we should need the police to maintain order.

The strawberry field was dangerous as a potential flying ground. It sloped badly, the earth was full of furrows and a deep ditch lay right across the centre. When the machine was nearly complete we selected a stretch for the take-off and boarded over the ditch, filling in the furrows, and making the ground as smooth as possible. We decided upon a Sunday morning for our first effort, and I sent a message to the police to let them know our intentions, but the message went astray, because no constables appeared. We made everything ready, and only when we were pushing the plane clear of the barn did I discover that a big crowd had gathered. The people were gathered right across the field, blocking the line of the take-off. When we asked them to move, we found that a public footpath traversed the field, and they reminded us that they had as much right to be there as ourselves, and refused to go.

The crowd was very obstinate, and would not make way even after I had explained that it would be dangerous to remain in the path of the machine. The only thing to do was to start up the engine and hope that they would run when they saw the plane coming towards them.

§2

It was my intention to try and take the plane off the ground without preliminary tests of any sort, although I had never flown before. I knew that when one pulled the control stick back, the machine should ascend, and that when one pushed the stick forward, the nose dipped. I knew, also, that it was necessary to gather flying speed before trying to take the plane into the air, and that lateral control was maintained by ailerons. But that was about the sum total of my knowledge.

The whole venture was, I suppose, very foolhardy, yet other experimenters were in exactly the same situation. The only thing a man could do, if he wanted to fly, was to build a machine and learn how to control it when he was off the ground, if he had the luck to make the plane rise. In any case, my enthusiasm was such that I would have given everything I had – as so many others actually did – for one real flight in the machine which I had designed and helped to build.

After various delays, I climbed aboard, the engine was started and, when the right moment had come, I waved to friends holding the wings. The plane was released and it began to run forward across the field, heading for the crowd, wobbling from side to side as it gathered speed. I was very thrilled at actually being under way, while I struggled to keep the machine as straight as possible, and I judged that I was travelling fast enough to get off the ground when I found myself almost up to the staring crowd.

I pulled back the control stick at once. The plane lifted a few feet into the air, hesitated, then flopped back with a crash, pitching half on to its nose before it came to an even keel, with the propeller damaged and the engine dead. A wing was broken, a wheel was smashed from the undercarriage and my first effort to fly was a failure.

There was nothing for it but to get the machine back to the barn, rebuild it and try again, but the damaged plane was too difficult for us to move alone, since it had to be lifted and balanced on the remaining landing wheel. I asked some of the crowd to help, but they were laughing and jeering and did not respond. They simply did not understand the months of work which we had put into the machine, nor could they appreciate the hopes we had entertained only a few minutes before, otherwise the attitude of the spectators would have been very different.

The only way to shift the plane seemed to be to start up the engine again, support the broken side of the undercarriage, and hope that the propeller would assist in dragging the craft across the rough ground. We warned the crowd that the damaged propeller was liable to snap off, and might harm some of them, but they still refused either to assist or to go. In the end, we restarted the engine and, at once, the propeller came clean away with its shaft, whizzing high into the air and disappearing over a hedge.

The evident danger startled the crowd, and most of them retreated. A few men, however, now relented and came to help us so that, somehow, we managed to get the plane back to the barn. We then discovered that, during our absence, thieves had rifled the clothes we had left hanging on the walls.

That was a blow, following what had already occurred, because I needed all the money that I could get for material to reconstruct the machine. We recommenced work the same day, trying to forget our disappointment, and I was buoyed up by the fact that I had actually managed to make the craft rise from the ground. It would be an exaggeration to say that the plane had flown, but it had certainly gone into the air under its own impetus and power.

We tried again and, in time, we achieved one or two quite respectable hops, then came news that J. T. C. Moore Brabazon had won the prize for which we had built our machine. He had accomplished a circular mile flight in an all-British machine, using a Short plane and he was the first 'Englishman' to fly; actually, he was an Irishman.

This came as a check to our efforts in the strawberry field, but there were other prizes for which we could try. *The Daily Mail* offered £10,000 for a flight from London to Manchester, and the Baron de Forest put up £4,000 for the longest flight from England to the Continent. It seemed possible that we could make an effort to win one of these, since our plane would need only a larger engine and a more efficient propeller. Henry Farman had shown that long flights could be achieved because, during the

Reims meeting, he had covered a hundred and eighteen miles without alighting, remaining in the air for over three hours.

We bought a bigger engine, and our efforts continued during 1910, while I secured propellers from the Continent, paying twenty-five pounds each for them. Again and again we took the machine out, but it never really flew. During the longer hops, I could feel the plane remaining in the air for a few moments under its own flying power, but these were not true flights.

Paulhan flew from London to Manchester in April, 1910, but we worked on, because the Baron de Forest prize still remained. The summer passed and winter came again, then, on December 18th, 1910, T. O. M. Sopwith flew a Howard Wright biplane from Eastchurch in Kent to Thirlemont, on the Franco-Belgian frontier, a distance of a hundred and seventy-seven miles, winning the de Forest prize.

He accomplished that just at the time when we had come to the end of our resources. I had spent over eight hundred pounds, and had no more money available, but, although the prizes for which we had hoped to try had been won, still others were put up. Ten thousand pounds was now offered for a flight around Britain and this lured us on; it was not, however, the money which we wanted so much as the opportunity that it would provide for more adequate experiment and equipment.

Since we could not continue without additional funds, I tried to raise them, but was unsuccessful. We decided to sell the machine, hoping that it might bring enough to enable us to make a fresh start, and I did discover a man who offered to buy, but at the last moment the deal fell through.

While I was still endeavouring to find a purchaser, I was approached by Friswells, a well-known firm of motor-car dealers. They suggested putting the plane up for auction with cars which they had for sale. They argued that it would be the first time in history that an aeroplane had been auctioned, and that this was certain to attract a great deal of attention.

I agreed, and their forecast proved correct. The saleroom was crowded, largely by people who had never had such a close view of an aeroplane. The bidding started at fifty pounds and rose in the most gratifying way until it reached two hundred and seventy pounds, then came a pause, and I decided to help matters on.

'And ten!' I called.

The man who had been making the price deliberated, but topped my figure with another ten pounds.

'And ten!' I said once more.

This brought the price up to three hundred pounds, and it also brought another long pause.

The auctioneer tried to conjure a further bid. There was no response. The hammer fell and, to my dismay, I found that I had bought my own machine. I at once went over to the man against whom I had been bidding and offered to sell the plane to him, but his enthusiasm had cooled.

'You bought it,' he said, 'and you can keep it.' His actual words were a little stronger than that, and his manner was altogether unfriendly, while he seemed relieved to know that he had not finally committed himself to the purchase. I realized that I had acted foolishly, and consulted the auctioneer. He indicated that I owed him twenty-two pounds and ten shillings, by way of commission, and suggested putting the machine up for sale again the following week.

I judged it better, this time, to stay away from the auction, and I did not go near Friswells until after the sale. I learned then that the plane had found a purchaser, and that the price was exactly twenty-two pounds ten shillings. As this sum balanced the commission that I had incurred at the first auction, I was virtually giving the machine away. It was a very unhappy moment for me, but the plane was sold and, since I had no finance for further experiments, my attempts to fly had come to an end.

I was depressed for a long time afterwards and, appreciating that I needed something which would help me to forget my interest in aviation, I turned to cars and to motor racing. I can see, now, that it was those two bids in that auction room which changed the whole course of my life. If I had not made them, I should probably have gone on trying to fly. I might have been one of the pioneers of aviation or, what is more than likely, I might have crashed finally near the strawberry field at Orpington.

§3

The first race I ever ran at Brooklands was during a gala day in 1908, when I rode a motorcycle and finished a long way behind the machines which were placed. The first time I ever raced a car was also at the track, during the same season. The machine was a twin-cylinder Renault which had run in the Paris-Madrid race of 1903; I paid sixty-five pounds for this car and I finished nowhere.

That was the total of my experience when I turned to motor racing again. I bought a Darracq which had taken third place in the Tourist Trophy race of 1908, when it had been driven by A. E. George, of George & Jobling, a Newcastle firm. The car weighed just under a ton, and it was capable of over 80 mph on the road; George would have won the TT but for the fact that his carburettor caught fire on the last lap, halting him for six minutes. The winner finished only five minutes in front of him.

In the first Brooklands meeting at which I drove this car, I won one race and finished second in another. This was encouraging, and it helped to overcome the disappointment in which my efforts to fly had ended. At this time, early in 1911, I could afford to own and race cars, because my business at Lloyds was prospering, and I now began to take motor-racing seriously.

I followed the Darracq with a Peugeot, growing very enthusiastic about this machine. It was then the fashion at Brooklands to give names to cars. *Delilah*, *Queenie*, *Yellow Peril* and *Pobble* were running while, until comparatively recently, *Whistling Rufus* and *Vieux Charles III* could be seen at the track.

I regarded it as essential to find a good name for the Peugeot and decided upon that of a horse which was racing on the day that the car was to make its debut with myself at the wheel. The horse was distinguished by a long tail, and was known as 'The Flapper'. The name appealed because it used to amuse me to pull the pigtails of 'flapper cousins'.

The horse did not win; neither did my Peugeot. Nothing that I could do to that car enabled me to score a victory that season, and the same thing seemed to apply to the jockey of the horse. Toward the end of the year I abandoned the Peugeot for another Darracq, which had originally been built for competition in the Gaillon Hill Climb, outside Paris.

It was a powerful car, and I completely reconditioned it, doing most of the work myself. I named it 'Flapper II', and when I began to race the car I experienced every possible kind of trouble. On the only occasion when it came within reasonable distance of winning an event, a control to the carburettor broke and put me out of the running. It seemed as if the machine was singularly unlucky, because the man who eventually bought the car from me was involved in a fatal smash at a crossroad three months later.

I sold 'Flapper II' partly because I was convinced that I should never be able to do anything with it, but mainly because I knew that another and much faster Darracq was available. This was the car with which Victor Hemery had won the Vanderbilt Cup, in America, in 1909. The engine was really big, with cylinders over six inches in diameter, and the car was capable of about 100 mph, which was a frightening speed in those days.

After arranging the purchase price, I went to collect the machine, and found it standing in the middle of a junk pile at a works in Kennington, with only its bucket seats and the top of its huge bonnet visible. The Darracq had been standing there for nearly a year, and some time was occupied in clearing away old wheels and tyres, lumber and bits of rusted metal before the car could be pushed out.

In spite of the battered appearance of the machine, I was

impressed by it and so, apparently, were the mechanics. When the tyres were pumped up, the engine primed and everything made ready for a start, I discovered that none of the men would do so much as touch the crank handle. All were afraid of the car, and the most I could persuade them to do was to push-start the machine after I had climbed into the driving seat.

The engine fired almost immediately, and presently I left in a cloud of smoke, beginning the long drive from Kennington to Bromley. The Darracq was not built for traffic work, and piloting that powerful old machine over the suburban roads of pre-war London had its exciting moments.

The car needed attention before it could be raced again, and I arranged with a local garage to build a body which followed my own ideas about streamlining. While this was being constructed, I overhauled the engine, and entered the machine for three events at the next Brooklands meeting.

Late on the evening before the car was due to race, and when I was actually preparing to paint 'Flapper III' on the bonnet, a friend pointed out that this name had brought me only bad luck, and that I ought to call the car something else. He then mentioned the title of Maeterlinck's play – *The Blue Bird* – which was having a wonderful run in London.

Everyone liked the play, the name sounded lucky, and I adopted the suggestion. I decided to christen the machine thoroughly and knocked up an oil chandler, from whom I bought brushes and tins of blue paint, working until long past midnight, colouring the bodywork and the wheels to match the name of the machine.

The paint had not dried when I drove the car to Brooklands the following day, and I was smothered with blue patches when I went to the starting line for the first race. The car won, and it came home first in another race before the meeting was over. The new name appeared to have changed my racing luck, and 'Blue Bird I' responded to all the experimental work which I did on it later, travelling faster each time I raced the car.

It was not an easy machine to handle, because shock absorbers were unknown in those days, while the tyres were built up on a basis of canvas, not cord as we have now. The car had wooden-spoked artillery wheels, and these had shrunk in their rims; rather than go to the expense of new wheels, I used to hose the spokes before each race. The water made them swell, so that they fitted tightly while the machine was actually running.

§4

I had tuned 'Blue Bird' to touch nearly 100 mph when the car involved me in my first motor-racing crash and gave me one of the narrowest escapes of my life. It occurred during the Brooklands August Bank Holiday meeting of 1912, in a race which I was particularly keen to win. In those days, races used to end down the 'finishing straight', which forks from the outer circuit at Brooklands, and the finishing line was indicated by a string of flags stretched high above the concrete.

The car was heavily handicapped but it soon gained on those ahead and was lying fourth when I came off the Byfleet banking at the end of the last lap. I could see that I was fast overtaking the three machines in front, and that I had every chance of winning. I approached the fork with my car moving flat out, going faster than it had ever run before, and it was doing fully 100 mph when the off-side front tyre burst.

Instantly, the car lurched, as if to continue around the main circuit. It went so far outwards that spectators, not knowing that a tyre had gone, imagined I had miscounted the number of laps and intended covering another. I wrenched on the steering wheel to bring the machine back to its course, but I made no attempt to slow. A tyre-burst can put a driver into serious difficulties if he tries to continue at speed, but the finish was now only the quarter of a mile away and, anxious to win, I kept the throttle wide open.

Although I corrected the skid safely, the car was carried directly towards the point where the track actually forked, and I had almost completely straightened out when the wheel with the burst tyre hit a low concrete kerb, placed where the finishing straight began and continuing down its length. One inch more, and I should have missed it altogether, but as it was, the impact completely shattered the wheel.

The tyre flew off, skimming above the head of a track attendant who was standing by the railings inside the kerb. The rim, bursting from the wheel, struck the iron rails a couple of feet from him, bending and twisting the metal, while fragments of wooden spokes were hurled into the air with tremendous force.

I knew that the rear wheel must also hit the kerb, since it was following the track of the front one, and it could not fail to smash in a similar fashion. This happened less than one-tenth of a second later, but it seemed an age before I felt the jolt. The wheel broke and the car tilted to an ugly angle, having now lost both wheels on one side.

With broken spokes flying, with dust rising behind, the car charged on along the edge of the track. My mechanic was pitched against me, so that I supported him as I clung to the wheel, our combined weight increasing the tendency of the car to turn over. I could actually see down into a ditch which lay behind the railings and I knew that, if the car did roll over, I should inevitably be impaled on the iron spikes.

Use of the brakes would have slung the machine round, when it must have turned upside down. All I could do was to kick out the clutch and hang on, holding the car to the course which it had set itself. As the first wheel broke, I had locked the steering over and it remained like this, the very speed of the machine keeping it straight, although I could feel the jarring of the bare front wheel hub as it ground against the concrete.

With the machine down on one side, skating along the edge of the track, it approached the crowd, which was packed behind the railings, opposite the finishing line. The people were standing stock-still, appearing to be spellbound. No one made any effort to run, and it was then that I began to worry.

I knew that the steering must eventually give under the enormous strain thrown upon it. Something must break, and the chances were that the car would then skid through the railings into the crowd. I was level with the spectators when the thing that I most feared actually happened. The steering broke, but by a miracle the car swung momentarily farther out on the track before, under now lessened impetus, it plunged straight at the crowd, the sound front wheel wobbling dangerously and the whole machine completely out of control.

Even then the spectators did not move, and only a few started back when the car, rapidly slowing, hit the kerb at an angle. The obstruction deflected the machine and it skated along for a little distance, finally stopping just clear of the railings.

No one was hurt and, from a photograph which I saw afterwards, only one man of all the hundreds who were there revealed any reaction; the picture was taken when the car was almost on the finishing line, and it shows him with both arms raised in the air. No one else had moved.

I was quite untouched, and the car took fourth place in the race. I realized that I was very lucky to have won clear and, largely because of this, I used 'Blue Bird' as a name for other machines which I owned and drove later. The car was repaired and I raced it again a month later, but the Darracq never showed its former speed, no matter how much I worked on it.

I ran several cars during the next season, 1913, and bought the Sunbeam with which Lee Guinness secured the Coupe de 'l'Auto' at Boulogne. I won on this car at Brooklands during the Whitsun meeting of 1914, and at the time I possessed a stable of five racing machines: the Sunbeam, a Schneider, Darracq, Peugeot and a Gregoire. My activities were almost entirely divided between business in the city and driving at Brooklands, and I was as much involved in motor racing as I had been in aviation not very long before. Life was very pleasant, when the Great War came.

I drove at Brooklands in the last race of the last meeting in 1914, taking the Gregoire into third place. When I dismounted from the machine I had no idea that I should not drive at Brooklands again for more than five years. Next day, war was declared and, like so many others, I rushed into khaki, locking my racing cars away.

§5

At the outbreak of war, I volunteered as a dispatch rider and, working in conjunction with the King's Messenger service, went to France in September, 1914. Before leaving England, I applied for a commission, but heard nothing more of this until I returned on leave in the following February. I then found that I had been gazetted as a second lieutenant in the Royal West Kent Regiment, and had actually been commissioned for nearly five months.

I sold all my cars during this leave, and parted with the splendid Coupe de 'l'Auto' Sunbeam for two hundred and fifty pounds. Immediately after the war, and over three years later, that machine changed hands for two thousand pounds, at a time when post-war prosperity had enormously enhanced the value of any kind of motor car.

On joining my regiment, I was able to make use of my knowledge of horses and took over the transport section, the service of which is to carry a battalion's heavier baggage on the march, and to deliver rations and ammunition to front line dumps when the unit is in action. Any infantry transport section is a hybrid formation, because the men are drawn from the ranks of the regiment and receive no particular training in horsemanship. The section is not a real mounted unit, neither does it belong to the line, with the result that most war-time battalions regarded it as a necessary evil, and one to be pushed well into the background. The discipline amongst the men usually became very ragged, although experience made all such sections efficient enough to do very valuable work when they entered battle areas, where they invariably operated under exceedingly dangerous conditions.

When I took over, I found my small unit slovenly and under strength, while the horses might have been in better shape. I began to build the section up according to accepted cavalry practice; I felt that a transport section ought to be a true mounted unit, properly trained to real wagon and riding drill. I abolished the infantry equipment which the men were supposed to wear, giving them bandoliers instead of ammunition pouches. I rigged them out like true cavalrymen, taught them riding drill and organized sports to keep them fit. I made them appreciate a well-groomed horse, and the fine appearance of clean harness.

We brought our horses to fully fifty per cent over strength, everyone kept in the finest possible fettle, and even acquired a trumpeter, using trumpet calls for the section instead of a bugle. In all this I was backed up by my commanding officer, who, although I was only a second lieutenant, gave me all the powers of a company commander. It was very unorthodox, but it gave us the smartest transport section in the divisions and brought a compliment from Lord Kitchener when he inspected us.

I remained with the Royal West Kents for almost a year, then opportunity came for a transfer to what was known as the Royal Flying Corps and, when I secured this, I was able to satisfy my earlier ambition and learn to fly. At that time, war pilots received a very sketchy training, while the machines we flew would be regarded as very dangerous now, but they were the best that could be produced and we seemed to do as well as any other nation.

Early in 1916, I was passed out at Gosport and, almost at once, became what was known as a 'ferry' pilot. My job was to take new planes across to France, and fly back others which were marked as 'Unfit for Further Flying Service'. These machines had either been condemned or needed comprehensive overhauls; often they had been badly knocked about by shrapnel and machine-gun bullets, and were in such indifferent condition that it was sometimes difficult to keep them in the air.

I met with the experiences which might be expected on such service, no different from those of dozens of other men. The work itself was interesting, particularly since it was impossible to guess what kind of machine one would have to bring back from St Omer, the landing ground to which we usually delivered new planes.

One particular machine I shall never forget, because it was the worst wreck that I ever attempted to fly. The fuselage was riddled with bullet holes, the spars had been chipped by shell splinters and the wings were ragged from split fabric. The whole condition was so bad that I determined not to attempt to fly the plane if the engine offered the least excuse; when the power unit was started up, however, it appeared to be in good tune, and I took off.

Flying weather was bad, and the air was full of bumps. The plane was in no shape to withstand rough usage, and I did not feel comfortable when I found myself over the Channel. I flew as carefully as I was able, but with every unavoidable lurch of the machine I expected something to break. I was halfway to the English coast when the plane dropped into an air pocket, and brought up with a deadening shock, which was followed by a cracking report that sounded clearly above the noise of the engine.

I could not bring myself to look towards the wing from which the sound had come; I imagined that one of the damaged spars had broken, and that I should see the wing crumpling up and breaking away, which would have meant a helpless plunge to the sea below. For seconds I sat rigidly there, waiting for something to happen, simply not daring to turn my head. The plane flew steadily on and when, at last, I found sufficient courage to give a sidelong glance I saw, to my amazement, that the wing was still intact. I tested the controls very carefully, first to one side and then to the other, but the machine responded satisfactorily.

I flew quietly on, wondering what had broken and expecting to find myself in trouble at any moment, but nothing happened and I sighted Lympne, the aerodrome from which we usually began cross-Channel trips. I made a careful landing, and the machine settled down safely enough. I reported what had occurred but, to this very day, I have never learned what it was that scared me so badly, because I had at once to take another plane across to St Omer. I imagine that a bracing wire must have snapped, which would be enough to have caused the explosive sound I had heard.

On ferry service we used to try and take machines over in everything short of absolutely impossible flying weather. It was very rarely that we were held up completely, although there was one spell when it appeared hopeless to try and cross the Channel. At the end of three days of thoroughly bad weather, between forty and fifty pilots and machines were held up at Lympne, when an urgent message arrived from the battle area, instructing the aerodrome commandant to ask volunteers to bring new planes over, but under no circumstances was anyone to be given orders to fly.

I happened to be with a group of four other pilots when the SOS came through. We volunteered to try and get across, and only when I had taken off did I appreciate just how bad was the weather. It was the most difficult trip I had ever known, but I reached Calais safely to find that only one of the others had got through, the rest having been forced to turn back. This was no credit to myself, because I was not a particularly good pilot, but I was always obstinate in trying to finish any job that I started. On this occasion I was rewarded by being detailed, on arrival at Calais, to fly another plane back to Lympne. I did it, and probably because no one else was foolish enough to try, I was the only man to cross the Channel both ways during that spell of bad weather.

The work always had some elements of danger, but frequently humour was mingled with it. Near the end of 1916, I had dropped a plane at St Omer one evening and was preparing to bring an old FE.2B back, when a man with an observer's wing on his tunic asked if I would give him a lift across the Channel. He was starting on leave, and if I flew him across he would gain what amounted to an extra day, because he could be in London soon after dark; the usual leave boat did not start from Calais until the following morning. He introduced himself as having passed out with me at Gosport, and I easily secured permission to take him.

'Look here, you'll promise not to stunt, won't you?' he asked.

That surprised me because, if he were an observer, he should have been used to stunting.

'I'm with the kite balloon section,' he explained, and added that he had never been in an aeroplane before.

He was nervous about flying, although his job was one for which I should not have cared very much; he had to observe the enemy back-areas from a captive balloon set up just behind our own firing line, forming a target for shrapnel and for any German airman who dropped out of the clouds.

I looked the plane over, then climbed in and warmed up the engine. When I opened the throttle, I found that the engine showed only seven hundred and fifty revolutions instead of the thousand necessary before it was safe to take off. The mechanics changed the plugs, and I made another test, with the same result. The carburettor was cleaned out and everything was checked over, but still the engine was unsatisfactory.

The only thing left was to change the magneto, which would take some time. It was then growing dark, and it seemed wise to postpone departure until next day. The observer agreed to this, and promised to be back at the aerodrome by six-thirty the following morning. He made his way into St Omer, and I spent the night at the aerodrome, turning out just at dawn to find two sleepy mechanics rolling the machine from its hangar. Work on the magneto had not been completed and this had to be done before I could leave; it was past eight o'clock when the engine was ready for another test. The observer had turned up, and he listened doubtfully when I opened the throttle, to find that the engine still showed only seven hundred and fifty revolutions.

I was tired of waiting about and decided to start, hoping that the engine would last out the flight. The observer, already very doubtful about making his first flight and appreciating that the engine was in a bad condition, suggested that, after all, he would prefer to go on the leave boat. I pointed out that, if he did, he would lose a complete day, since the boat had already gone and, finally, he made up his mind to come with me. We took off and, once in the air, the engine picked up, running well until we were almost directly above Calais, then, for no apparent reason, it stopped. I headed towards the aerodrome, dropping in a steep spiral and landing comfortably, to discover my companion very white and looking a little shaken.

'I thought you promised not to stunt!' he exclaimed. I had not been stunting, and explained why I had come down. Mechanics tried the engine, and almost at the first swing of the propeller it started again, still showing only low revolutions, but enough to take the plane into the air. My only object, by this time, was to cross the Channel and see the last of the machine, and I left immediately, not troubling to gain height, but sending the plane away at a low climbing angle.

It was a beautiful morning, and the Channel was busy with shipping; I had, during bad weather, crossed when not a vessel was in sight. The engine began to run more smoothly as we gained height, and levelled out at four thousand feet. Nothing happened until we were over mid-Channel, when, without warning, the motor stopped as abruptly as it had done before.

It was impossible to glide back to Calais, nor could I reach the opposite shore; since I had to come down, the obvious thing was to drop the plane as near to a ship as possible. There was no danger, because we should be picked up at once, and should escape with no more than a wetting.

A forced landing of this sort meant a week's leave, according to normal usage in the service. I thought of this as I selected a big ship, half-hoping that it would be bound for India because, if it were, I should be able to enjoy an enforced sea voyage before returning to duty; I had been working as a ferry pilot for more than a year, and so far had had no leave at all.

The plane glided towards the ship, while I tried to reassure my companion, who was holding grimly to the side of the machine, staring downwards and looking badly scared. I saw people on deck looking up at us while I shaped for a landing ahead of the vessel. We had come down to three hundred feet when, just as suddenly as it had stopped, the engine fired again, and my ideas about a trip to India vanished. I flattened out, flew over the vessel and on to Lympne without a fault.

I landed, and the machine had barely stopped when my companion jumped out and went running away towards the aerodrome offices. He vanished amongst the buildings without a word; I never set eyes on him or heard of him again. Undoubtedly, he was convinced that everything had been deliberately designed, and that I had broken my promise not to stunt.

As with this incident, the majority of unusual happenings occurred in bringing planes back from the battle areas, and the most outstanding of these, so far as I was concerned, occurred near the end of my time as a ferry pilot. I had flown two new machines over to St Omer and had brought two old ones back, when I was asked to take another plane across. As I neared the French coast, I noticed a heavy bank of mist coming down from the direction of Dunkirk, obscuring the shoreline. I forgot about this while I flew on, landing safely at St Omer fairly late in the evening. When I reported, I was asked to ferry back yet another craft marked unfit for further flying service, making the sixth plane I had flown that day. It seemed unlikely that I should reach Lympne before darkness fell, but I was told that flares would be put out for me.

This plane had been badly knocked about, but the engine seemed in fair condition when I tested it, so I waved the chocks away and headed for Calais and the Channel. When I reached the French coast, I noticed that the mist which I had seen earlier had rolled so far south that it completely obscured the shore. My aeronoid showed five thousand feet when I sighted Calais, but I was unable to tell when I left the land behind and flew out over the sea, because the mist and the evening shadows hid everything below. I travelled for some distance before the mist fell away and I sighted water, and it was when I had left Calais five or six miles behind that the engine stopped dead.

I turned the plane round at once, because I could never have covered the remaining distance across the Channel. I knew that I could reckon upon being able to glide about a mile for every thousand feet of height which the machine held, and this meant that I could glide for some five miles; with luck, I might reach the French coast.

The moment that I brought the machine about, however, I remembered the mist. It hid the shore, and covered all distinguishing features beyond. I saw it as a long, grey wall which made it impossible for me to do anything more than head the plane in the direction of Calais aerodrome, or where I thought the aerodrome to be; there was nothing to guide me towards it.

The machine lost height steadily, and at just under a thousand feet I ran into the mist. I realized now that I should probably drop into the water and, if that happened, I was almost certain to lose my bearings in the smash, with every chance of swimming in the wrong direction when I tried to save myself, assuming that I was able to swim at all after hitting the sea. If the plane dropped on the shore, I was certain to make a crash landing, when the chances of escape were just as remote.

When the aeronoid showed five hundred feet, I gave up all hope, believing that I had only a minute more to live. The height dropped to four hundred, three hundred, two hundred feet, while I looked overside and saw only the mist streaming past. Two hundred feet showed, then one hundred, and the aeronoid registered no height at all when suddenly, out of the haze in front I saw two huge humps, and recognized them as hangars on the edge of the Calais aerodrome.

Sir Malcolm with his sister Winifred.

Photographed whilst in the Royal Flying Corps.

Malcolm Campbell posing with his first aeroplane.

A young Malcolm Campbell in the first 'Blue Bird', a Darracq, with Godfrey Waters.

Napier 'Blue Bird' seen from the front.

Sir Henry Segrave in his Sunbeam at the 1922 French Grand Prix.

Campbell watches as a mechanic works on the 1920 Sunbeam.

At the wheel of a 1901 car on the beach at Daytona in 1933.

Sir Malcolm Campbell in his 4 litre Sunbeam leading the Hon Brian Lewis (winner) in his Alfa-Romeo – PA Images: Alamy Stock Photo.

1912 Lorraine Dietrich 'Blue Bird' at Brooklands with Malcolm Campbell – Heritage Image Partnership Ltd: Alamy Stock Photo.

Malcolm Campbell driving a Monoposto car at Brooklands circa 1924 – PA Images: Alamy Stock Photo.

Absolutely by chance I had glided straight for the landing ground, and the plane could not have been more than fifty feet up when I saw the hangars. It was impossible to fly between them, because they were so close together that they would have caught my wings. My only chance was to bank the machine steeply, and this I did, clearing the hangars safely. When I tried to level the plane out it would not answer; I had lost flying speed and, consequently, the controls were soggy; I hit the ground with a crash, wrecking the undercarriage.

I was very badly shaken, but not physically injured. That I should have been able to glide directly back through the mist and gathering darkness to a landing ground that I could not see was extraordinarily good luck. It was a providential escape, but the shock of the crash remained with me for a long time afterwards. Somehow, I could not shake it off, and at last I decided to apply for leave. I had worked for eighteen months without a break, and the application resulted in my appearance before a medical board, as a result of which I was given leave and, at the same time, removed from ferry service. The tension of constant flying had taken temporary toll of my nerves, and at the end of my leave I was appointed flying instructor at Coventry.

I had learned quite a lot about aviation under war conditions, and knew many of those little errors which can cost a pilot his life. In the hope of helping cadet airmen, I wrote a little book which I called *Hints to Beginners on Flying*. I had five thousand copies printed, passing them to as many men as I was able. I filled the pages with anecdotes which, I hoped, would encourage a man who was nervous and help him on his way. The war dragged on and I was transferred to Denham, where I gained a captaincy. Then came the Armistice, and I took off my uniform in 1919, returning with others to a world that was much changed.

§6

I have tried to sketch something of my war-time days, although conscious that my experience cannot compare with that of many men.

The war taught me many things, and I was left with a great respect for those who fought in the trenches, who ran greater risks and endured far more than I was called upon to face. With them, I shared profound relief in a return to more peaceful ways, and for myself this meant a return to motor racing.

I was thirty-five years of age when next I drove a racing car, and this proved to be the real beginning of the career that I had sought so long.

THE THIRD CHAPTER

§I

AFTER THE WAR I RETURNED to Lloyds, where I had left a very fine business in 1914, only to find that most of the clients interested in my libel insurance policies had gone to other brokers. To build up the business again would have taken a long time, and I decided to leave the City, although I still remain a member of Lloyds.

I felt the need for some active interest, and considered entering the motor business, fulfilling a desire which I had expressed to my father fifteen years before. I wanted, also, to take up motor racing again, but Brooklands was still in the hands of the War Office, and for almost the whole of 1919 I followed out certain ideas concerning a motor agency.

I felt that the general public did not know very much about motor cars, and that they should be able to put as much trust in their motor agent as they did in their insurance broker. It seemed to me that the same thing could apply to motor cars, that a man should be able to secure an agent's assistance and co-operation in finding the right vehicle, and that he should be a man of high integrity.

I worked things out on these lines, then sought an agency for the right type of car. I read the specifications of a new chassis which was to be put on the market; it appeared an ideal machine, and I went to see the man behind it. He agreed to let me have the London agency, and I paid ten thousand pounds as a deposit against cars which would be supplied to me, then rented showrooms in Albemarle Street.

No cars had been built by the time of the motor exhibition in 1919, but in spite of this, I sold no less than five hundred and eighty machines. I took cheques for fifty or a hundred pounds with each signed order form, arranging for the customers to accept their cars in strict rotation, according to the delivery schedule which I had been promised. Some of the orders could not possibly be filled for months, but the customers were perfectly agreeable to wait.

This seemed an excellent start for my new business, because I had sold every machine for which I had contracted, and that is an ideal situation. I expected cars to begin to arrive soon after the motor show, as had been promised by the manufacturers, but none came through. Time passed, and still there were no deliveries. Customers grew impatient but, taking up agencies for other machines, I was able in some cases to supply cars other than the ones originally ordered. Weeks ran into months, and still none of the new chassis appeared. In actual fact, no production models were constructed until years afterwards.

The manufacturer found that, in order to build his cars, he would be obliged to import machinery from America, which involved very large sums of money. More important than this, however, he foresaw the slump which followed the post-war boom, and it was this which made him decide to abandon his plans. He returned my ten thousand pounds, adding interest at the rate of five per cent; I returned the deposits of disappointed customers, also with interest, and so the matter was settled without loss to anyone.

Had the cars ever materialized, the transaction must have been exceedingly profitable to myself, and would have formed the foundation of what might have grown into a splendid business. As the affair turned out, it provided an instance of the misfortune which followed all my efforts to run a motor agency. I gave it up in the end, and this brought to a finish efforts to occupy myself in the motor business.

It was through the agency, however, that I secured the car with which I returned to motor racing. The last machine I had driven in a Brooklands race had been the old Gregoire, and during the year after the war I got out designs for an improved car, taking them over to Paris for discussion with the makers. The conference came to nothing, but while I was there I saw one of the most famous of all racing machines. I bought it on the spot, and drove it at Brooklands on the day the track reopened.

§2

The car was a Lorraine-Dietrich, which had been raced by Victor Hemery in the Grand Prix of 1912, over the Dieppe circuit. It had appeared at Brooklands afterwards, when Hemery had used it to lower no less than eleven world's records; he covered nearly ninety-eight miles in one hour on the track, and broke the two hundred miles record at 95.5 mph. Those were very high speeds, and I was further impressed by the fact that my first really good racing car had also come from Hemery's hands, the Darracq, which had been the original 'Blue Bird'. It seemed fitting that the famous Lorraine-Dietrich should also be painted blue and be given the same name because, in some measure, I was starting motor racing all over again.

At that time, early in 1920, it was not permissible to import cars from abroad, but the difficulty of bringing the Lorraine-Dietrich into England was overcome by declaring that the machine was a staff car, returning from France after use in post-war affairs. Even this involved certain difficulties, but we overcame them, although the customs officers expressed certain doubts about the machine, since it had only two bucket seats and an enormous petrol tank. It was not in the least like the kind of car used by Staff Officers.

Once the machine was safely in my hands, I put it into racing trim for the first post-war Brooklands meeting; this was due to be held on Easter Monday, April 5th, 1920, after a long time had been spent in repairing the track. The organizers were the Essex Motor Club, and the day proved to be so wet that the officials would not admit spectators, who formed a queue outside while argument went on concerning the postponement of the meeting. It was put off until the following Saturday, the track was thrown open to anyone who cared to come in, and a few spectators drifted towards the paddock. After a time, the rain stopped, upon which it was suggested that one or two match races might be arranged to lessen the general disappointment.

In those days, both cars and motorcycles appeared at the same meetings, and I agreed to race the Lorraine Dietrich against a Matchless motorcycle ridden by Major J. W. Woodhouse, over a distance of one lap. The concrete was flooded with great pools of water, and I won at 78.9 mph, gaining the distinction of securing victory in the first event held on the reopened track, although one could hardly call the match an official race. However, I did win one of the two important events run off during the postponed meeting the next Saturday.

This opening meeting was not an important one, and the one arranged for Whit Monday was altogether bigger. In the short interval between the two holidays, I sold the Lorraine-Dietrich, but the car has always remained at the track, renamed 'Vieux Charles III'. It is sometimes put on show as a veteran from the pre-war Grands Prix, and soon it will be a quarter of a century since Hemery first drove the car in a race on the road.

This Whit Monday meeting has some importance, in the light of later events. The late Sir Henry Birkin appeared for the first time at the track, driving a Peugeot during the opening event, and in the big race of the day, the 100 mph Long Handicap, H. O. D. Segrave was at the wheel of an Opel. The race showed something of his quality as a driver, and it was the first in which he ever ran.

His machine had been driven by Karl Joerns in the 1914 Grand Prix, and it was on scratch when Segrave turned out at Brooklands. He had to give six seconds start to three other cars; one was a French Alda, also a Grand Prix machine, another my old Lorraine-Dietrich, with Hawkes at the wheel, while the third machine was a Schneider which I had bought only a few days before.

Hawkes took the lead in the first lap, and Segrave came roaring past me. The Schneider did not show the speed that I had expected, and I tailed away behind; Hawkes took the lead and Seagrave came up to pass him on the second lap. He was driving splendidly when, just beyond the Byfleet bridge, the tyre left his off-side rear wheel. He must then have been travelling at fully 100 mph and was very close to the upper edge of the banking, but he held the machine straight, slowing down steadily. The Lorraine went on to win, and Segrave limped into the paddock on three wheels and a rim, the crowd applauding his fine driving. He took the Opel out again in the last race of the day, and won.

Looking back on those early post-war meetings, it seems as if each one of them served to introduce some man, or some machine, destined to play an important role in the years that followed, when the world's land-speed record became the most coveted honour that motor racing could offer.

During the week prior to the next Brooklands meeting, in June, a machine came to the track which had been specially built for attacks on world's short-distance records — that is, records lying between one mile and ten miles. This car was known as the 350 h.p. Sunbeam, and it had a twelve-cylinder, V-type power unit developed from the aero engines which the Sunbeam people had been making during the war. It was a single-seater, with a cowled radiator and a stumpy, rounded tail, while the engine had a capacity of 18,322 c.c.

This term, 18,322 c.c., is a technical one, and indicates both the size of an engine and something of its power. The average family car has a power unit of between 1,500 c.c. to 2,500 c.c., and comparison makes it easy to realize that the big Sunbeam was a most impressive machine. It was to be driven at the meeting by W. G. Hawker. He took the car out for a final practice run during the morning, and burst a tyre behind the Members' Hill. He kept the machine under control until he was halfway down the railway straight, then the car slithered off the track and carried away ten yards of the corrugated iron fencing which stands between the course and the railway embankment. Hawker was unharmed and, although the car was not seriously damaged, it could not run during the afternoon.

I regarded the Sunbeam as a real racing machine. It was so big, and so powerful, that it seemed as if it could be made to travel just as fast as a man dared drive it. The only really high-speed cars available at that date were from pre-war days, but this was a thoroughly modern machine, out to achieve a pace far greater than anything which had yet been attained.

Everyone was disappointed when the car failed to turn out, in view of news which had come from America just a month earlier. The report said that Tommy Milton, a prominent American racing driver, had taken a sixteen-cylinder car through a measured mile on Daytona Beach at a speed of 156 mph. The car was said to have caught fire during its run, but he held the machine until it cleared the timing tape, afterwards deliberately driving into the sea and extinguishing the flames.

No one in England really believed Miller's reported speed, because 156 mph sounded phenomenal. The highest pace hitherto recorded in Europe had been 125.95 mph set up by Victor Hemery. In any case, Milton's figure could not rank as a record, since it had been agreed, in 1913, that world's records for short distances should be taken from the average speed of two runs, made in reverse directions of the course. Additionally, the timing apparatus had to be of a type approved by the Commission Sportive, representing the International Association of Recognized Automobile Clubs.

The mile record was then of interest only to men who built cars or who raced them, joining issue in friendly rivalry. The news about Milton, however, did lend greater interest to the attack which the Sunbeam was to launch, but the machine had to overcome those preliminary troubles which invariably present themselves before a new racing car can produce its true form.

§3

I drove at most of the Brooklands meetings during the remainder of the 1920 season, also giving some attention to hill climbs, a branch of motor racing into which I had not previously ventured. During 1921, I competed somewhere every weekend, either at the track or in hill climbs, at meetings held on sandy beaches or in speed trials at seaside resorts.

All the time, the 350 h.p. Sunbeam was being developed, and it was during this season that a car appeared which had an even bigger engine. This machine was owned and raced by Count Louis Zborowski, and he called it 'Chitty-Chitty Bang-Bang', a name derived from the sound of its exhaust note. He built the car up from a Mercedes chassis, constructed in 1910, while he used a Maybach aero engine of 23,000 c.c. which had been taken from the Z 17, a Zeppelin brought down in England during the war. He handled this truly huge machine well, and used to lap Brooklands at speeds around 110 mph.

Zborowski had a love of big cars, and he intended to use 'Chitty' for attempts on world's records, but the machine became involved in a particularly disastrous crash, when he replaced it with an even larger and more powerful car which actually did raise the world's record, although Zborowski did not drive it.

The significance of 'Chitty' is that the car's engine had been built for a Zeppelin, while the Sunbeam had a power unit developed from aeronautical practice. These aeroplane engines were employed in big racing cars because they could be adapted very easily, and because they could be obtained at far less cost than would be involved in the construction of a special motor. Instead of turning a propeller, they required only relatively minor modifications to enable them to turn a pair of rear wheels. In addition, they were built in such a way as to secure the greatest possible horsepower from a minimum of weight, which is an asset in a car. Almost every successful attempt to attain high speed on land has been powered by an aero engine.

It was not long after 'Chitty' appeared that still another car fitted with an aeroplane engine came to Brooklands. This machine was a Fiat, owned by E. A. D. Eldridge, and named 'Mephistopheles'. In 1908, it had been handled at Brooklands by Felix Nazzaro, a magnificent Italian driver, who had set up a lap record of 121.64 mph, which still stood.

'Mephistopheles' remained idle during the war and was brought from retirement to run in the 1921 International Speed Trials at Fanoe Island, Denmark, after which it had passed into Eldridge's hands. He rebuilt the machine, putting in a new engine, and the car proved so powerful that it was impossible for him to open it out fully on the track. Obviously, so fast a machine could not be limited to racing at Brooklands, and it was not long before Eldridge was driving it with a view to securing recognition for the Fiat as the fastest car in the world.

About this time, there became active at the track one more driver destined to set up new records. This was J. G. Parry Thomas, a splendid engineer who always drove the machines on which he worked. He lived in a bungalow built at the inside of the course, and all his waking hours were spent either in his workshop or out on the concrete. He took racing very seriously, and I ran against him on so many occasions that we seemed constantly to be striving against one another. He was a splendid man, and always held my admiration for his fine work and equally fine driving. Our rivalry, always very sporting and friendly, became even more acute when Thomas also made the one mile record his aim.

When the racing season of 1922 arrived, it found the 350 h.p. Sunbeam ready to attack world's records, while most of the men who were to figure in efforts to raise land speed were on the scene: Segrave and Parry Thomas and Eldridge, with myself in the background. Then, over on Daytona Beach, a man of whom none of us had ever heard made the first move in a campaign which was to continue ceaselessly for many years.

This was Sig. Haugdahl, who had built a car with a 250 h.p. Wisconsin hydroplane engine, mounted in bodywork which was streamlined to the last degree and which, it was said, had all external nuts and boltheads faired to streamline form. Haugdahl worked this machine up to about 150 mph, only to be troubled with serious vibration which, eventually, he found was caused by unevenly balanced tyres. It took him six weeks to get wheels and tyres balanced, when he made another effort and claimed to have covered a measured mile at 180 mph.

That speed was set up as an American record, but it was made along one way of the course only, and was not recognized in Europe. Frankly, no one believed his speed, and although this may have been an injustice to Sig. Haugdahl, the pace that he claimed appeared impossible in the light of what we knew of high speeds in Europe.

Following Haugdahl's effort, and in May,1922, Kenelm Lee Guinness drove the big Sunbeam in a practice burst at Brooklands, and hand timing showed the the car to have achieved 144 mph over a half-mile dash down the railway straight. Even allowing for any error in timing, the figure showed that all existing records could be broken by the car, and shortly afterwards Lee Guinness made an official attempt. The highest speed that he registered was over the kilometre, which he covered at 137.15 mph after a flying start; his pace through the measured mile was much lower, being 129.17 mph. However, he had done enough to mark the Sunbeam as officially the world's fastest car, while he smashed the Brooklands lap record with 123.39 mph.

It was obvious to anyone who saw the car that it could achieve still higher speeds on a more suitable course, one which would give the Sunbeam room to get up speed before crossing the timing tape; there is not a straight mile on the Weybridge track, and this had handicapped the car.

I was ambitious to drive the machine in an effort to get nearer the limit of its speed. I thought that its pace could be shown on Saltburn sands, where the Yorkshire Auto Club were holding speed trials a month later, and I was able to persuade Louis Coatalen, the director of the Sunbeam company, to lend me the car.

The machine was tuned up, and on the 17th of June, 1922, I found myself at Saltburn with everything ready for my first attempt on the world's record. The course was marked out along the beach between Saltburn and Marske, where low cliffs stand at one side of a fairly wide stretch of smooth sand, long enough to allow a run of two miles before the car entered the measured distance. There was a fairly strong wind blowing south-east from Marske, and this was behind me on the first run.

I took the car away steadily, then put my foot hard down. The engine was in splendid tune, and its acceleration was really impressive. The machine handled well, and I knew that I was moving fast when I passed the first timekeepers. No timing apparatus was employed, synchronised stop watches being used to register the Sunbeam's speed, and I was clocked as travelling through the measured distance at 130.6 mph.

I turned the machine about, and on the second run, against the wind this time, the pace was much higher; the car achieved 134.76 mph. In all I made six runs, the fastest being at 138.08 mph. It was a curious fact that the car was always faster running towards Marske than when it had the wind astern, while my revolution counter more than once registered the Sunbeam as travelling at over 160 mph. The difference between this and the recorded pace was due to wheel slip.

The mean speed of the two best runs was an improvement on

the figure which Lee Guinness had set up at Brooklands, and as I drove home from Yorkshire, I congratulated myself upon holding the world's record. This feeling of satisfaction did not last for very long, however, because the Commission Sportive would not admit timing by stop watches, and the record was disallowed.

My disappointment was very keen. There was not the slightest doubt that the car had actually achieved the speed claimed, and taken the record. The attitude of the Commission Sportive was perfectly correct; rules governing record attempts had been agreed upon by international representatives and had to be obeyed. I determined to break the record again, and to break it over a course properly timed, so that there could be no question of the car's performance. Still further, I determined to do it only for the satisfaction of proving the truth behind the claim which had been disallowed.

Having made this decision, I offered to buy the 350 h.p. Sunbeam, but Louis Coatalen would not even consider selling the car.

§4

At intervals, in the months which followed, I repeated my efforts to buy the big Sunbeam, because I felt that there was no other car in England with which the record could be pushed higher, but Coatalen would not sell the machine.

I was racing continuously now, and became particularly successful in hill climbs; there was a period when I held records for Holme Moss, Spread Eagle and Caerphilly hill climbs, and I still have credit for the fastest run up Thundersley Hill. I was not so fortunate at Brooklands that season, but I drove in the 'speed championships' which were organized at the track towards the end of September, 1922. On the day before these events, Zborowski had one of the most remarkable escapes in the history of motor racing, and this escape had an influence on the later land speed record attempts.

He was practising with 'Chitty-Chitty Bang-Bang' and burst his off-side front tyre as he came out from behind the Members' Hill; he was then moving at above 120 mph. The car shot towards the upper rim of the track, and hit a low parapet where the course runs above the River Wey. This diverted the machine, and sent it skidding broadside down the banking. Here it left the track and jumped a ditch, then struck a timing box on the edge of the course, completely shattering it; a telegraph pole was cut down, the front axle was torn away from the car and sent spinning through the air, while the 'Chitty' charged on over the grass inside the track. When the machine finally came to a stop it was still right way up, and Zborowski was seated quite unhurt behind the wheel. Within a few minutes he was travelling round Brooklands at speed again, using a borrowed car, in order that the accident might leave no impression on his nerve.

'Chitty' had been badly damaged and, during the winter, Zborowski began rebuilding it, then gave up the task and constructed another machine instead. He called this new car the 'Higham Special', and fitted it with a 27,059 c.c. twelve-cylinder Liberty aero engine; the machine made its first appearance at Brooklands early in 1923, and must have been about the biggest car ever to have run on the track until that date. The following year, Zborowski lost his life on Monza speedway, during the Italian Grand Prix, and it was then that the 'Higham Special' was acquired by Parry Thomas, who eventually used it for attempts on the world's short distance records. At the time of 'Chitty's crash, Parry Thomas was collecting international class records with a Leyland car, and it was the knowledge which he had gained in tuning this machine that enabled him to develop the 'Higham Special' to phenomenal speeds.

When the 1922 racing season ended, I renewed my efforts to buy the 350 h.p. Sunbeam. The machine was standing idle at the track, and it was still there when Brooklands opened again for racing in 1923. Early in the summer, I saw a possibility of making a really effective record attempt if I could secure the car, because the Danish Automobile Club was again organizing speed trials at Fanoe, where the Fiat, 'Mephistopheles', had already competed. A German car had achieved 125 mph on the sands in 1922, and I believed that the Sunbeam would have an opportunity of showing its real pace at the next meeting.

The fastest of Continental machines had entered, handled by very fine drivers, and I wanted to take out the best car we had in England. I approached Louis Coatalen once again and, as a satisfactory outcome of my persistence, he agreed to sell the Sunbeam. It was then hardly a fortnight before the Fanoe event, and I collected the car immediately, arranging for it to be sent by train from Brooklands to Horley railway station, near Povey Cross, where I had established what was regarded as quite an efficient workshop and garage, in the grounds around a house which I had bought after the war.

Waiting for the car to arrive were two mechanics who have shared, since I bought that old Sunbeam, every racing experience that I have known, and both work with me still. They have played a great part in my life, and deserve an adequate introduction.

§5

One of the mechanics, Leo Villa, came to me through the kindly agency of Jules Foresti, a driver who often raced at Brooklands, and who agreed to bring over from France two racing cars which I had bought: a Ballot and an Itala. I told Foresti that I needed a first-class mechanic, and he mentioned Villa, who had been Foresti's mechanic during various races, and who was then in Paris. On Foresti's recommendation, I arranged for this young mechanic to come over to England with the cars, and work for me during the season.

Villa duly arrived with the Ballot and the Itala. He was short and curly-haired, and I found that he could speak both French and Italian, his father's native language, although his mother is English. Villa had started in life as a pageboy at Romano's, in the Strand, where his father was head wine-waiter; he had an uncle who acted in a similar capacity at Pigani's, while his only brother is second butler at the Savoy. Villa never liked his first job; he was in constant trouble with the other pageboys, and his father judged it wise to withdraw him when, as the result of a disagreement, Villa emptied the contents of an ink pot over the head of the hall porter.

Villa had always wanted to be a motor mechanic, and a job was now found for him in the London firm which handled Gregoire cars. Later, his uncle spoke to Jules Foresti, a relative of the family; incidentally, Foresti's real Christian name is Guilo, but this has become altered to the French form, Jules, as a result of the time he has spent in France. Foresti agreed to give Villa a trial, finding him so excellent about his work, and so keen, that he took him as mechanic in two Targa Florio races. This event, held over a mountain circuit in Sicily, was regarded as the most arduous of all races, and it provided a real test for any mechanic.

Later, Villa went to the Ballot works as a member of the experimental department. The factory straddled the city limits of Paris and, because by-laws forbade the running of engines after a certain hour at night, the shed where racing engines were tested was set just outside the city walls; its location thus overcame the by-laws, and no official objection could be made to noise. Villa was working on an engine one evening, preparing it for a car on which he was to act as Foresti's mechanic in the French Grand Prix, when the lights failed.

The shed had its own lighting plant, driven by a petrol-fed motor. The belt between the motor and the dynamo had broken and, flying upwards, had torn out the bottom of the petrol tank. Villa, investigating the trouble, reached the plant just as the leaking petrol exploded. He was very badly burned, and had to spend six weeks in hospital, while the experience left him with a dread of fire, which he was still trying to master when he came to me, a year later.

The other man who awaited the arrival of the 350 h.p. Sunbeam was Harry Leech, and he had been introduced to me by Major Nixon, a very old friend who had worked on war-time airships at Pulham, in Norfolk. The Sunbeam's engine was an offshoot of those used in these aircraft, and I had mentioned to Major Nixon that I felt the need of a mechanic who was familiar with this type of power unit; he suggested that Leech would probably be willing to help tune up the machine.

Pulham had been the centre of airship activity, but all work there had stopped. The Air Ministry had not decided, at that time, to continue the construction of such craft. Major Nixon told me that Leech was a competent draughtsman and engineer, but he had so firm a belief in the future of airships that he was staying on at Pulham – sweeping out offices and doing odd jobs, earning no more than thirty shillings a week – solely that he might be on hand when work began again.

I expected to see an unusual man, with characteristics beyond the ordinary, and when Leech came down to Povey Cross, I found that he was very powerful physically, while he bore out all the good things that Major Nixon had said of him. After he had been working with us for a little while, I made him a substantial offer to join Villa and myself, but he would not accept. He preferred to go back to Pulham, and wait for airship construction to begin again. Work recommenced soon afterwards, and, later on, he was a member of the crew aboard the R.101 when the airship crashed at Beauvais, in France.

He was in one of the gondolas when his spell of duty ended, and he went into the men's smoking-room for a cigarette. He had barely lit it before the craft struck the side of a hill and immediately burst into flames. Leech was alone in the smoking-room, trapped by fire, and only his strength saved him. He tore a padded bench away from the wall, using it to smash a hole through the side of the airship.

As he clambered through, he heard a cry from the gondola

where he had been working, and remembered the two engineers who were there. Escaping gas was alight all round it, but Leech ran through it and dragged one of the men clear. For this act of bravery he was rewarded by a medal for conspicuous gallantry, and anyone who knows the heat of hydrogen flames will appreciate what he faced.

He was one of the few men who survived the crash, and when airship building ceased, he went to the engineering department of Southampton University, where the authorities allow him to take his holidays, just as the people at Pulham had given him leave, whenever I ask him to join me and help with a machine. Which means that, for years, Leech has sacrificed his holidays in order to be with Villa and myself.

§6

Villa accompanied me to fetch the 350 h.p. Sunbeam from Horley railway station, one Monday evening. We then had less than a week in which to put the machine in trim; it had to be entrained for Harwich by the following Saturday, in order to catch the boat for Denmark on the Monday.

I drove the car from the station, and it ran very badly. Great clouds of smoke poured from the exhaust and from under the bonnet and, obviously, something serious was wrong. Once we got the car into the garage, it did not take long to discover that the scavenging pump was broken; this meant that oil was being driven from the oil tank into the engine sump, and was not being returned.

Louis Coatalen had lent me a mechanic named Webster, who now hurried off to secure spare parts. When he returned, we began a race against time, repairing the broken pump and raising the compression of the engine to give greater power. We worked continuously during the following week, and on the Friday I went up to London about various matters, returning late in the evening. I expected everything to be ready for departure; instead, I found the car pushed halfway out of the garage, while the three mechanics greeted me with very glum expressions.

Villa's first remark was that the car would be unable to run at Fanoe, and all three were definite about this. They had examined the gearbox as a matter of routine, and Leech now produced the shaft which carried first, second, and third gears. The gearwheels and the shaft had been machined from one solid block of steel, and all three gears were stripped, the pinions being flattened and 'chawed', making it quite impossible to race the machine. 'It's no good, skipper,' Villa said. 'We're done.'

He had every reason for making the remark, because it was a special gearbox, and no spares were in existence. Within twenty-four hours, the car had to be on the railway truck which was waiting for it, and there was hardly time to effect a repair even if a new gear-shaft had been available. Since no spare shaft existed, it was natural to regard the whole undertaking as quite hopeless, and to give up any idea of running the car.

Being confronted with such a situation, just at that time, provided a worthwhile experience. From what followed, I learned that, no matter how formidable a difficulty may appear, there must always be some way to overcome it, and it was the disappointment of the three tired men which made me determined that, somehow or other, we would run at Fanoe.

The most reasonable thing seemed, first, to call up the Sunbeam people. Fortunately, I was able to get into touch with a man whom I knew well. I explained the situation, and told him that we must have a new gear-shaft, no matter what the cost. He said he would do anything in the world to help us, but pointed out that a special block of steel would be required from a foundry in Sheffield; if it could be obtained, however, he would see that men were in readiness at the Sunbeam factory, in Wolverhampton, and promised they would work without break until a new shaft and its pinions had been cut.

When they saw that there might be some chance of repairing

the car, all three mechanics cheered up. Webster volunteered to go to Sheffield, and started immediately, driving all through the night. At eleven o'clock the following morning, Saturday, he was at the Sunbeam works with the steel, and men began work on it at once. We towed the car from Povey Cross to the railway station and loaded it on the waiting truck, with spares, tools, and tyres, after which there was nothing more we could do. Webster remained at Wolverhampton, ready to bring the shaft away the moment that it was completed, while I advised him of my movements for the Monday, so that he could meet me right up to the moment when the boat was due to leave Harwich.

During the weekend, it was uncertain whether the shaft could be made in time. Men worked on it all day Saturday, all the following night, all Sunday and Sunday night, and on Monday I went with Leech and Villa to Liverpool Street railway station to catch the train for Harwich. If Webster did not turn up there, I knew that the position was almost hopeless, because he would hardly be able to get to the boat in time.

There was no sign of the mechanic until the guard was actually waving his flag, then Webster appeared, racing up the platform. It was something of a triumph when he unwrapped the gleaming steel shaft which, at one time, it had seemed impossible to acquire, and when he had recovered his breath, we started to plan the work necessary to refit the gearbox and get the car finally ready.

We arrived at Fanoe on Tuesday night, and attacked the gearbox next morning. The Sunbeam was housed in a shed which had no artificial light, so that we were able to work only by day, and it was not until Friday afternoon twenty-four hours before the car was due to run that we had the machine in proper trim.

The sound of the engine was very heartening when we started up, and I took the wheel with the intention of driving down to the sands and trying the machine out. Fortunately, we had also brought over a 24–60 h.p. Sunbeam which had been entered in various events and, using this, I had been able already to familiarize myself with the course. I sent the big car away, but covered hardly five hundred yards before every one of the shock absorber brackets broke, and I was obliged to turn back.

We had laboured all day and half of every night on the car while it was at Povey Cross; this had been succeeded by a period of anxiety about the gear-shaft, and now the broken brackets robbed us of all confidence in the machine. We began to make new ones, but we felt that, when they were ready, something else would fail on the car.

§7

The speed trials were being held along the foreshore of Fanoe Island, which is opposite Esbjerg, on the Danish coast. The island is long and narrow, and a course some six miles in length had been marked out over the firm sand. The entry was international, and our chief opposition was formed by a big, four-cylinder Opel, driven by Karl Joerns who, the previous year, had made fastest time of the day with this car. Another rival was a Stower, from Czechoslovakia, and there were other cars from Italy, Sweden, Austria, Norway and Denmark, as well as machines which, like the Opel, came from Germany. The German drivers and their entries were formidable, and they had won nearly every prize offered the year before.

The outstanding event was the attempt on the flying mile, and the driver who made fastest time won the title of 'speed champion'. The trials for the flying mile and kilometre were to be held on the Saturday, and the Sunday was to be devoted to races between the same machines. It had been provisionally agreed that, for Sunday, cars would be handicapped according to the times they had set up on the previous day, and the drivers were called to a meeting on Friday evening to ratify this arrangement.

All competitors in the small classes agreed to it, after which the officials approached the men in the unlimited car class; that is, those who were expected to set up new figures for the world's speed record. I was asked whether I should prefer the Sunday's races to be on a handicap basis or from scratch; I answered, in company with others, that I was willing to leave the decision to the German drivers, since they were in the majority. They promptly asked for scratch races in the big-car class.

The decision made me wonder what the Germans had up their sleeves. They knew that the Sunbeam had done 138 mph at Saltburn, and I knew that Karl Joerns claimed to have done 150 mph on Fanoe Beach during practice, but I did not take this speed too seriously, because there is always a good deal of exaggerated talk before an event of this nature. Thinking it over, I came to the conclusion that, since they obviously knew I was having difficulty with the big Sunbeam, they thought they would stand a better chance during the races if we all started from scratch. They had every justification for this because, had I been asked, I should have been obliged to admit that I had very little hope of doing anything with the car.

I went back to the garage, and work had to be continued on the Sunbeam until an hour before it was due to appear, and when I did run down to the sands the machine was turning its wheels along the beach for the first time.

The first event in which I drove the car was over the mile from a standing start, and any doubts that I had about the machine were quickly dispelled. The Sunbeam won easily, covering the distance at 82.19 mph; the next best was 75 mph, set up by Karl Joerns on his Opel.

The big machine was rewarding us for our work by running magnificently, and I felt altogether more confident when I took the car down to the start for the outstanding effort of the meeting. There was a side wind, but the sand was in very fair condition, and I had a run of about two miles before entering the measured distance. I accelerated steadily then, in top gear, put my foot hard down.

The car was much faster than it had been at Saltburn although, on that opening run, I had no time to register my impressions. I can remember only the work of holding the car, and that it was not easy to keep the machine straight. When I entered the start of the mile, the Sunbeam was travelling flat out, and I was moving more quickly than I had ever done before, while two thoughts flashed through my mind.

'This is fast!' Then, near the end of the mile, I thought, 'It can't be possible to go much faster than this!'

At that moment I must have been touching 150 mph, because I clocked 146.4 mph over the distance. The machine was not so quick on the return run and, having become a little more accustomed to the pace, I was able to study the car's behaviour. It weighed only about a ton and a half, and it seemed too light for its power; also, it had a tendency to slide to the right, travelling crabwise, and this felt very dangerous. Other than this, the car gave no trouble at all, and the mean speed of my two best runs, either way of the course, worked out at 137.72 mph, which was the fastest of the day. Joerns put up a very good show with 132 mph, but the Sunbeam was too much for him.

Following this success, I took out the smaller car, and this also beat everything in its class, with the result that officials and crowd were most enthusiastic, while the German drivers were certainly surprised. When the day's events ended, they approached the Danish officials and said that, after all, they would prefer to have the Sunday's races on a handicap basis, and not from scratch as they had agreed on the Friday. The officials, however, refused to make any alteration in the arrangements, and the following afternoon found the big Sunbeam on the line again, now matched against its rivals in a straightaway event.

I drew a bad position, near the sea and so close to the water that it was washing the sands only a few feet from the Sunbeam's wheels. As I sat there, I considered starting off with a rush, and leaving the rival machines as far behind as possible, because I felt confident that the Sunbeam would win the event; but this seemed a churlish thing to do and, when the flag fell, I accelerated carefully and the rest got away from me. The car soon picked up speed, however, so that I overhauled the rest one after the other, catching Joern's Opel some distance before the finish and winning the race handily.

In other events that afternoon, the 350 h.p. Sunbeam and the 24–60 h.p. machine won everything there was to win, sweeping the board clean of all prizes, very much as the Germans had done a year earlier.

I was naturally elated, because I now held the world's record with the car. The Germans took their defeat very sportingly; they had done their best to win, but they had been fairly beaten and they showed no regret. I was invited to a banquet in the evening, and I agreed to attend if I could take my mechanics with me. There was no objection to this, and I think it was Villa who found himself seated next to a German duchess, quite unable to exchange a word with her, but enjoying himself nevertheless. The mechanics had an excellent evening, and I know that, when we came away, I found Webster sitting on the steps of the hotel, reading a Danish newspaper which he was holding upside down.

We came away from Fanoe with a blue and gold pennant issued by the Dansk Motor Klub, bearing 'Fanoe Champion – 1923'. This time, we felt, there could be no doubt about our having set the world's fastest speed, because the runs had been properly recorded. Shortly after our arrival in England, however, I learned that the Commission Sportive would not accept the Dansk Klub figures, the objection being that they had not been registered by an electrical apparatus of which the Commission approved.

The Danish authorities protested, and took the trouble to send their apparatus to Paris, where it was demonstrated before the Commission. It was proved to be absolutely accurate, and this was admitted, but the international regulations governing timing apparatus could not be changed, and the submitted speeds were disallowed.

For the second time I had broken the record, and for the second time official recognition had been refused. I had resolved, after Saltburn, that I would break the record, and this unexpected setback only made me the more determined to break it officially and definitely under such circumstances that there could be no possibility of dispute.

THE FOURTH CHAPTER

§ 1

IT IS ONE THING TO set up the world's land-speed record as a personal objective, and quite another to find a suitable opportunity for attacking it. The next attempt required some consideration, because it was necessary to be quite sure that nothing more could go wrong. By the time that the authorities in Paris had definitely refused the figures proffered by the Danish club, it was too late in that season to do anything more with the 350 h.p. Sunbeam, and I concentrated upon what proved to be my first important long-distance race.

This was known as the Two Hundred Miles race, organized the Junior Car Club, and run at Brooklands. I had driven in the opening event of the series two years before, but it was not until this year – 1923 – that the race became outstanding, largely because two Fiats were sent over from Italy to compete. These machines had been most successful on the Continent, and their engines were fitted with superchargers, or 'blowers'. A supercharger compresses an explosive mixture of petrol vapour and air, 'blowing' into the engine a quantity much greater than the pistons can draw into the cylinders by normal induction. Roughly, the device increases the horsepower by thirty per cent, although everything about the motor has to be strengthened to withstand the additional power output.

These victorious Fiats were the first 'blown' racing cars ever to appear at the track. They were short, sleek red painted machines with stumpy tails shaped like a wedge, very compact and efficient in appearance. One was to be driven by Carlo Salamano, and his machine was entered by D'Arcy Baker, who represented the Fiat organization in England. He chanced to be an old friend of mine and, through his influence, I was able to persuade the Fiat company to send over a second car, to be entered and driven in the race by myself.

This made me the first man outside the official team ever to handle one of these cars, and Fiats insisted upon providing the necessary mechanics and pit staff, and on doing all the work of preparing the machine before it was sent to Brooklands from Milan. Even Villa played no part in making ready for the race, and during the event he was an ordinary spectator.

Salamano had a great reputation as a driver and, long before the cars appeared for practice, he was marked as almost certain to win. When the machines arrived, we did no more than half a dozen laps, enough to make quite sure that everything was in order, after which the Fiats were sheeted over and put away until the day of the race.

We lapped at 103 mph in practice; even at this speed, the Fiats were capable of moving still faster. The fastest lap ever made during any previous Two Hundred Miles race was at about 95 mph. Since the Fiats were easily ten miles an hour faster than their opponents, it was obvious that they had only to maintain what was, relatively, touring speed in order to win.

Naturally, I was very pleased with my car; it handled well, and was fully as fast as Salamano's. It was interesting to see the effect of this performance upon other entrants, who began working night and day, striving to bring their machines to perfection and make some reply to the Italian challenge. The track was busy from early morning until late in the evening, and no less than fifty-six cars were down to run. The event was actually formed by two separate races, one for 1,100 c.c. machines run off in the morning, and the other for 1,500 c.c. cars due to race during the afternoon, when the Fiats were to appear. Interest lay chiefly in the later event, in which twenty-six cars finally came to the line.

I endeavoured to learn as much as possible about the Fiat, and was particularly anxious to discover what speed the car could safely maintain during the event. I was assured that the engine would stand up to anything that I cared to ask from it; in other words, I was told that it was impossible to over-drive the machine.

It may, perhaps, be as well to explain how a racing car is handled. Instead of a speedometer, the instrument board usually carries a revolution counter, recording the rate at which the engine is turning over. An engine may be able to run all day at five thousand revolutions per minute, and it may be possible to lift this figure to 6,000 rpm, but it is obvious that reliability will be lessened at the higher speed. The machine may be doing ninety miles an hour at 5,000 rpm and one hundred and ten miles an hour at 6,000 rpm; from this it will be appreciated that the higher the engine revolutions, the faster the car is travelling. And the faster the machine goes, the more chance there is of some mechanical failure.

It is very necessary for a driver to know exactly when he is taking a risk with his car – not a driving risk, but a mechanical one. In order to indicate this, most revolution counters have coloured sections and, with an engine capable of the speeds indicated, the dial would have a green sector at 5,000 rpm, a yellow patch at 5,500 rpm, and a red sector at 6,000 rpm

It is not always possible for a driver, when his car is moving fast, to see exactly the position of the needle on the dial, although he can pick out its position in relation to the bands of colour. He would know, when the needle was over the green, that he was not stressing his engine, and that his pace was about 90 mph. If rival cars, or signals from his pit, forced him to go faster and lift the needle on to the yellow patch, his speed would be about

100 mph, and he would know that he was putting some strain on his engine. If the needle went up into the red he would, assuming the needle to be well across the sector, be moving flat out at 110 mph, stressing his power unit and running the risk of engine trouble bringing him to a stop.

Racing cars run very much faster than the speeds indicated, and engine revolutions go considerably high, but the pace of a car in relation to its engine is all a matter of gearing, a technical aspect of no immediate interest here. It will, however, be understood that a driver's sole purpose in a race is to force his competitors to maintain a speed which will keep their engines turning over at the limit, increasing their chances of cracking up, and yet to save his own car as much as possible.

The Fiat people told me that I could drive my car just as fast as I liked. They assured me that it was absolutely reliable, and they would not raise the gear ratio when I suggested it, so that the strain on the engine would be lessened. The Italian *équipe* was full of confidence, and I gradually came to understand that the Fiats hoped to run through the race as fast as possible, setting up new records for the event and generally creating a very fine impression of their capabilities.

During the practice period, I also tried to secure some decision regarding race tactics between Salamano and myself, because the situation was a little peculiar. Although the cars were in the same team, we were rival drivers, each anxious to do his best to win.

If we raced directly against one another, there was a possibility that we might take too much out of the cars and have trouble. Both Fiats were so fast that they were likely to leave the rest of the field behind after a few laps, and one of them seemed certain to achieve a runaway win. In short, a Fiat victory appeared so sure that we had to find some way of deciding whether Salamano should win or whether I should take that honour.

Nothing was arranged until the cars were actually being made ready for the start. It was then agreed that whoever took the lead on the first lap should be allowed to retain it and should make the pace until ten laps from the finish, the second Fiat sitting on the tail of the leader. Over the last ten laps Salamano and I were to fight it out between ourselves. This was a good plan, because we would not actually come to grips until the cars had almost done their work; assuming they held the lead, one would then take first place and the other second.

The general impression seemed to be that I stood little chance against a driver like Salamano; those who had seen him in races on the Continent assured me that he would be able to leave me behind any time that he cared to do so. Salamano himself showed no consciousness of such superiority; he was always very helpful and friendly. At the same time, I was ambitious to make as good a showing against him as possible. Although I had no experience of Grand Prix road racing at that time, I did know the Brooklands course very well indeed, while I had accomplished a good deal of very useful work in hill climbs and speed trials. I looked forward to a steady, high-speed run, followed by a real fight over the final ten laps of the race.

§2

Twenty-six cars lined up by the Fork at Brooklands on a chilly October afternoon, and many of these machines represented *marques* which no longer exist: Warwick, Marseal, Crouch, Bertelli, Marlborough-Thomas. But amongst the rest were three Bugattis and three Aston Martins; these names still appear in motor racing.

The cars were lined up in three rows, with both Salamano and myself in the last line. While we waited, I considered my chances of making a racing start and, perhaps, taking the lead on the first lap, setting the pace for the Italian driver throughout the race. I was so intent upon this that, when the flag fell, I let up the clutch too suddenly, and stalled my engine. The rest left me behind, but mechanics ran to the tail of the Fiat and the car went off from a push start. The delay lasted only two or three seconds, but it enabled the rest to get well ahead, and I saw a Bugatti taking the lead on the banking around the hill, with an Aston-Martin close behind. Other cars were spread out across the track, Salamano using the fierce acceleration of his red machine and streaking through them.

I opened up right from the start, overtaking one or two machines before I reached the railway straight. The track in front was filled with cars, but the Fiat passed them one after the other, and not many remained ahead when I ran on to the long Byfleet banking. At the far end of this, near the finish of the first lap, I saw that Salamano was lying second to the Bugatti and that only two cars lay between us.

I passed them both on the rush back to the Fork, so that the first lap ended with the Bugatti leading, Salamano second, and my Fiat in third place. We both went in front of the French car before the railway straight was reached and, after that, the superior speed of the Italian machines began to show. We drew well away from everything else and, towards the end of the second lap, I expected Salamano to ease the pace a little; the Bugatti, our only challenger, had been left far behind and was steadily falling further back.

Salamano, however, increased his speed as his engine grew thoroughly warmed up. I kept my Fiat on his tail, and by the end of the fourth circuit we were averaging 101.64 mph, fully ten miles an hour faster than any other car, and already lapping slow machines. In order to hold the pace set by Salamano, I was forced to drive with my foot hard down on the throttle pedal.

Although I remembered that the engines were supposed to be able to stand up to any amount of hard work, it seemed unreasonable to keep them at what was virtually flat-out speed. I felt, however, that Salamano was more experienced than myself; all I could do was to hold the pace he set, because I dared not slow. Had I eased the throttle he would have raced far ahead, which meant that I should have had no chance at all when the time came to fight it out over the final ten laps of the event. Another, and quite personal aspect of the matter was that, if I fell behind, the watching Italians, and others, would think that I could not drive well enough to hold Salamano.

Common sense should have made me slow; I should have known that no car of those days was capable of standing up to such speed for seventy-three laps of the track, the distance we had to run. On the other hand, it is not easy to be quite cool and calm in one's first big race, particularly when one has a famous Continental driver as an immediate rival. I accepted Salamano's speed, and we continued round the track, riding high on the bankings, constantly overtaking other machines.

We gained ground to such an extent that, at the end of twelve laps, we came up with the Bugatti which had first held the lead. We caught him near the Byfleet Bridge and I saw Salamano place his Fiat to pass the French car. Instead, he suddenly slowed and I eased the throttle for a moment, watching the Fiat drop towards the bottom of the banking, the mechanic looking back and waving me on. I shot past and, with my foot hard down again, overtook the Bugatti.

This machine was so near the upper edge of the banking that there was barely room to go by, and the Fiat's off-side tyres were almost touching the rim of the concrete as we passed. My mechanic was looking back all the while, watching Salamano; following the curve of the banking, I glanced over my shoulder and saw that the other car had slowed right down and was already far behind.

Something had gone wrong with Salamano's machine, and I eased my own speed, then watched for him when I came round on the next lap. Approaching the Fork, I saw smoke rising from the side of the track opposite from the pits. Salamano had halted his car there, and I saw him sprinting across the course to the Fiat depot. His mechanic was standing by the car with a fire extinguisher in his hands, while oil lay on the concrete under the machine, which was smoking badly.

It looked as if Salamano had met serious trouble, but I forgot his difficulties when, only a few seconds later, I heard a noise from my own engine. It was a thin, rattling sound and, at the same time, the car slowed, the revolution needle dropping. I rammed my elbow into the side of my Italian mechanic, nodding towards the instrument. He looked at it, then patted my shoulder and laughed reassuringly.

Evidently he had not heard the noise, and seemed to think that I was asking if we were going too fast; it was impossible to talk in the car, because of exhaust roar and supercharger whine. I drove on, listening for a repetition of the sound and, along the Byfleet banking, I put my foot hard down, hoping to make sure that everything was all right.

The engine sped up for a few moments, then came an abrupt clattering, while smoke poured from the louvres of the bonnet, gushing into the cockpit, half-blinding us and accompanied by choking gases. I stamped on the clutch pedal and took my foot off the throttle, pushing my head over the side of the machine, staring through the thick smoke and gasping for breath while I tried to keep the car straight.

The rattle continued while the car slowed, then the engine went dead and we coasted off the end of the banking towards the pits, the smoke clearing all the time. Other cars in the race came from behind and roared triumphantly past us when I pulled up at the pit and climbed out. Salmano was standing there, and it was easy to see from his attitude that his car was out of the race. I reported what had happened, and received orders to try and start up again. My mechanic swung the starting handle, although I knew that something serious must have occurred.

He jerked on it again and again. At last, the engine fired brokenly, rattled wildly and stopped. We unstrapped the bonnet, and there was no need to look any further; a hole had appeared in the side of the crankcase. Both Fiats were out of the race. Salamano had completed thirteen laps while I had covered only fifteen, a disappointing result after the hopes in which the event had begun.

The machines had found trouble because they had been driven too hard at the outset. Salamano was a road racing driver, accustomed to events in which all-out speed is impossible for very long, because of corners and bends. Finding himself in a Brooklands track race, where a car could be driven with the throttle wide open all the time, he had simply put his foot hard down and had kept it there.

When the Italian cars were pushed off the track, their bonnets were secured so that no one outside the team discovered the cause of their failure; I never learned what had happened in Salamano's engine. Immediately after the race, the cars were shipped back to Italy, and not until they reached Milan were the bonnets opened again.

This race brought home the fact that a high-speed car is a delicate instrument, requiring careful handling; I had appreciated this before the event, but the experience drove home the lesson. I learned, also, to rely upon my own opinion concerning the driving of a car and, afterwards, I wished that I had allowed Salamano to go ahead from the start. I might then have continued in the running after he fell out; on the other hand, he might have secured an unassailable lead, slowing up before trouble could develop.

It is never very much use trying to guess what might have happened, after a race is finished.

§3

The racing season came to an end with the Two Hundred Miles event, and I considered preparing the 350 h.p. Sunbeam for yet another attack on the world's record. I decided to have a special streamlined body built for the machine, and the car went up to the premises of Messrs. Boulton and Paul, in Norwich; they supervised wind-tunnel tests, decided upon the lines of the body, and started work.

The Dansk Klub asked me to make my next effort during their speed trials, in August, 1924, and it was for this that the special body was prepared. The work occupied some months, and when the racing season came round again I ran several times at Brooklands, using cars from the stable of racing machines which I had accumulated.

Early in June, the Sunbeam was ready and, although its frontal appearance was not much altered, the reconstructed body showed several new ideas; we put discs on the rear wheels, and these were so arranged that they formed a casing designed to help streamline the brake drums, while a fairing for the driver's head was placed behind the cockpit and moulded into a longer tail. Altogether, the car looked very promising, and when it had been returned to Povey Cross we tuned up the engine in readiness for another effort at Fanoe.

We were working on the car when I was asked to take it to Saltburn Sands and try for the record there, as I had done a year earlier. This seemed to offer a good opportunity for testing the new body before going to Denmark; on the other hand, I felt that the course did not offer the same opportunities as Fanoe Beach, and that it might be better to reserve the machine until August. I was on the point of refusing the invitation when I heard that Eldridge intended to compete at Saltburn with his huge Fiat, 'Mephistopheles', and that Parry Thomas was turning out with his Leyland, which he had also provided with a new streamlined body.

Both were to try for the record and, in view of this, I decided to compete, although with some misgivings. I was doubtful whether the runs would be electrically timed, but I understood that an official electrical apparatus was being employed. On arrival, I found that this consisted of a silk thread stretched across the course which, when broken by the passage of a car, actuated the timing apparatus. In theory, the idea worked well, but in practice the result left a lot to be desired.

It was a windy, stormy day, and the meeting opened with various sprint events, following which came attacks on world's records. I took the Sunbeam into the measured distance after a long, flying start, but the silk thread failed to break, although the car hit it at about 140 mph; the thread simply passed under the machine's wheels. An adjustment was made, but the same thing happened to Eldridge's Fiat, and it occurred again when Parry Thomas brought his big Leyland down the sands. On that first run, hand timing registered the Sunbeam's speed as being 145.26 mph.

I made a return run and, this time, the thread broke, but the electrical apparatus was not working properly. According to my revolution counter, the car touched 156 mph. By hand timing it registered 143.39 mph, and the electrical apparatus showed its speed as 138.08 mph.

All this was very unfortunate, because the Sunbeam was going really well. I felt that it was much faster than it had ever been before, while the new bodywork made the car far steadier than I had ever known it.

There was some delay while the officials checked their apparatus, and when it had been announced as in proper order, Eldridge made another run and clocked 135 mph. Parry Thomas then tried again, but, unfortunately for him, the thread slipped over the nose of the car when he entered the mile at above 130 mph and, whipping along the bonnet without breaking, caught his face. Watching his run, it was obvious that something had happened, because the machine swerved, and he cut out, slowing down. When he halted, his face was streaming with blood; he carried the scar left by the slender silk thread for the rest of his life.

So far, each run by any one of the big cars had been followed by a long delay, and I now grew very doubtful concerning the possibility of any satisfactory outcome to the afternoon's work. The weather was threatening and unpleasant, the sand was anything but good, and it seemed unlikely that the apparatus could be made to work sufficiently well to permit the claiming of official records. I had, in any case, actually broken the world's record, but my runs could not count.

Eldridge and I discussed matters with the timekeepers, and it was when we had agreed to make another attempt that a thunderstorm broke, driving away the spectators and leaving the beach almost deserted. Under a drizzle which followed the storm, with grey skies overhead and the tide creeping in, the whole scene appeared so desolate that I gave up all hope of being able to do anything, and instead of running again, packed up and made for the hotel where I had stayed overnight.

Sometime after I had arrived, an official came to me with the news that Eldridge had actually taken the world's record. Apparently he had driven his Fiat down the beach again, and had been timed at 134.81 mph. His speed was much below that of the Sunbeam, but it had been taken officially on the apparatus. At a dinner that evening, I was given a medal to commemorate the fact that, actually, I had set up fastest time of the day, while Eldridge was awarded a similar trophy for securing the record. He, however, was not altogether satisfied, since it was obvious that his figure would not be accepted by the Commission Sportive. He must have left Saltburn actuated by much the same feelings as myself on similar occasions, imbued with a determination to secure the record under official conditions. I know that I might never have continued my attempts, but for the way in which I was constantly thwarted.

In any case, Eldridge made another effort within the next three weeks, this time at Arpajon, about twenty miles from Paris, where there existed four miles of absolutely straight and perfectly surfaced road. This highway was specially fenced in on either side, and the car offered an amazing sight as it approached the measured kilometre in the centre of the stretch. The Fiat was painted dull red, catching the sunlight as it roared down the road, skidding and swerving from side to side and travelling at very little short of 150 mph.

The crowd bolted from the fencing, taking shelter behind the trees until the machine had passed. Eldridge held it safely over two similarly dangerous runs, achieving 146.8 mph only to have an objection lodged against him. According to the regulations, a car running for world's records must be fitted with a reverse gear, and the Fiat was without one. Eldridge was accordingly disqualified through a technical fault.

How he felt about this may be gathered from the fact that he and his mechanics worked solidly for the next two days and nights, fitting a reverse gear, following which they brought the machine back to the Arpajon road at dawn one morning. Gendarmes diverted all traffic for three hours, and Eldridge tried again.

He made several efforts, but carburation was bad, cutting down the machine's speed. During one attempt, he threw the tread from a rear tyre, but made his return without bothering to change the wheel. Finally, when he thought he had worked the car up to approximately the speed demonstrated during his disqualified efforts, and when the road had to be opened for normal traffic, it was discovered that spectators had unwittingly walked across the electrical timing strips, upsetting the recording of the apparatus. Then, when Eldridge was about to make one last run, the apparatus itself broke down.

§4

For all his very real endeavour, Eldridge was without reward, but these experiences with ineffective timing apparatus taught something to all drivers who were interested in the record. It was becoming obvious that such efforts had to be thoroughly organized, and that absolutely nothing must be left to chance, while the experience of the big Fiat at Arpajon made me the more determined that nothing should go wrong when I went to Fanoe.

In resumed correspondence with the Danish officials concerning the Fanoe Beach trials, I told them that I would run only if correct apparatus was provided, with responsible officials controlling it. They were ready to accept any suggestion which I made and, in the end, it was arranged that Colonel Lindsay Lloyd, then clerk of the course at Brooklands, should go to Fanoe Beach, accompanied by Mr E. V. Ebblewhite, the official Brooklands timekeeper, and that they should take with them apparatus belonging to the Royal Automobile Club, and which had been approved by the Commission Sportive. This made it certain that any speeds the Sunbeam might attain would receive official recognition.

The general public knew very little about the world's record at this date. It was not until speeds began to reach figures which would have been impossibly fantastic ten years earlier, that people other than those in motor racing circles demonstrated any interest. Even racing men showed little more than mild curiosity, but the fact that the world's record might become a real objective was suggested by the announcement of a special car constructed in Paris. I heard about it just before we took the 350 h.p. Sunbeam over to Fanoe.

This machine had been designed by an Italian engineer named Moglia, and financed by an Egyptian, Prince Djelaleddin. It had cost about £4,000 to build, and was actually the first machine ever erected solely for attempts on the measured mile. The engine was a straight eight, and developed about 400 h.p.; it was supercharged, because forced induction was then in its infancy, although provision was made for a 'blower'.

The car was known as the 'Djelmo', from a combination of the names of the two men principally concerned, and it was beautifully streamlined, with a blue body, a white radiator cowl and a red front axle – carrying out the French national colours. The intention was to run the machine on Daytona Beach, and it was expected to achieve 180 mph then regarded as a phenomenal speed. The 'Djelmo' was very unfortunate because, by the time that the machine had been brought to its proper tune, the record had been pushed so high that the car was outdated; it actually made only one attempt, and then not under the control of those who were responsible for its creation.

The existence of 'Djelmo', however, was an added spur to my mechanics and myself. The big Sunbeam was shipped over to Denmark, and we arrived at Fanoe three days before the trials were due to start. At the first opportunity I went down to look at the beach, finding it in very bad condition. Heavy storms had swept Fanoe Island during the preceding week, and the sand was scattered with broken boxes, sodden rags, masses of seaweed, lobster pots and heavy wreckage. It was the effect of this litter on the beach which really mattered, because the sea had formed holes around the larger objects.

The Dansk Klub officials agreed that the beach would have to be cleared, and that it would require several tides to bring the sand into smooth condition. They promised to attend to this, but not very much had been done when I brought the Sunbeam down for a test. The beach was still rough, and I could do no more than learn how the car was running. Before leaving England, we had carried the air intakes of the carburettors to a position behind the radiator, the idea being that, at speed, the rush of wind to the intakes would lend a mild supercharging effect. This scheme proved a failure, and we decided to remove the device.

We saw Karl Joerns on the sand with his big Opel, and I noticed that he was running without an exhaust pipe. There was no reason why the Sunbeam should be burdened with one and we removed ours on returning to the shed, cutting off the pipes from the exhaust ports so that they jutted as little stumps from the side of the bonnet. Probably the removal of the exhaust did not help the car very much, but any saving in weight might mean a little gain in speed.

On the morning before the car was to run I went down to look at the beach again. The actual course had been cleared, but its fringes were still littered with flotsam, and this was likely to make matters difficult if, by some mischance, the car should skid out of the marked area. A huge piece of wreckage remained in the middle of the course, sticking out of its attendant hole, and officials were putting red flags around this as a warning to competing drivers. During the afternoon, I had to skim the edge of this hole when the Sunbeam was moving at anything up to a hundred and forty miles an hour.

I believed that I should be able to keep the car in hand and, as long as the sand was reasonably smooth and clear, I did not worry. But I knew the chance always existed that something might go wrong and put the machine out of control; for this reason, I did not like the way in which the crowd would be allowed to come right up to the edge of the course. While I was driving, people would be standing within fifteen or twenty feet on either side of the car, and it would not require very much of a skid to send the machine into them.

In addition to all this, the timekeeper's box was set within about ten feet of the timing tape at the end of the measured mile. This wooden structure would be full of officials when I crossed the tape. As the Sunbeam would then be travelling just as fast as I could make the machine move, and as it had a tendency to run crabwise at maximum speed, there was a possibility that it might go sideways into the timing box, with disastrous consequences.

Plenty of steering room is absolutely essential for a machine travelling at very high speed, and I suggested to the officials that spectators should be placed further back, and that the timing box could be set in a less dangerous position. I can remember being somewhat insistent about this, and the whole thing has some importance in view of what followed.

When we brought the car down to the beach in the afternoon, I found the timing box still in its old position, and the spectators were crowded right up to the flags marking the course. Nothing at all had been done, and had I then known all that experience has since taught me, I should never have run the car until the arrangements had been altered. As it was, we took the machine down to the far end of the beach and made everything ready.

The majority of the spectators had, naturally, gathered near the timing box, and only a few were along the lower end of the mile. This was fortunate.

From the moment that the Sunbeam got under way, I knew that the car was in really fine condition; it gathered speed magnificently and entered the mile at well above 140 mph, still accelerating. I felt the machine start to 'crab', as it always did, and it was as I began to bring it straight that both tyres were torn from the rear-wheels.

They left the rim almost simultaneously. The off-side one flew clear, but the other slipped inside its wheel, crashing against the body and just missing my left elbow, which jutted over the side of the cockpit. The tyre then jammed against the brake-arm, ramming on the brakes.

Instantly the car pitched into a 140-mph skid, but by good luck it was this skid which threw the jammed tyre clear. It flew away from the wheel in one gigantic leap, releasing the brake and overtaking the off-side tyre.

All this happened in the fraction of a second and, with the brakes off, I was able to straighten out the car. While I did so, I could see both tyres rolling ahead, travelling almost side by side and looking like great hoops as they plunged towards the sea. The soft sand near the water's edge diverted them and, with the Sunbeam still skidding and sliding, the tyres shot across the front of the car in the direction of the sand dunes. When they hit rough ground they jumped high into the air again and again, finally vanishing from sight and eventually coming to rest without doing any damage.

By that time I had the car under control and slowing down. I drove on to the depot which the mechanics had established, and during that short journey I had plenty of time to appreciate the narrowness of my escape. If the tyre had caught my arm I should have been left with the task of trying to straighten the machine one-handed, which at that speed would have been impossible. Luckily, it did not hit me, and another piece of good fortune lay in the streamline fairing formed by the discs where they shrouded the brake drums. This projection had prevented the tyre locking the brake-arm completely; had it been able to do so, the Sunbeam must have spun in circles, running into soft sand and turning over.

The car itself had not suffered at all, and required only a wheel change before we could try for the record again, but we decided to use different tyres. Those which had been thrown off were known as 'beaded edge', and were held on to the wheel by security bolts; these bolts were fitted in order to prevent the tyre creeping around the wheelrim and tearing out the valve to the inner tube. If that happened, the tube would deflate, and the tyre would fly off the wheel. I had lost the two rear tyres because, owing to the way in which the car 'crabbed', a side-strain was set up, nipping the inner tubes and bursting them.

A second type of tyre existed, known as 'straightsided', and we had brought over a set, with their attendant wheels. These tyres could not be thrown off, and if they had security bolts, they could not creep and pull out the valve. We fitted two of them to the rear of the car, but it seemed safe to leave the beaded-edge tyres on the front wheels, because they were not subjected to the same strain. While Leech and Villa were working on this, I spoke to the officials, once again asking them to have the crowd moved further back.

If the rear tyres had come off where the spectators lined the course, some of the people must inevitably have been hurt. I had never seen tyres leave a car in the impressive way those two had flown from the Sunbeam; the velocity behind them had been very great indeed, while the tyres themselves were heavy. I told the officials this, but they felt certain that no real danger existed, when I remarked that if anything did happen, the blame must rest with them. All I could do was to make ready for another run.

We took the Sunbeam back to the starting point, which was

indicated by tall, slender poles carrying flags; quite a crowd had gathered here now, watching while the engine was warmed up. With everything in good trim, I sent the machine away and it gathered speed magnificently, travelling at 100 mph when I changed into top gear. Still accelerating, the car roared towards the start of the measured mile, down the length of which more thin flag-staffs were set, with ranks of spectators showing darkly between them, standing on either side of the cleared course.

Near the peak of the Sunbeam's speed, the car tried to 'crab', and I had as much as I could do to keep it straight. Aiming the machine between the narrow line of people as it came off the breadth of the empty sands was very like entering a narrow road, and when I sent it squarely across the centre of the timing tapes, I was wedged down in the cockpit, with my foot rammed hard on the throttle pedal so that it could not be shaken off by the bumps. The car was doing 140 mph then, increasing its speed as it dashed between the gradually thickening spectators on either side.

I picked out the banner at the end of the mile, whipping under the steady wind, and saw a big crowd just before the timing box. I was two hundred yards short of this, travelling at a genuine 150 mph, when the car suddenly lurched, its tail swinging outwards so that the machine headed straight towards the crowd, exactly as though some enormous force were thrusting it round.

For a moment I imagined that the steering gear had broken, then, as I instinctively tried to correct the skid, I saw something rolling and leaping beside the car. The machine was catching up and passing the blurred shape, and I thought that it was the off-side front wheel. I expected the Sunbeam to get completely out of hand, and it seemed inevitable that it must crash into the timing box. I was using all the strength I had in an effort to wrench the machine back on to its course, easing the throttle at the same time, and the car skidded for a hundred yards before I was able to bring it straight, when it crossed the timing tape safely and ran clear of the crowds.

The tyre that was to kill a young boy detaching from the wheel rim of the Sunbeam at Fanoe Beach.

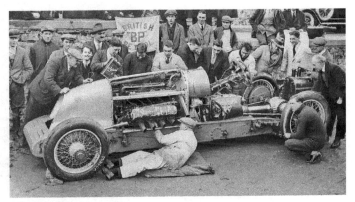

Napier 'Blue Bird' being worked on in 1927.

Campbell with Sir Henry 'Tim' Birkin: Courtesy of Brooklands Museum.

Front view of the tyre about to fly into the crowd with tragic consequences.

Record-breaking at Spread Eagle Climb driving a Sunbeam in 1922.

Campbell on race day in his Bugatti at Brooklands.

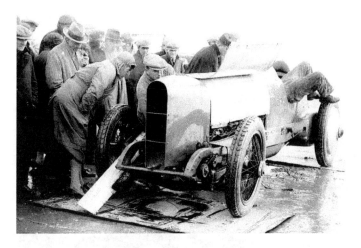

The 1924 350 HP Sunbeam record-breaking 'Blue Bird' at Pendine Sands. Campbell looks on anxiously as mechanics try to repair a fault prior to his attempt at the mile record.

On a return run on a wet Pendine Sands.

George Eyston at the 1926 Boulogne Grand Prix.

Campbell and Leo Villa with Napier 'Blue Bird' in 1928.

Campbell in Sunbeam 350 hp after test run on Pendine Sands.

It skidded again, then slowing down, I saw that it was not a wheel which had gone; the off-side front tyre had flown off. As I brought the machine to a stop, a crowd which waited at the end of the cleared course came running towards me, cheering and waving; they knew that something had happened, and were expressing relief, as people do when they see disaster averted. But I knew that the tyre must have been thrown into the packed spectators, and it seemed certain that some damage had been done.

Looking back, I saw people swarming across the course at the end of the measured mile, and it was not long before I learned that the tyre had struck a boy standing near the timing box. The boy was severely injured, and the mishap meant that my worst fears had been realized. Further record attempts were cancelled immediately, and the unfortunate boy lived only a short while.

We took the car back to the shed, all of us very upset at what had occurred. Later on, I learned that the car had been timed through the mile at 139.81 mph, in spite of the lost tyre; the record would have been sure if I had made a reverse run, although that was out of the question.

Presently I was shown two unusual photographs of the incident; one had been taken by a photographer kneeling on the sand, who had clicked his camera just as the car passed him. Until he developed his negative, he did not know that he had actually secured a picture of the car and of the tyre flying from it. The other photograph had been taken by a man standing a few yards from the timing tape; this picture showed the first photographer on the sand and the tyre spinning away from the car, while it also revealed the boy who was hit the fraction of a second later, just on the corner of the timing box. As had occurred at Brooklands, in 1912, when the Darracq crashed, the crowd remained immobile, with the exception of one man who stood near the boy. He had his arms upraised and was running from the tyre.

An inquiry followed the accident; the investigation lasted a long time, and it was something of an ordeal. It was not that I expected to be blamed, but I could appreciate the feelings of the boy's parents and felt inexpressibly sorry. This accident affected me all the more when I realized that, had the officials taken my advice, it would never have occurred. To have been the means of killing the little fellow was too terrible for words.

I believe we were all under some sort of arrest, and we were not allowed to leave the island until after the inquest, but the investigation resulted in complete exoneration for myself and my mechanics, after which we packed up and came home again. It took me a long time to forget the tragedy.

For the fourth time I had attempted to break the record, and still again I had failed. The circumstances surrounding the effort certainly became a warning to all promoters of similar events, while the tyre trouble made it quite clear that, for high-speed work, a new type of tyre should be used.

Dunlops began a thorough investigation of the whole tyre question, because they saw far enough ahead to realize that speeds would become still higher; finally, they evolved an altogether different type of tyre, which eliminated the faults even of the straight-sided type. But for what happened at Fanoe, their investigations might have been postponed for some time; coming when it did, the work achieved by Dunlops lent an added factor of safety, not only to record attempts, but to normal motoring, because the new type of rim was eventually used on all touring cars.

§ 5

When the Sunbeam rolled into its garage at Povey Cross, the car was still a failure, so far as I was concerned. It now had a special body and had been the subject of much expense and trouble, but still the machine had not gained the record. Soon after our return, we began to prepare for another effort. Although I had no idea of where the car could run, I was determined to try again before winter made further attempts impossible.

It was at this time that I discussed the Sunbeam with C. Amherst Villiers, a very clever designer who was interested in racing-type engines and, more particularly, in superchargers. We agreed that still more power could be gained from the Sunbeam by fitting special camshafts, the design of which he worked out. During these discussions, we also talked over the question of building a special car for world's record attempts, in much the same way as 'Djelmo' had been constructed.

Villiers pointed out that, whatever was done to the engine, the big Sunbeam must be already very close to the limit of its speed, and he considered that a car could be designed which would far surpass anything of which the Sunbeam was capable. The idea was most interesting, and we talked it over many times.

These conversations were the actual beginning of the 'Blue Birds' which were built later, but, at that time no active steps were taken towards the creation of this ideal car. We went ahead with our work on the Sunbeam, and the new camshafts were machined; when they arrived, we found that, by some unfortunate error, they had been cut in such a way that everything was reversed and the shafts were useless. They had to be scrapped.

Before this happened, however, I had been looking for a course on which to run the car. A venue was desirable in England, but since it was not permissible to use a road, as at Arpajon, I had to try and find a suitable beach course. There were sands at Southport and at Saltburn, but I wondered if it might be possible to find an even better stretch of coast. I made inquiries, and was told of a long, flat beach in Carmarthenshire, near the village of Pendine. It proved to be a very remote spot, with hardly more than a score of houses in the village, but the sands were as good as anything I had ever seen.

When the tide was out, it left a very broad stretch some seven miles long, and the surface was quite firm except that, under certain conditions, a stationary car had a tendency to sink in the sand; at speed, however, there was no danger of this. It seemed to me that the beach was ideal, not only because of the good surface but because there would be no risk of big crowds of spectators.

I communicated with the Royal Automobile Club, and they agreed to send their apparatus to Pendine. I took the car up there in the middle of September, 1924, and when the timing officials arrived they went to infinite trouble to make certain that their apparatus was in proper order, finally measuring a course and marking it with absolute accuracy.

These precautions occupied some time, and we had to wait a few days before everything was ready. Bad weather developed, and rough seas threw a great deal of wreckage on the beach. Conditions were not good when on Wednesday, September 24th, 1924, we decided to make a start. The local people gave us friendly assistance in placing the marking flags and clearing away the wood and fish baskets, litter and seaweed from the beach as the tide ran out.

When everything was ready, I took the Sunbeam down the course, making several runs, but although the car behaved well it could not develop maximum speed. Patches of soft sand dragged on the tyres, and gusts of wind materially reduced the machine's pace. The weather improved overnight, and in the morning the wind had steadied, but it had become very strong, blowing at between thirty and forty miles an hour. The sand was much firmer.

As the tide went out we ran the Sunbeam on to strips of metal sheeting to prevent it sinking, waiting while our local assistants completed the work of placing flags along the course, and the timing apparatus was made ready. The tide was still receding when I received the word to go.

When I sent the Sunbeam away I knew that, for the first time in any attempt that I had ever made, everything was in excellent order. There could be no doubt about the timing, there was no hampering crowd, and the car had only to beat the wet conditions of the sand and the heavy wind. On my first run, however, I discovered that there were long, soft patches down the course, and when the car reached them the effect was exactly as if a brake had been applied. The Sunbeam slowed, but the moment the wheels reached a firmer surface the car shot forward again.

The way in which the machine checked was visible to those who watched, and was still more apparent to myself. Each time I had to hold the car up against a possible skid, trying at the same time to avoid wheel spin. In spite of all this, the Sunbeam was very fast, working up speed with each successive run. In all, I covered the course three or four times in each direction, going flat out every time.

Holding that big machine was exhausting work. It was necessary to grip the wheel as tightly as possible, virtually hanging on to it with all my strength, while the mental tension of constantly guarding against skids, combined with the physical strain, provided a limiting factor to the number of runs I could accomplish.

I finally brought the car back on to its metal sheets, then interviewed the timekeepers. They were smiling, and the little crowd which had gathered began to cheer. The mean speed of my two fastest runs proved to be 146.16 mph – definitely the world's record.

In that lonely spot, and at the fifth attempt, we had succeeded; there was no doubt about the figures, and official confirmation by the Commission Sportive was merely a matter of form. The occasion seemed to warrant some sort of celebration, and everyone who had assisted was invited to a dance at the only hotel in Pendine. The local people helped to make the affair an occasion which would live for a long time in the memory of the villagers.

Next day we left for home, elated and satisfied. The record was soon confirmed, marking the 350 h.p. Sunbeam as officially the fastest car in the world. I had achieved my ambition, but now there developed an aspect of the matter which I had not considered before. In actually setting up the record there had been no plaudits, no excitement, and no particular honour existed. But we had tried for it for so long, and had been disappointed so many times that now I held the record I found that I wanted to keep it.

At the same time, another objective seemed within easy reach – the round figure of 150 mph. It was not much faster than the speed we had already achieved, but it represented two and a half miles a minute, and that captured the imagination. I thought it would be an honour worth having if I could be the first man in the world to travel at this pace on land.

I knew that Parry Thomas wanted to try for the record, 'Djelmo' was then being tuned up, and I heard that the Sunbeam people were thinking of building a special car for Segrave. If these machines turned out, and if they were successful in surpassing the speed I had recorded, they were almost certain to push the figure up to 150 mph.

I decided to try and achieve 150 mph, and I talked it over with Amherst Villiers. We agreed that the special car we had discussed before I went to Pendine would certainly be more successful than the big Sunbeam, and I suggested that he should get out designs for this machine.

We thought this new 'car' would be ready to run during the next season. As events proved, two and a half years were to pass before the machine ever turned a wheel under its own power.

§6

During the winter of 1924, we worked on plans for the new 'Blue Bird', and one of the first questions concerned the speed for which the car should be designed. It soon became evident that the car would cost a great deal of money and, in that case, it would be foolish to aim at only 150 mph. It seemed wise to plan a machine which would lift the record to a very high figure. We looked past 150 mph to the next round figure, and our ideas jumped from two and a half miles a minute to three miles a minute –180 mph.

Such speed appeared enormous, but Amherst Villiers believed that a car could be built that would reach it. We went into matters thoroughly, and agreed upon a chassis fitted with a 450 h.p.

Napier-Lion aero engine. It was further decided not to make use of any existing parts or material, but to have everything made solely for this car. The machine was to be hand-built throughout, erected carefully and with no margin left for error.

When this had been determined, initial drawings were made and work was commenced. Villiers attended to the detail work when the racing season of 1925 came round, and I began to run again at Brooklands. All this time there was at the back of my mind memory of how the Fiats had run in the Two Hundred Miles race the year before, and I conceived the idea of building a special car for the 1925 event. I actually began work on this, planning a 1,500-c.c. machine with a supercharged engine; the car was partly constructed, but later I abandoned it in order to concentrate on the new 'Blue Bird'.

During the early part of the season, I expected to hear that 'Djelmo' had been made ready, or that Parry Thomas was trying for the record, but nothing happened. The big Sunbeam remained idle in its garage until June when, just to give the car a run, I took it up to Skegness sands and drove in some trials, and a month later I entered it in more speed trials held on Pendine Sands, which had now been recognized as an excellent setting for such events.

I made no attempt on the record, but the fact that the car was regarded as the fastest in the world created interest amongst the spectators. Also, driving the Sunbeam brought back my earlier wish to reach 150 mph. It had become evident that the special machine which we were building would certainly not be ready to run that season, because construction was very slow, and it seemed reasonable to make just one more effort with the big Sunbeam.

I decided upon this, and the necessary arrangements were soon completed. To my surprise, a number of newspaper correspondents arrived at Pendine, where the runs were to be made, on July 21st, 1925. Apparently the fact that we were to attempt to lift the record to 150 mph interested the general public, because it sounded so much faster than 146.16 mph. For the first time, people other than motoring enthusiasts gathered to watch, and a scattered crowd was lined up along the sand dunes when we brought the car out.

A stretch of sand six miles long was selected, allowing two and a half miles on either side of the measured distance. The beach had a number of shallow depressions, and there were wet areas, but the sand was fairly firm and weather conditions were as good as any under which the car had ever run. Short flag posts lined the course, and a banner was stretched as an additional guide above the electrical timing tapes.

Before bringing the car to Pendine we had tuned the engine very carefully, fitting new pistons and raising the compression, while a cushion was clamped to the back of the driving seat so that I could press against this and make certain that my foot was hard down on the throttle pedal.

When I started it was with some sensation of adventure. Even though I knew that the difference between the speed I had already attained and what I hoped to do was only fractional, I could not but feel that I was actually trying to do something no one else had ever done before. This may have helped to register very clear impressions during the half-dozen runs which I made.

My chief concern, after I had changed into top gear, was to keep my foot on the throttle pedal, so that I had to brace myself in the seat all the time, to be sure that the throttle was held wide open.

The sensation of speed was more intense than anything that I had ever known, and it was quite unaccompanied by any attendant indication of danger. The marking flags seemed to be rushing to meet me instead of, as at more moderate speeds, appearing to be approached by the car. The beach raced away beneath the front of the machine, while spray and sand was flung high in rear, almost hiding the car from those who watched.

The pressure on my eardrums was very heavy, and the air, droning past, felt solid, very much as water feels when one is coming to the surface after a dive. I was conscious of some bumps, and little patches of soft sand occasionally checked the car slightly; when this happened, the wet sand slashed upwards from the front wheels, so that my goggles were obscured at the end of each run, making vision difficult.

The whole run was quite free from trouble, and I set up a new record for the mile with 150.766 mph; the kilometre worked out at 150.869 mph, while the greatest speed which the car attained on any run was 152.833 mph.

All this was, actually, only a little better than the car's earlier achievement, but it had an altogether unexpected effect. To my surprise, the run was reported in newspapers all over the country, achieving headlines in the London evening papers, while the dailies carried photographs and accounts the following morning. It was not the matter of a brief paragraph here and there, but was reported everywhere.

Overnight, attempts on the world's land-speed record became news. Apparently it was not ordinary news, but something suddenly discovered to be exciting. From that moment, it became evident that these attempts were passing beyond the sphere of ordinary motor racing, and were presenting interest to people who had never driven a motor car.

The effect was stimulating – and it meant that the record would never be allowed to remain where it was. Real activity followed amongst those drivers who had, as it were, been standing on the edge of making record attempts. The Sunbeam firm at once became energetic about the new car they had planned for Segrave to drive. Parry Thomas, who had been consistently taking class records with his Leyland during the year, decided that this car was not big enough, and he bought the 'Higham Special' which Count Louis Zborowski had built.

It must be confessed, that as a result of this, I became even more reluctant to lose the record that I had won, and I was committed to defending it, because the 'Blue Bird' was now well under way. Progress was still slow, however, and I gave up everything in order to concentrate upon the car and to help tackle certain problems which had arisen.

The question of transmission gave us a good deal of trouble, but this was solved by Villa. He mentioned that he knew an Italian engineer named Joseph Maina, who was working on a new type of epicyclic gearbox, which, if it proved all its designer hoped, would be capable of dealing with the tremendous stresses set up at the speed the car was being built to reach.

Villa introduced Maina and he explained his new gearbox. It was apparent, from the outset, that it was precisely the thing needed for the car, so Maina joined the little group of experts already busy on the machine.

The car was still far from completion when Parry Thomas took the Higham Special up to Pendine and attacked the new record. He had renamed the car, calling it 'Babs', and unfortunately for him the beach was in a bad state; he could not make use of the machine's speed, and was forced to abandon his attempt.

This brought the 1925 season to a close, with the record still standing to my credit. Towards the end of the year, the 'Blue Bird' reached the stage when it appeared that only detail work was required to complete the machine. It seemed that I should be able to take the car out early in the following summer, and there was no need for me to remain by the machine during the final construction. Accordingly, I accepted an opportunity to realize a boyhood dream. I joined an expedition bound for a Pacific island in search of hidden pirate treasure.

THE FIFTH CHAPTER

§ I

THERE IS CONSIDERABLE DIFFERENCE BETWEEN driving racing cars and seeking buried treasure, but from the days when, as a boy, I read Rider Haggard's books, anything with a hint of romance appealed to me greatly. It was this which eventually brought me to Cocos Island, in the Pacific ocean, where gold and precious stones to the value of over twelve million pounds are supposed to be secreted. That island, I firmly believe, is haunted, and the expedition brought an experience which I shall never forget.

The enterprise was partly the result of a story told me by the captain of a liner, while I was on a pleasure cruise to Madeira in 1924. According to him, the crew of a Spanish treasure ship had mutinied in 1763, and had hidden thirty million pounds worth of silver above high-water mark on one of the Salvage Islands, which lie between Madeira and the Canaries. Incidentally, they had buried their dead captain above the treasure.

While the liner was in port at Madeira, a yacht named *Adventuress* steamed into the harbour; it was owned by Kenelm Lee Guinness, who had been first to break records with the 350 h.p. Sunbeam. During a visit to his yacht, I related what I had heard from the captain. This tale captured the imagination of Lee Guinness and his companions to so great an extent that they proposed seeking the treasure without delay, suggesting that I should join them and start immediately for the Salvage Isles.

I accepted the invitation and we went ashore, buying picks and shovels, sailing the following morning. The Islands proved to be deserted and rocky, set in a coastline so rough that, owing to heavy seas, we found it impossible to land, and we lay off the island all night. Next day, a gale broke, and as the bad weather looked as if it would last for some time, we agreed to return to England, fit out a proper expedition, and come back to the islands at the first opportunity.

This plan was never carried out because, on returning home, we investigated the captain's story, finally coming to the conclusion that there was very little to confirm the authenticity of the yarn, or, alternatively, if ever the silver had been buried there, it had long since been discovered and carried away.

In the course of these inquiries, I stumbled upon the story of Cocos Island; this was inevitable, because this Pacific isle has acted as a magnet for treasure hunters for the past two hundred years. I collected proofs that treasure was still hidden there, consisting of gold bars, jewels and a gold image of the Virgin, stolen from the cathedral at Lima, the capital of Peru, and secreted by Captain Thompson, a merchant skipper who had turned pirate.

Additional to this, and as an added incentive, two other treasure hoards are hidden on Cocos. One had been placed there by Captain Edward Davis in about 1690, and the other had belonged to Benito Bonito, known in his day as 'Bonito of the Bloody Sword'.

I gathered all the information that I could, and talked it over with Lee Guinness. As a return trip to the Salvage Islands appeared useless, he was quite ready to go to Cocos. He had, however, contracted to sell his yacht, and had to deliver the vessel to its new owner by the end of March, 1926. At this date, near the end of 1925, there was just time to sail for Cocos and return, and we made immediate arrangements for departure, collecting a crew and equipment.

Before this, we had tried various devices designed to locate hidden gold, most of them working on the same principle as that employed in water divining. None of them were successful, but three days before we were due to sail, we were put into possession of information provided by an old map and a letter, which completed our clues to the location of at least one portion of the treasure.

The relics had once been the property of a man who had befriended two sailors; these men had not only landed on the island, but had actually seen part of the treasure in a cave. One of the two was a seaman named Keating, and evidence suggests that he murdered his companion, leaving his bones with the treasure.

Lee Guinness' yacht was a converted Liverpool pilot boat, very comfortable and seaworthy. She had a cruising range of nine thousand miles, and we carried a crew of twelve, with a ship's mascot in the form of a little mongrel dog named Pinto; he had been born aboard ship, and was exceedingly sharp, full of real courage. We sailed by way of Madeira, where we bought an old, cockleshell of a boat for use in ferrying between the yacht and Cocos, then we headed across the Atlantic, passing the edge of the Sargasso Sea, that strange area of floating weed which is supposed to be the graveyard of many ancient ships. Eventually we reached Jamaica, afterwards using the Panama Canal to reach the Pacific, now headed directly for Cocos.

The voyage was pleasant, marked throughout by those incidents which invariably accompany a trip of this sort. We were all eager to reach Cocos, and the island was sighted at dawn, on February 17th, 1926. It had a skyline of harsh peaks, and its coast is formed by ugly rocks. Watching, as we steamed nearer, I remembered that the ancient Incas had once lived here, and that the island had seen piracy and murder; morning mist made the whole place seem eerie and unreal.

It was unsafe to take the yacht too close in-shore, and we dropped anchor three quarters of a mile out to sea, in what was charted as Chatham Bay. The boat bought at Madeira was lowered and six of us crowded into it, taking spades, compasses and revolvers. The boat was so heavily laden that its gunwale rode barely three inches out of the water, and we had hardly left the yacht when, at the side of the boat, we saw a green-black shape rolling over and the head of a shark appeared, snapping at one of the oars.

The fish was longer than our boat, and it followed us all the way to the shore, two others accompanying it. I sat ready to use a revolver if one of them attacked, as seemed likely, but they sheered off when we reached shallow water, and soon we were ashore.

According to our clues, we had to locate a creek and, pausing at high-water mark, pace towards the north, which should bring us facing a slab of rock, at one side of which was a hole. If a bar was inserted in this, the front of the rock could be levered away, opening the entrance to the cave in which the treasure was hidden.

Before leaving the yacht, we had used field glasses to search the coastline, and had picked out what we thought was the creek. We made for this at once, located highwater mark, and began pace towards the north. The ground was thick with undergrowth and cluttered with boulders, and when we came to the end of the prescribed distance there was nothing at all to be seen, which gave us our first hint that finding the treasure would not be the comparatively easy matter that it had appeared before we sailed.

We split up into two parties, seeking other creeks and finding none, after which I decided to try and climb up to the cliffs at the foot of Observation Hill, a rocky height which rose at one side of the bay. From these cliffs, it seemed possible to command some view of the island.

I started off, accompanied by one of the crew. We had to use bush knives to hack a way through the thick undergrowth, and at the end of three hours we had made very little progress. It was then growing dark, and we were obliged to return to the yacht, where we held a long consultation. It was decided that Chatham Bay was not the one referred to in the clue, which gave the bay no name, and that our search should commence from Wafer Bay, farther along the coast.

Next morning, we sailed round to this, and found that here the jungle grew right down to the high-water mark, the ground beyond rising very steeply. When we landed, we discovered the ruins of huts which other treasure seekers had erected during similar expeditions. They stood derelict in little clearings, and on the bark of a tall palm tree showed the names of ships which had visited the island during the past century, many of them manned by crews attracted, like ourselves, by the store of pirate treasure.

We made use of our clues again, but they led us nowhere. The only spot which looked as if it might be the rock we had to find was well inland, on the hillside; although it was not anywhere near the bearings given by the clues, we decided to investigate. We had to cut our way through the undergrowth, where creepers hung like a network from the trees or trailed along the ground, continually tripping us.

The heat was intense, insects plagued us, and the jungle was so dense that we had to keep to our route by compass bearings. We had climbed for some time when we suddenly discovered three twelve-foot pits which, we decided, must have been dug by earlier treasure seekers. We struggled on, and when we reached the top of the height we were scaling we found the big rock still beyond us, appearing just as far away as it had seemed from the shore.

We learned that this was typical of Cocos; impossible to judge distance. One was continually lured on, only to be disappointed in the end. We retraced our steps, returning to the yacht at nightfall for another conference. This decided us that we should find nothing at Wafer Bay, so we returned to the spot at which we had originally landed.

So far, we had spent two days on Cocos, just time enough to make us realize that the island would not readily yield its secret. Sharks guarded its coastline, and its shores were thick with jungle; its hills lent an uncanny air of solitude to the interior, while the heat-haze made all objectives as elusive as mirages. But we had come to find the treasure, and were determined not to admit defeat so easily.

§2

On deck next morning, and while the shore party was preparing to land, I used field glasses to study Observation Hill. The summit seemed quite flat, and I picked out what appeared to be a zigzag path running upwards from the coast at the side of the bay. It looked a simple matter to follow this path and gain the crest of the height.

Before investigating it, however, we decided to examine a rock which rose from the sea some distance off-shore, and which might be the one that we had to find. We learned nothing from it, however, and one of the party cut his foot on a sea shell while clambering up the rock; this put him out of action for a fortnight, and was the first mishap which Cocos Island brought us. There were others to follow; it is a fact that ill fortune attends all who search for treasure on that island.

That afternoon, I felt the reaction from the excitement and anticipation of the two previous days, and I was tired out after the exertions of the morning. I rested aboard the yacht, thinking things over, and came to the conclusion that much time could be saved if we camped ashore. Landing from the boat was not easy, and the state of the tide suggested that it would grow more difficult as the days passed.

It was arranged that I should camp ashore accompanied by two volunteers from the crew, Elmer and Packham. They were fine fellows, with exactly the right temperament and stamina for the job, and next morning we landed with a tent, picks and shovels, dynamite and crowbars and rations, and accompanied by our little dog, Pinto.

Before making camp we investigated the zigzag path which I

had seen the day before. We had to cut a way through the jungle to reach it, and it proved to be a beaten track which, however, was soon lost because it was badly overgrown; it was easy to discern from a distance, but hard to follow when one was actually on it. We were forced to turn back, but on our way we found the bed of a dried-up creek. It was just such a creek which formed our first clue in the search, although pacing out distances from highwater mark led us nowhere.

We hunted round for some time, but discovered nothing, and returned to the beach. We had to cut away overhanging branches and clear jungle undergrowth before we could pitch the tent, and in levelling the ground we disturbed two ants' nests. In order to clear the insects away, we lit big fires; the ants appeared completely fireproof, because they were still there when we kicked away the ashes, although the stones beneath were almost red-hot.

After making camp we decided again to try and trace the path to the top of Observation Hill. I felt certain that this track was a relic either of the pirates or of the Incas, and if we could reach its summit it seemed likely that we should be able to see a good deal more than we could from the beach. We followed our former route, and after some searching managed to pick up the path beyond the point where we had first lost it. We followed it, hacking our way through creepers and grasses all the time, often losing the path but always discovering it again, until we were two-thirds of the way up the hill.

We were unable to go farther, because the sun was getting low and Cocos was no place to wander about in after dark. When we began the return journey, we found the wind in our faces, and it occurred to me that if we could set fire to the dry grasses, the wind would carry the flames up the hill, burning away the undergrowth and making access to the summit quite easy next day.

I set a match to the grass and we hurried down the hill. Flames spread rapidly, but the fire burned downwards as well as upwards, so that we soon found ourselves pursued by a blaze which travelled with amazing swiftness. We almost fell down the hillside in our efforts to escape, reaching the shore just at sunset; the whole hillside above us was then one mass of roaring flames which flared to the sky and, as the darkness deepened, lit everything with a blood-red glare. The heat was so intense that stones and boulders cracked, exploding like gunshots.

We watched the blaze reach the top of the hill and spread down to the shore. Luckily for us, the undergrowth here was too green to burn, otherwise we should have been forced off the island. The fire raged until midnight, scaring everything on the island. Birds wheeled screaming in the darkness; in the jungle wild pigs stampeded, and the wings of disturbed insects created a humming sound which formed a background to all other noises.

We turned in when we were sure that the fire offered no danger to the camp, and next morning I was amazed to discover that it had actually done very little damage. Patches of grass were burned out where the ground was very steep, but only the drier parts of the jungle had been set alight although, in the darkness, it had seemed as if everything was aflame. We soon saw that the fire had not helped us at all, while the zigzag track had not been cleared in the least. We followed it once again and this time managed to reach the summit; the fire had swept over the plateau, burning grass here and there in little patches, but not clearing the ground as we had hoped.

We now had a complete view of our side of the island, and could actually discern sharks swimming above patches of sand in the bay, but we found it impossible to see far inland. Other hills and ridges were just high enough to cut off the interior; with the strange perversity of Cocos, all our work in getting to the summit of Observation Hill availed us nothing, just as the fire had proved useless.

The clue which concerned the creek on the beach had led us nowhere, but there still remained the possibility of locating one of the other treasures. There was a great slab of rock about a mile inland, and in its face was a cleft in which treasure had been hidden. I hoped to sight this rock from the summit of the hill, and this was a reason for our continued efforts to climb it. There was no sign of the rock, but at the back of the plateau was a low hill, and we struggled to the top of this. Once again, our view was blocked by other hills, all tantalizingly low, yet just high enough to make it impossible to see anything.

Climbing down again, we began a search of the plateau, and suddenly discovered a path. It was very faint and very old and was much overgrown, but it led us to a narrow waterfall which dropped for a hundred feet down the side of the hill. Obviously this had formed a water supply for the buccaneers, and it was all we discovered just then.

It was now noon, and in making our way back to the camp, we struck off the zigzag path that we had followed, soon to find ourselves on very dangerous ground. The hillside was steep and, although trees grew here and facilitated our descent, their roots had so little hold that the trees were liable to be torn out if any weight was put on them. In addition, there were defiles and precipitous gulleys, their edges shrouded by creepers and under-growth; an incautious step invited a dangerous fall.

Once back in the camp, we made a midday meal, then began another search of the rocks in the undergrowth about the bay, looking for the cave. For three days we worked ceaselessly, scrap-ing moss and ferns from huge rocks in the hillside, searching in all directions. The heat was so great that our shorts and shirts were soaked from perspiration, while our faces and arms became livid as the result of insect bites. Eventually we located a huge rock completely covered with ferns and moss; when we cleaned this, we found a crack stretching around three sides of the rock, appearing to form part of a door.

This was exactly what we were looking for, and our excitement was intense as we worked on, hoping to reveal a fourth fissure and the hole in which a crowbar could be inserted to lever out the face of the rock. We felt certain that we had discovered the hiding place of the treasure, but there was no opening, and there was no fourth crack. For all that, we drilled holes all round the rock, plugged them with dynamite, and then exploded it.

The top of the rock was blown completely away, and it proved to be solid right through. We used dynamite to blast other rocks which seemed as if they might cover the entrance to caves, but without result.

Lee Guinness now said that we could remain only three days more on the island, because he had to return to England in time to hand the yacht over to its new owner. After this, accompanied by Elmer and Packham, I began a systematic search of small areas of the interior. We had met no dangerous animals, there were no snakes, and we had seen only a few wild pigs, and we went armed only with our now much-blunted bush knives when we started this new phase of our search. It was when we were investigating a ledge, beyond the outer edge of which was a sheer drop of three hundred feet, that a wild boar emerged on another shelf immediately above.

He was a huge brute, with red-rimmed eyes and ugly tusks, kicking loose stones down as he ran along his ledge, seeking some way to attack us. Pinto had accompanied us, and the little mongrel was so full of courage that he tried to leap upwards and attack the boar; had he succeeded, the animal must have plunged down on us, when we should have been bowled off the ledge and over the precipice.

No animal is so blindly vicious as a wild boar, and we were quite helpless. Blunt bush knives would have been useless against him, as I realized while I held Pinto back.

It looked as though we were completely trapped, because the boar was working himself into a rage, while Pinto was barking furiously. Then, seeking some way to get at us, the boar vanished momentarily into the undergrowth, and we took the chance to bolt, scrambling along the ledge and running down the hill, not breathing freely until we were back in camp.

The happening may serve to illustrate the courage of Pinto,

and this gives point to what occurred that night, after we had spent the afternoon in further fruitless search. Tired out, we turned in, but I found sleep difficult because of stings and insect bites. The two men were sound asleep and I was dozing, with Pinto curled up at my side, when the dog gave a wild howl and suddenly darted to the tent flap.

He paused there, barking wildly. By the light from the fire burning outside, I saw that the dog was trembling. I grabbed my revolver, shouting to the men, who were already rousing. The three of us crouched together, staring outside while Pinto remained at our feet, quivering and yapping, obviously beside himself from terror, and actually foaming at the mouth.

He became quiet for a moment, standing with his fangs bared, while he gazed into the surrounding darkness, and I have never known so uncanny a feeling as that which came to me then. There was nothing to be seen, yet I knew that someone or something stood there in the fringe of the surrounding jungle.

We could hear nothing, but something had frightened and alarmed the dog, something of which the courageous animal was so much afraid that he would not venture beyond the tent. The two men seemed to be affected by the same terror, and neither would move.

The dog began to bark madly once again, and I stepped to the opening of the tent. Pinto's hair was standing on end, his eyes bulging as he stared straight ahead, and, with the revolver cocked, I went forward, following the direction that he indicated. I stopped at the edge of the undergrowth, conscious of a sensation that I was very close to something which was dangerous and unnaturally evil.

I stepped into the bushes, my finger on the trigger. If it had been a wild boar that had disturbed us, the creature would have attacked me on the instant, but I heard no sound other than Pinto's barking, which now began to die down to a series of terrified yelps.

I searched all around the camp. There was no physical indication of any intruder and yet, when I returned to the front of the tent, I felt that whatever had come there had now gone away.

I comforted Pinto, but there was little sleep for anyone until dawn came, and never had daylight been so welcome. I searched the undergrowth once more, but I still found no trace of man or animal. We started work again, after a sketchy breakfast, making our way up Observation Hill, because I felt certain that this formed a central point for the activities of the pirates. We soon found ourselves on the summit once more, and, prowling about here, discovered the foundations of what had once been a stone-built house. Searching around this, I came across an old, rusted ringbolt, which looked as if it might have come from a sea chest.

This was the first object that we had discovered on Cocos which formed any sort of relic, and it was succeeded by our finding a faint path which ran from the house to the edge of the plateau. It brought us to a ledge on the steep hillside, and here was a stone-built shelter which must once have been a look-out. On the flagstones inside lay a spade; the wood crumbled to dust when we picked it up, while the spade itself was so rusty that flakes fell away at a touch. It was peculiarly shaped, and must have been very old.

Our spirits rose at these discoveries, and we hunted on along the ledge. Trees sheltered the far end, and here we found a stretch of ground which, obviously, had been dug up; the trees had kept the earth dry, and evident traces of digging remained. The spot was a remote one, and a likely place for treasure, and we started to dig at once, using our bush knives and our hands, burrowing furiously. We had cleared only a few feet when sunset came. Night always seemed to arrive on Cocos at the most inconvenient moment, and we were forced to abandon our work and hurry back to camp while daylight remained.

Although no clue that we possessed suggested that treasure was hidden on this ledge, it seemed a very likely spot. Elmer and

Packham were as excited about it as myself, and we spent the evening wondering what we should find when we returned with spades in the morning. We were some time in getting to sleep, then, just about midnight, I was once again roused by Pinto's wild barking. I jumped up, and the uncanny experience of the night before was repeated.

There was something in the darkness outside the tent, something which terrified Pinto and gave us all a sense of being in the presence of the supernatural. I searched around the camp as I had done before, but had discovered nothing at all when I returned to the tent.

What it was that spied upon us from the darkness I do not know, but I have since wondered if it were possible that a scout from the supposed descendants of the Incas, said to live in the interior, had come down to look at us. Yet, being spied upon by some remnant of a long-gone civilization could hardly have scared Pinto as much, or have produced so real a sensation of fear as that which came to my companions and myself.

We did not sleep again, and at daybreak we were off, loaded with tools and ropes, and taking food with us. The sun came up while we were still struggling towards the ledge, and the heat was so great that we were exhausted by the time we had hauled our heavy burdens to our objective. We rested a while, then began a methodical digging of the area we had started upon the afternoon before.

When we had dug down for four or five feet, we came upon a very old sheet of corrugated iron, so brittle that it broke when the shovels touched it. The earth above the sheeting was loose, but it was hard-packed below, and had never been touched by a spade. We dug deeper, however, then gave it up and began to trench along the ledge. We uncovered sheet after sheet of rusted corrugated iron, but we found nothing else by midday.

We had worked so hard that we were all dizzy and shaky from fatigue, and after we had made a meal, both men fell asleep. I dozed for an hour and commenced digging again. Elmer wakened and joined me, while Packham slept on. We found more soft ground on another ledge lower down the side of the hill, and investigation disclosed still more of the corrugated iron. Here and there we dug below it until we reached solid rock, but at no time could we find any hint of why the iron sheeting had been buried. Elmer and I gave it up after a while, and sat down to rest.

The ledges were now scarred by holes and trenches, and mounds of earth showed everywhere. We were very tired and had nothing to show except a ringbolt and the head of a rusted spade. Presently Elmer wandered off by himself, going down the hill, and after a few minutes I heard him shout, then came the sound of rocks falling through the undergrowth. I ran in the direction of the noise, scrambling and sliding downwards, expecting that he had fallen into some rocky gully. Instead, I broke through bushes on to a ledge which was paved with cobblestones, and which seemed as if it had been hacked out of the side of the hill. On the inside of the ledge was a rampart of big cobbles, placed as if they were designed to block the entrance of a cave. Elmer was tearing at these, pulling them out and flinging them over the edge of the ledge, so that they rolled down the hill and formed the crashing sound which I had heard.

It appeared obvious that the stones must hide a cave, and we attacked them furiously. The terrace was quite artificial, and could have been constructed only at the expense of much labour, because the ledge was well below the top of the hill, and every stone which paved it must have been carried down.

Packham had been awakened by the uproar, and he came to help. The deeper we dug into the stones, the bigger they became until, when we had tunnelled into these boulders to a depth of eight or nine feet, they were so large that even our crowbar could not exert sufficient leverage to shift them.

We had to pause, all three of us gasping and thirsty. We had no water, we were soaked from perspiration, now so tired that we could hardly stand. Such reserve of energy as we had possessed

after our exertions of the morning had been expended in the furious attack on the boulders. In any case, we could do no more,
because the sun began to set.

We rested for a few minutes, then packed up, starting down the
hillside, so tired that we lurched as we scrambled along, constantly
dropping the tools that we carried. We struggled on, slipping and
sliding, each making the best pace that he could, separated by the
rough going. I reached camp first, and Packham arrived shortly
afterwards. We had both taken a drink before it occurred to us
that Elmer was a long time in joining us, although we imagined
that he must be resting on the way down.

A quarter of an hour passed, and it was beginning to get dark
when I started back to look for Elmer. At that moment, he stag-
gered out of the undergrowth, dragging his shovels; he was deathly
pale, and his face was twisted from pain.

He had fallen two hundred feet down a rocky slope, wrenching
the muscles and ligaments of one leg so badly that it was as much
as he had been able to do to drag himself along. In spite of his
pain, he had crawled back up the slope, recovering the shovels
and then, burdened with them, had made his way on to the camp.

The dinghy came from the yacht while Packham and I were doing
what we could for him, and we carried him to the boat, which came
with a message that our time was up, and that the return voyage
to England had to begin before dawn. The treasure hunt ended
when we struck camp and rowed with Elmer back to the ship.

I looked back at the shore as we went. The island was cloaked
by darkness, and the black lines of trees along the beach gradually
faded. That was the last I saw of Cocos Island, and we sailed away
in the night. Our expedition had been futile, visited by the misfortune which comes to everyone who seeks the treasure which, I am
still convinced, is hidden there. Others have been to Cocos since to
be baffled by the peculiar mystery of the island and by its haunted
atmosphere, and to meet with the bad luck which came to us.

When I came on deck next day, Cocos Island was no more

than a memory and, as the voyage drew on, I turned my thoughts towards the car which was still being built at home, and which I hoped would raise the land-speed record still higher. But, in the months which followed, it seemed as if the ill luck of Cocos Island remained with me.

THE SIXTH CHAPTER

§1

WHILE I WAS AT COCOS, the car with which Segrave was to attack the world's records was completed, and it proved to be quite a small machine compared with the cars which it rivalled. It had a twelve-cylinder, supercharged engine, which gave about 300 h.p., and this was very high in view of the fact that the engine was only 3,977 c.c., less than a quarter the size of the 350 h.p. Sunbeam.

I had known for a long time that this car was being built, and fully appreciated that Segrave was more likely to break the record, because he was the finest of British racing drivers. He had won the French Grand Prix, and had performed remarkably well in other Continental road-racing events; he had scored many victories at Brooklands and had achieved his successes because his whole attention was concentrated upon motor racing. He had started without any real financial support, winning fame and popularity solely through his own ability. Later on, he was to become still more appreciated.

His new car was known as the 'Four-litre Sunbeam', because of its engine size, and he took the machine to Southport Sands. His first effort was unsuccessful, but he made another attempt a few days before I had returned to England and lifted the world's record to 152.336 mph. He attained this speed over the kilometre, and would have taken the mile record as well had he not been troubled by misfiring after he had cleared the kilometre during his fastest run.

It might, perhaps, be as well to make clear the difference between kilometre and mile records. The kilometre is, of course, a shorter distance and, for this reason, higher speeds may sometimes be achieved over it than over the mile. Usually, a car is timed over both distances during a single run, one electrical timing tape being set at the start of the measured distance, another at the end of the kilometre, and a third at the finish of the mile. Under this arrangement, a car making an attack on the mile automatically registers a speed for the kilometre as well. The machine may, if it is still accelerating, prove faster through the mile than through the kilometre. On the other hand, if it crosses the first tape at the limit of its pace, the speed may fall away all through the distance; the kilometre will then be covered in faster time than the mile, because the car is slowing down.

In Segrave's case, his car eased up after the kilometre so that, although he secured the actual land-speed record with 152.336 mph, I still held the record for the mile with 150.766 mph. This, however, was merely a technical point; the fact remained that Segrave had travelled faster than any living man, but I hoped that he would hold the title only temporarily. I expected to regain the record without difficulty when 'Blue Bird' was completed.

I was disappointed to find the car still far from ready. It was being erected at the Robin Hood Engineering Works, near Kingston, where K.L.G. sparking plugs are made. These plugs had been designed by Kenelm Lee Guinness, whose initials provide their name, and he had been good enough to loan us part of one of his workshops for 'Blue Bird'. It was convenient to keep it at a place near London, obviating long journeys with material which would have been necessary had the car been in my own garage at Povey Cross.

I found that the back axle and the gearbox were delaying completion. These two components were largely experimental; parts were scrapped over and over again, while Maina found it necessary to alter the design of the gearbox to a considerable extent. Every time a new part had to be machined, replacing some discarded item, work was held up, but it was vital that construction should not be rushed. It was better to continue steadily, overcoming each difficulty as it appeared, and so make certain that, when the car was ready, it would do all that we hoped.

I was not greatly concerned about the delay. We now knew what Segrave's car could do, and it appeared unlikely that his four-litre could be made to travel much faster. I guessed that, now he held the record, Segrave would rest content until someone made an attack on his figures. I assumed that, eventually, I should be able to take 'Blue Bird' out and lift the speed to somewhere near three miles a minute; it was of no real consequence whether this was done at the beginning of the racing season or at the end of it. Accordingly, I made a return to Brooklands racing, and it was during practice for a meeting in mid-April that an accident occurred, and I experienced an escape as strange as it was providential.

Villa and I were practising with a Bugatti which I had bought, and were trying to improve the carburation. We covered several laps, stopping frequently to lift the bonnet and make further adjustments. The bonnet was secured by two straps, following the usual racing practice, one strap being at the front and the other at the back. The alterations to the carburettor setting brought some improvement, and after our last halt the car began to run very well indeed.

I watched the revolution counter while I drove. I could see the dial through the spokes of the steering wheel and, at the same time, I was able to look along the bonnet and keep the track in view. Driving like this, we came off the banking to the railway straight at about 110 mph when, without the least warning, the bonnet lifted, forced upward by the wind; the strap at the front had not been properly secured after our last stop, and the buckle had slipped, while the second strap acted like a hinge.

The bonnet rose and slammed completely over, catching me squarely on the head. The cover was a heavy one, backed by what amounted to a hundred miles an hour gale, and the force with which it struck was very great. The result was a complete blackout for myself.

I was knocked unconscious. That was inevitable, and it is necessary to stress this in order to explain what followed. Although I was knocked out, insensibility lasted only for the fraction of a second. I came round again at once, and in my mind was one clear thought that I must keep the car straight and bring it to a halt.

When my eyes opened, the track ahead was masked by the bonnet, which was jammed over my head. I was aware of Villa trying desperately to drag the engine cover clear, but he found this impossible, because of the wind and the weight of the metal. Then, jammed down in the seat, I saw a narrow opening directly in front, formed where the bonnet curved from its hinge. It was no more than a slit, but it gave me a constricted view of the track; I was able to keep the car straight, while I slammed on the brakes as hard as I could.

I felt the Bugatti slow right down, then I lapsed into unconsciousness again and the car pitched into a short skid which brought it to a halt broadside across the track; I learned this afterwards.

When I came round, I had been carried into the paddock for attention, and I had not the least recollection of anything that had occurred, except that we had come down to Brooklands that morning. I had not the most remote idea of taking out the Bugatti, or of being struck by the bonnet. As the days went by, however, recollection returned a little at a time until, at the end of some eight weeks, I had regained a complete and most vivid memory of every detail of the accident.

The point of the incident lies in the extraordinary way in which I came round after first being stunned, returning to consciousness for the few seconds necessary to stop the car, then collapsing again. By all the laws that we know, my mechanic and I should have been killed that day, just as I ought to have crashed disastrously when I lost two wheels from the old Darracq, or when I turned to glide back to France during the war, with the sea and shoreline obscured by mist and the engine of my plane dead.

On each of those occasions I had a providential escape, and it was this third experience which made me a fatalist. It is my belief that no man dies before his time, and I have never been able to explain these things. I know only that they actually happened.

§2

Within a fortnight of the mishap at Brooklands, something occurred which was very disconcerting, as far as our hopes about the unfinished 'Blue Bird' were concerned. My attention had been concentrated upon Segrave and his four litre Sunbeam, and I had half forgotten about Parry Thomas. Suddenly, I heard that he was at Pendine, and that his big car, 'Babs', was the centre of a really well-organized attempt upon the new record.

The preparations were the most complete that had ever been made. There were fifty assistants in his *équipe*, using ten cars and half a dozen motorcycles and four or five lorries, while the car was transported to Pendine on a big six-wheeled wagon. A medical man was in attendance, R.A.C. officials were on the scene, and there was a squad of police to help maintain order; public interest had grown to such an extent that a big crowd was expected on the lonely beach.

Everything was carried through in the most efficient manner possible, the course being marked out by flags strung between posts driven into the sand, while tall masts were placed in buried oil drums to indicate the start and finish of the measured distance.

On April 27th, 1926, Parry Thomas lifted the land speed record from Segrave's figure of 152 mph to the astonishing speed of 168 mph for the flying mile, actually registering 172 mph during one of the runs. Not satisfied with this, he took 'Babs' out again next day, and set up 171.09 mph for the flying kilometre, and 170.6 mph for the mile.

Unexpectedly, he had raised the land-speed record until it was within measurable distance of the 180 mph for which I was aiming, and which we had regarded as a phenomenal figure. His success was a real blow to our hopes, because 'Blue Bird' had been designed for a maximum speed of only three miles a minute; Thomas had almost achieved this and our car had not yet turned a wheel.

This was not all, however. After his effort, Thomas said that 'Babs' was quite capable of 180 mph, and that he would make an effort to reach this speed after overhauling the machine. He was not a man who boasted, and I knew that he meant what he said.

If he succeeded, 'Blue Bird' would be useless. The only thing we could do was to push on the completion of the machine, hoping that we should at least have the chance of making a run before Thomas brought 'Babs' out again.

The new record had a natural reaction upon Segrave; like myself, having once held the record, he was reluctant to lose it. He wanted an opportunity to regain it and, following a discussion with Louis Coatalen, it was decided to build a far more powerful Sunbeam car. They began to design a machine calculated to raise the land-speed in much the same way as we had intended that 'Blue Bird' should do. When we began work on our car, the record stood at 150 mph, and we wanted to do 180 mph. The figure was now 170 mph, and the new Sunbeam was to aim at over 200 mph.

Only a year earlier, I should have regarded two hundred miles an hour as impracticable but, in view of what had been accomplished, it was now more than merely possible. It was obvious that the contemplated car would take a long time to build, and that 'Blue Bird' would be out before this Sunbeam was finished; if only we could get our machine running before Thomas appeared again, I might recover the record, although the chances were that I should hold it only for a short time.

Thomas either remained content with the laurels he had gained, or else he found that preparing 'Babs' for three miles a minute was a greater task than he had anticipated. This gave us a respite, and we continued to work hard over 'Blue Bird' while, as an interlude to worrying about the car, I entered for the first Grand Prix race ever held in England.

This was the British Grand Prix, run off at Brooklands on August Bank Holiday, 1926. It was to be a real, Continental-type race, and in order to make the event as much like a road-race as possible, artificial turns were built from sandbanks, forming a bend halfway down the finishing straight, and another where the straight ran on to the outer circuit; the section of the track round the Members' Hill was eliminated. The race proved to be the finest that Brooklands had ever seen, and was certainly the most important in which I had yet driven.

At first I intended using the Bugatti which had been involved in the mishap during April, but an opportunity came to acquire a 1,493 c.c. straight-eight supercharged car of the same *marque*, which was altogether faster. Bugattis of this type had won every Continental race in which they had been entered and, since I should be running against a group of the finest road-racing drivers in the world, the machine at least offered a possibility that I might finish well up in the event.

I did not receive the car until the day before the race, and it was the first of this model ever to appear in England. It was raining when the machine arrived at the track, and the only practice I had was eight or ten laps over wet concrete. The engine had been tuned at the Bugatti works, and was in excellent fettle, but the brakes were not good. After I left the track, I drove the car down to Povey Cross, accompanied by a Bugatti mechanic who had been sent to help with the car. This man, with Villa and another mechanic, worked throughout the night, relining and adjusting the brakes, and they had not been to sleep at all when we returned to Brooklands next morning.

I determined to do my best in the race, if only to back up their

good work, but the odds were against me because, quite apart
from the calibre of the drivers, competing cars were the finest
machines available.

Three Delages had come over from France, one of which was
handled by Robert Benoist. Louis Wagner was at the wheel of
another; he had been racing cars for over twenty years, his experience being wider than that of any man living. Segrave was driving
a Talbot, and a second car of this *marque* had Albert Divo at the
wheel; he was an ex-racing mechanic who, at that time, was rapidly
building up a fine reputation for driving skill. Captain G. E. T.
Eyston was on an Aston-Martin, and Parry Thomas had entered
a car of his own design, but was unable to bring the machine to
good tune in time and withdrew. In all, nine cars came to the line,
which seems a very small field, but they were the fastest of their
type, backed by factory organization.

The event was run over a distance of a hundred and ten laps
two hundred and eighty-seven miles, while the artificial bends
made it necessary to corner eight hundred and eighty times before
the race was done; a fairly good test of endurance.

It was a glorious afternoon when the machines lined up, at two
o'clock, and the scene at Brooklands was a little unusual because a
bridge had been built across the finishing straight between the two
bends. It was supported by metal piers, the bases of which were
guarded by sandbanks, and, during the race, cars had to shoot
between these piers. It was safe enough, because machines could
come only one at a time out of the bend just before the bridge.

When the flag dropped, Divo was first away, but my Bugatti
kept almost level with him until we reached the railway straight,
then Segrave swung past me, with Benoist on a Delage following
him, and I clung to fourth position. The opening lap was fast, all
the cars keeping close together then, as we came off the Byfleet
banking on to the finishing straight, the front axle broke on a
Talbot driven by Moriceau.

The machine was travelling at nearly two miles a minute

when this happened, and was close to the tail of my Bugatti. I had a glimpse the Talbot skidding across the track behind me, and, luckily, it stopped just at the edge of the concrete, Moriceau climbing out unhurt.

The leading cars were all close together when we reached the first bend, and Segrave entered it just ahead of my Bugatti, flame streaking from his exhaust pipe as he took the turn. I clung to him and to Benoist for another lap, then the Bugatti began to misfire, and I stopped to change plugs. The delay dropped me back to sixth place, and I had hardly restarted when Divo lost the lead and Segrave went in front, with Benoist hounding him on a Delage.

Now and again, I saw something of the 'dog fight' which followed between these two. Segrave was faster on the straights, but the Delage gained on all bends. Both appeared to be driving flat out, setting a pace which made every man behind them use full throttle, and I found myself in a race quite different in character from anything that I had previously known.

The standard of driving was very high, altogether keen and finished. I was forced to concentrate on every movement, and there was never a moment in which I could relax. Since my attention was given to the car, incidents which occurred during the race were viewed only momentarily, and one happening was very curious.

I saw Wagner's Delage halted in front of its depot, and the driver was jumping with both feet into a shallow tub filled with water, which splashed over the concrete around. This seemed extraordinary, and, afterwards, I learned that the Delage exhaust pipe had been carried too near the pedals, and Wagner's feet had been scorched. He was simply trying to cool them. All the Delage drivers had this experience, and, in one case, the pipe set fire to the bodywork of the car.

Later, I saw Segrave pulling up for a wheel change, and he got away just as I came round again. For a few laps we rode together, struggling to be first at the corner each time we raced down the straight. Usually I managed to beat him, only for him to come level and pass me when we reached the Byfleet banking. He got away from the Bugatti after half a dozen laps, but presently I caught him up at the first bend; his brakes had jammed, stalling his engine.

Benoist had taken the lead by this time, and I received a signal that I had come up into third place. At the end of sixty laps, I pulled in to refuel and change the rear wheels, and this delay dropped me back to sixth position once again.

I drove the Bugatti hard after that, taking signals every few laps from a control station which we had set up along the railway straight. It is more usual for a driver to be signalled from his pit, but a separate arrangement is better because it relieves the depot of congestion, while there is less risk of the signals being masked by other cars. I knew, all through the race, my exact position, my lap speeds, and who was in front of the Bugatti.

Following my stop for fuel, I was signalled that Segrave lay immediately ahead, and I picked up a place when I caught him. He had slowed down, and I next saw him at his pit, with smoke and flames coming from his car. He restarted, but was forced to retire after one or two laps more.

Presently I saw another cloud of smoke at the pits. Benoist's Delage had stopped, and men were squirting the contents of fire extinguishers on the engine. He had gone on when, not long afterwards, I saw another Delage halted, and I knew that all these checks meant regained ground for the Bugatti. The Delage drivers were forced in because the heat from their exhaust pipes made the cockpits like ovens, and reserve drivers had to carry on with the cars.

The control station was now signalling me to go faster, and I had my foot on the throttle pedal when Divo's Talbot retired. I took third place then, but I was still given the 'Faster!' signal. I could not answer it, because the Bugatti was gradually slowing; the car had been driven hard, and the pace was beginning to tell. I could see from the scoreboard that Wagner was now in the lead, with Benoist second, and I knew that the signals which I received meant that I had a chance to win, if only the car would show more speed.

'Faster' was showing each time I came round, and I put all my weight on the throttle pedal, ramming it down until it seemed likely that it would be forced through the bottom of the car, but still the Bugatti would not pick up speed, although it was relatively very fast.

It was near the end of the race when I saw Benoist in front. I chased him for two or three laps, closing down all the time, then overtook and passed him. The control station told me that I had taken second position, and they still asked me to go faster. The car was not capable of it, and I was tiring. The jolting of the machine on the rough surface and the corners which came with every lap were telling, and although I still drove with the throttle opened at its limit, the Bugatti's speed steadily fell away. I could not catch the car that lay in front, and, in the end, Wagner's Delage came home first, the Bugatti was second, and Benoist arrived third. These were the only machines to finish the race.

My Bugatti had given no trouble, and it was encouraging to have taken second place against men who could be classed as Grand Prix drivers, and the success of the car persuaded me to enter it for a road race held over a circuit outside Boulogne, just a month later.

§3

After the British Grand Prix, the Bugatti went back to the London depot for an overhaul, when it was found that most of the valve springs had broken. It was this that had slowed the car during the latter half of the race. Had they not given way, there was a reasonable chance that the machine might have won, which promised well for the Boulogne event.

This meeting included speed trials, a hill climb, an event under the official title of Grand Prix International des Voitures Légères,

and another road race called the Georges Boillot Cup. I entered
my supercharged Bugatti for the first of the two races, and in the
same event Captain George Eyston entered the 'unblown' Bugatti
which I had originally owned, and which I sold to him after buying
the supercharged model. Segrave was down to drive a Talbot, and
he also took over his record-breaking four-litre Sunbeam, which
he was to run in the speed trials.

These were held along a four-mile stretch of quite ordinary
road which, although straight, switch backed for part of its length.
In these trials, Segrave showed his unusual courage and skill,
breaking all records for the meeting by taking the Sunbeam over
those four miles at just above 140 mph. His performance was the
finest feat of driving yet accomplished, because the speed was only
twelve miles an hour below his former world's record; it was carried out on a quite normal road and was sustained for four miles.

The excitement created by his achievement was followed by
tragedy during the hill climb in the afternoon. One of the entrants
was a popular Brooklands driver named R. B. Howey, and fast cars
had already attacked the hill when he started on his white Ballot.
The course was a mile in length, set along a road running up Mont
Lambert, just outside the town. It had three bends, the first two of
which Howey took in splendid style. He entered the third bend
at what must have been 75 mph, and the machine was well under
control until it slid a little too far outwards. The tail struck a low
bank at the side of the road, the impact pitching the machine into
a four-wheel skid that sent it broadside. Howey tried to straighten
but, all the time, the machine was sliding down the camber to
the outside of the bend. Here the tail caught a car parked just off
the course; the Ballot bounced off, crashed headlong into a tree
and turned over. There was no hope for poor Howey. The smash
injured a gendarme and four spectators, and the rest of the events
for that day were cancelled.

All this occurred on the Thursday before the race in which I
had entered, and during practice my Bugatti appeared to be the

Foresti works on the engine of 'Djelmo' prior to a run at Pendine Sands.

Giulio Foresti's horrific crash in 'Djelmo' in November 1927.

Sir Henry Segrave at Brooklands in September 1925.

The Napier 'Blue Bird' at Daytona Beach in 1928.

Malcolm Campbell with the 1933 'Blue Bird' in which he set a world land speed record of 272.46 mph at Daytona, Florida in 1933.

Campbell before another record attempt at Pendine sands.

Campbell entertains the onlookers.

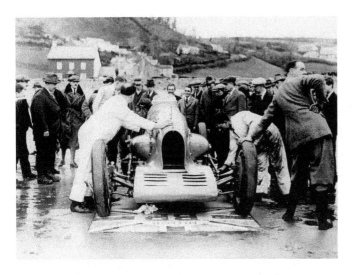

'Blue Bird' getting some attention during a 1927 record attempt.

Malcolm Campbell in the 350HP on Saltburn Beach in June 1922.

Parry Thomas driving 'Babs' at speed at Pendine in April 1926.

fastest machine in the event; the car was in excellent tune, and on Friday I took it round the circuit, not intending to travel fast. Villa was with me, and we were doing about eighty miles an hour along a straight when there was a sudden blow-back from the carburettor, accompanied by a clatter from the engine.

I pulled up and we lifted the bonnet, to find a connecting rod sticking out through the side of the crankcase; one glance was enough to tell us that the car would not run, because repairs could not possibly be made in time. I was so keen to race that I endeavoured to buy another car, solely that I might take part in this, my first real road event. There was no machine available, and I had to remain a spectator, while the race was actually won by Eyston, who drove the Bugatti which I had sold him only a few weeks earlier.

§4

Before leaving England for Boulogne, I had entered the Bugatti in the 1926 Two Hundred Miles race, which was dated a fortnight after the French event, and my first concern was to get the car repaired. When I made inquiries it appeared as though it would be quite impossible to deliver the machine to the Bugatti works soon enough for the extensive attention required to bring it into racing trim. These works were at Molsheim, over four hundred miles away, and sending the car by train would involve a delay of more than a week.

The only solution was to take the car by road. Immediately after the Boulogne meeting, we hitched the Bugatti behind a Mercedes, and a friend towed me all across northern France. This was as uncomfortable a journey as I have ever undertaken, because the Bugatti had very hard springs and we were obliged to go slowly, so that I felt every bump on the road, while the unguarded wheels smothered me with mire from the highway.

We arrived safely, and the Bugatti mechanics began work

immediately. Ettore Bugatti – the creator of the cars, and whom I knew well – did everything to give the machine a chance of success in the Brooklands race, even sending it back to England by one of his most trusted men.

The car, however, was very unfortunate. It arrived about four days before the date of the race, and on my first practice run the engine 'blew up', holes appearing in the crowns of four pistons. Men worked day and night fitting new valves, new pistons, and a cylinder block, and I tried the machine out again.

From then until the day of the race we had endless trouble with carburation and plugs, finding it hard to discover a suitable fuel for the machine. By virtue of night and day work, the machine was sent to the line in what appeared to be good trim, but the race had hardly begun before the Bugatti was visited by a series of small and annoying troubles.

First an oil pipe broke under the dashboard, necessitating a stop to secure it. Then the welding on the exhaust flanges broke away, and Villa burned his hands badly in trying to make a repair. Sparking plugs constantly burned out, and other difficulties arose until, after fifty laps, the machine was forced out of the race.

This ended my racing for the season. We pushed on with 'Blue Bird', and it was now that I heard stories of unceasing work at the Sunbeam factory on Segrave's new car. Details concerning it had been released, and it was known that the machine was to have two 500 h.p. engines, placed one behind the other, with the driver seated between them. This gave the car a total of 1,000 h.p., making it the biggest machine ever built. With so much power backed by the clever and excellent design of which Louis Coatalen and his colleagues were capable, it was almost certain that the 1,000 h.p. Sunbeam would come very close to the speed they had set out to reach.

Thomas had let 'Babs' stand idle all through the summer, but he was beginning work again, and so far as I knew, Segrave might attack with the Sunbeam at any time. If either he or Thomas turned out before I was ready, the probability was that they would set the record out of reach of 'Blue Bird' altogether. It was then actually two years since the car had first been contemplated, and we had been actively engaged in construction for eighteen months. We could not allow all that time and all our endeavour to be completely wasted, as it must have been if either of these other cars went for the record before we were ready. The only way of avoiding this was to work harder on the job than ever before, and this we did.

We brought the machine down to Povey Cross, and increased the number of mechanics. We were now able to live with 'Blue Bird', as it were, and the men worked in shifts, so that, during every hour in the twenty-four, mechanics were busy on the car.

§5

As November slipped by, we engaged still more mechanics, until there were no less than eleven on the job. They slept in huts behind the house, and we used an old granary as a mess room.

Everything at home was completely disorganized. Work overflowed from the garage and was carried on in the house. The panel beaters, who came down to build the body, worked mostly at night, hammering their aluminium sheets and creating a continuous din, which made sleep difficult for those off duty.

We worked solidly until Christmas Eve, stopped for twenty-four hours, and restarted on Boxing Day. The car was completed just before the end of the year, and we spent New Year's Day in preparing the car.

The machine was quite definitely 'home made.' It had been constructed according to the ideas of Amherst Villiers and Maina, and myself, backed by the advice of interested experts. The panel beaters had fashioned beautiful, streamlined bodywork, which was painted blue, with a small Union Jack on either side of the scuttle. There was a fairing for my head, behind the cockpit, from which the tail dropped to a wedge, and the car was about fifteen feet in length. The front wheels were wider apart than the rear; the latter had a track of 4 feet 9 inches, while the front track was 5¼ inches. Such an arrangement was common to very fast cars, and it made for stability at speed.

The brake-drums had been turned out of solid steel, and we had introduced a hand-lever for the clutch, in addition to the ordinary pedal. The lever was designed completely to free the engine from the new epicyclic gearbox; unless this were done when the car was stationary, the machine would start moving under the drag of the gearbox.

Our initial attempt on the record was planned for Sunday, January 2nd, 1927. There was an unpleasant drizzle during the whole of the night before, and at dawn the beach lay under heavy mist. Presently the mist cleared, revealing a desolate stretch of silent and empty sand.

At nine o'clock, as the tide receded, assistants marked the course with flags. Rain was falling then, and it continued until nearly eleven o'clock, when we made ready to bring the car out. The sands were very sloppy and wet, thin mist still hung about, and the prospect was altogether bleak and chill. We had waited so long, however, that I was anxious to make the attempt whatever the conditions.

The car was rolled on to boards placed at the starting point, and these prevented the wheels sinking in the sand. We started the engine and everything was warmed up. I was told that all the timing arrangements were in order, and, at last, I revved up the engine and let in the clutch.

The car lurched a couple of feet forward, then the engine stalled. I made a second attempt, but the gearbox was faulty, and again the engine stopped.

We spent an hour making adjustments, then I tried once again. This time the car jerked forward, lunged off the boards and rolled on to the sand, halting with the engine dead. At once the machine began to sink in the soft, wet surface. I climbed out of the cockpit, while the mechanics called to the driver of a lorry which stood near. It was rolled on to the boards and, using a tow rope, we tried to drag 'Blue Bird' back. In the minute or so which had elapsed, the machine had already sunk until the sand was above its tyres, which meant that it was six inches deep in the sand. The lorry was powerless to drag the car out; each jerk on the tow rope only forced the wheels deeper, while the efforts of the lorry kicked the boards in all directions.

We shouted to the spectators who had gathered, and they crowded around the car until fifty or sixty pairs of hands were thrusting on the machine. By this time, 'Blue Bird' had sunk until the frame was touching the sand, and our first attempt to move the car failed. The situation was desperate, as the tide was fast coming in; we heaved again in unison and, reluctantly, the wheels rolled out of the troughs they had formed, mechanics thrust planks under them, and we were able to run the machine safely back to the boards.

Owing to the state of the tide, nothing more could be done. At the end of more than two years' work, we found ourselves pushing the machine back to its shed, conscious that it had not yet run under its own power. We spent the remainder of the day, and nearly all night, in making adjustments to the gearbox, bringing the car out again at noon next day.

'Blue Bird' roused willingly enough and, this time, mechanics and helpers gathered at the tail of the car, pushing it off the boards when I started. The machine went away with a roar, greatly to my relief. I had no intention of doing more than try the car out on that first run, but I reached 135 mph through the mile, making one or two unpleasant discoveries. The front wheels sent sand streaming at my windscreen and, shooting past its edge, this stung my face, smothering my goggles. Wind, rushing through the radiator and past the engine, blew under the leather jacket which I was wearing, chilling me to the bone and actually lifting me upwards in my seat. When I reached the far end of the course and applied the brakes, I found them almost completely ineffective, and there were some moments when I feared that I should be unable to stop the machine.

Fortunately, 'Blue Bird' slowed before running in to really bad sand, and I was able to turn round for a run in the reverse direction. I opened up once more and soon came to the conclusion that the engine was not giving off enough power. I returned at about the same speed, then decided to make a second practice run in order to confirm my first impressions. This time, however, the car stopped after covering fifty yards, the gearbox giving trouble once again. The machine immediately began to sink, but there were plenty of people to help roll the car to safety, and amongst those who ran over was Parry Thomas. He had come up to watch the attempt, and he was the first to commiserate with us upon our hard luck when we decided to abandon the effort for the time being, and to take 'Blue Bird' back to Povey Cross for the attention which was obviously needed.

That afternoon the car was put on its lorry, and the long journey of nearly three hundred miles begun. Before leaving, I made provisional arrangements to return in a fortnight's time, a date which coincided with the spring tides, which always left a broader and smoother beach than at ordinary times. I was anxious to make a second effort with as little delay as possible, because Thomas told me that he was working hard on 'Babs' and would soon be coming up to Pendine himself.

I consulted the makers of the Napier-Lion engine concerning an increase of the power output. When the engine had first been tested, it had given off 525 h.p., and they had then suggested that it would be impossible for me to make use of all this power. I had been doubtful about this at the time, because I knew that even slight increases of speed demanded greatly enhanced power. It had been proved, roughly, that 300 h.p. was required for 140 mph, and 500 h.p. was necessary to reach 170 mph. I considered that

600 h.p. would be needed to reach 180 mph, the speed at which we were aiming. These figures are not accurate, but they are sufficient to suggest how more power was needed, most of which would be absorbed in overcoming wind resistance.

High compression pistons were fitted, and special tuning brought the output of the Napier-Lion engine to 635 h.p. The gearbox was overhauled, and we investigated the brake trouble. We found that, although the drums had been milled from solid steel, they were too thin, and flexed when the brakes were applied at speed. We scrapped the drums and fitted others which were heavier.

The newspapers were filled with the story of that unfortunate first attempt, and it created more interest than any previous record effort. It was generally known that Thomas was getting ready and that Segrave's 1,000 h.p. Sunbeam was nearing completion, and it was obvious that the record had become a straight fight between the three of us. Thomas and I believed it to be inevitable that Segrave would best whatever figure either of us might achieve, although a chance did exist that his car might not be so fast as was anticipated. Segrave's car was being designed to do 200 mph, and many new factors might become apparent when he attempted this speed.

Quite apart from all this, we had begun work with the idea of reaching three miles a minute, and I was determined to achieve this if the car made it possible. I did not worry about what Parry Thomas or Segrave might do afterwards. Everything seemed well with the machine when we started for Pendine again on January 16th. A crowd was waiting in the village to see the car, and the local people were only too ready to render any possible assistance. They agreed to help in marking out the course for practice runs, because I intended to spend three or four days with the machine before making an official attack. I hoped, during these runs, to test the car thoroughly and to drive quite fast, and I was a little concerned about the effectiveness of the new brakes. Accordingly,

I arranged for assistance to be available at both ends of the course so that, if I found myself unable to stop the car, I could run it into the sea; the water would act as a brake, and helpers would be handy to drag the machine back to the sand.

We arrived at Pendine late on Sunday afternoon, and we took the machine out on Tuesday morning. The weather was very poor; an exceedingly strong wind was blowing, while sheets of water lay over the course. However, we intended to run, whatever the conditions, and it was not long before 'Blue Bird' got going. Clutch and gearbox proved satisfactory, but I handled the car carefully during the first dash down the course.

The machine flung a great stream of water and sand behind, and the wind kept catching the car. There was one point when it produced a nasty skid which brought 'Blue Bird' almost sideways. The drag of the wet sand was something that could be felt, and on some patches the car slid badly, but no wind now came into the cockpit, because we had an extended shield on the side of the body to deflect the wind, while the brakes proved to be moderately efficient.

In view of the state of the beach, the car ran very well. I held it at a steady 140 mph over two runs, then decided to try the course again and, this time, to open up a little more, although there was no chance of bringing 'Blue Bird' to its maximum speed. I went twice through the mile at 160 mph and, as everything seemed satisfactory, we made arrangements for an official effort two days later.

I had observed a very wet stretch of sand which, upon investigation, proved to be half a mile in length. The water came from a stream which ran through the dunes, and it seemed feasible to try and dam this little river. This was done next day and, as a result, there was promise of a much drier course during the record attempts.

Wind continued high, and it was squally on the morning when 'Blue Bird' was to come out again. There were alternate showers of hail and snow which, fortunately, passed off towards midday, when the course was marked and everything was made ready once again. The sun began to shine weakly, gleaming on thin stretches of seawater which lay over the sand.

'Blue Bird' was rolled out, the engine was warmed up, and I sent the car off. Immediately after the start, the sand was anything but good. The drag was tremendous, and I felt that the car would never touch real speed. I kept my foot hard down, but I was not going fast enough to change into top gear until I was barely half a mile from the timing tape which marked the measured distance. The sand was firmer here, and I rammed the throttle well open as I approached the tape.

Until then, the car had been sliding and slithering on the treacherous surface, but now it steadied, accelerating splendidly, and was still gathering speed when I entered the mile. I drove through it, and at once made a return run, but I felt that the beach would not allow the car to reach record-breaking speed. When I stopped after that first double run, I doubted whether I had recorded even 150 mph, and I was surprised to be officially informed that the speed was 166.38 mph for the double run and that, with the wind, I had done 171.3 mph.

This was so near the record that it was very encouraging, and I tried again. On the second run, the car did not do so well, and when I heard the figures, barely 160 mph, I grew a little desperate. I decided to make one more effort. This time, the car got away to a really grand start, and I entered the mile with the revolution counter showing well above 180 mph. I knew that, even allowing for wheel spin, I must beat the record and that it required only a similarly fast return to secure it. The car held its pace through the mile, but slithered a little on the bad sand just clear of the distance. I stopped safely and turned, starting back again, determined to drive the machine flat out every yard of the way, knowing that it would have to be my last effort of the day, because the tide was now coming in.

'Blue Bird' gathered speed, and I steered to avoid wheel marks made on previous runs. The machine was travelling at over 170 mph when, just before reaching the mile, the wheels ran on to the patch of soft sand across which I had skidded a little earlier. At once, the car shot sideways, sliding off the course, chopping down one of the flag posts as it went. It skidded for half a mile, while I struggled to keep it under control, with the tail pitching first one way and then the other, sand shooting outwards in great streams from the wheels. By the time I brought 'Blue Bird' back to the course, the car had slowed right down. The skid spoiled the run completely, and I drove on to the end of the beach, wondering what damage had been done.

We found that the broken post had made a great dent in the side of the bonnet, and one of the rear tyres had been badly gashed. With the tide coming in, there was no chance of trying again. 'Blue Bird' returned to its shed, and we examined the figures set up during the day. When the times of the car's two fastest runs were checked, it was found that we had been within one-third of a second of breaking the record which Parry Thomas had set up.

It was bad luck to come so near success, and still to fail, although the speed would not have been the 180 mph at which we were aiming. It was still more unfortunate that, owing to the state of the tide, it would not be possible to make another attempt until a fortnight had passed. In view of this, 'Blue Bird' was loaded on to its lorry and we returned to Povey Cross once more, where we worked on the machine for a week, then went back to the sands on Sunday, January 30th.

This was our third visit to Pendine and, if anything, the weather was now worse. We prepared the car during Monday, and that night a storm raged. In the morning, we found the beach strewn with little shells and debris. Local people and visitors walked over the beach as the tide went out, picking up shells and doing their best to clear the sand so that I could make a practice run. They made an extraordinary collection, including forty feet of wire hawser, two dead sheep, and endless pieces of timber.

While they were working, half a dozen cars raced out with marking flags. Men travelling on the cars placed the flags, while the drivers kept the machines moving, otherwise they would have sunk in the sand, although the surface was actually firmer than it had ever been during our previous visits.

They were still busy when we brought the car to the beach, and the moment that the last flag had been placed, I started. I was not trying for the record, but 'Blue Bird' was timed at 175 mph through part of the mile. I knew that the machine was travelling very well, and I was so elated that I drove flat out over the return trip. Five hundred yards short of the timing tape, I felt a lurch and the machine pitched into a furious skid; one rear tyre had been cut by the razor-edged little shells which still lay on the beach.

I straightened and kept my foot hard down, risking a worse skid in my eagerness to learn what 'Blue Bird' could really do. I held the car all through the measured mile, but the deflated tyre was a handicap, and the machine clocked only about 160 mph. When I stopped, Villa and his companions began to change the wheel, because I intended to run again. Most unfortunately, it started to rain and it was not possible to go on.

Flying spray and sand were bad enough to contend with during a run, but rain would foul my windscreen, sand would cling to it, and I should be blinded. We were forced to give up for that day, and the rain continued all night, ceasing only at eleven o'clock the next morning, when we decided to make another practice run.

At such short notice, it was impossible to get much help in laying out the course. We had half a dozen cars, but only one man was available to drive each machine and place the flags; at least two helpers had hitherto been on each car, one to mark the course and the other to keep the machine moving.

We solved the problem by sending the drivers out with instructions to put their cars in bottom gear and lock the steering over, so that the machines would run in circles while the drivers placed the flags. They started off and the arrangement produced the most astonishing sight that I had ever seen. When I looked along the beach a little later, the cars were going round and round with no one in them while, between the machines, the drivers were frantically busy, splashing through the water which still covered the sand, and hammering home the short flag posts.

Later, I surveyed the beach, and it became apparent at once that all the work was wasted; there was far too much water on the sand to make fast driving possible, and it was useless to bring 'Blue Bird' out. Disappointed, I stood watching as the tide flowed out, and noticed that the only dry places on the beach were the huge circles drawn on the sand by the wheels of cars used in marking the course. In constantly turning around while their drivers set the flags, the tyres had formed ruts which now drained off all the adjacent water. This suggested an idea.

If a plough were employed to cut a furrow along the beach, it might drain water from the entire length of the course. It was worth making an experiment, and mechanics raced off to find a plough. They returned just as the tide began to come in and, hitching the plough behind a lorry, a test furrow was run for some distance. Very soon, water was seeping into the furrow, vanishing from the sand on either side and leaving it dry. It would be difficult to express our elation at this discovery, because dry sand meant a firm surface, and 'Blue Bird' had done enough to prove that this would materially assist the car to beat the record.

We made our plans that evening, securing a second plough and the use of a tractor to draw it. Yet again it rained through the night, but the weather cleared in the morning, although the wind was then blowing off the sea, slowing the ebb tide. The moment that sand began to show through the water, the two ploughs started off, the idea being to cut a furrow on either side of the course. The plough drawn by the tractor ran along the sand on the seaward side, and the other, hauled by a steel cable attached to a lorry, worked on the inside of the course.

Unluckily, this second plough threw the man who was working

it after he had gone a little way, and the ploughshare itself was broken. The other carried on, however, running down the six-mile course. It progressed very slowly, and its work was not done by the time that the tide had run out and, backed by the wind, began immediately to turn.

We had the car warmed up and ready. I could wait very little longer if I were to drive the machine before the sea hid the beach again, and only now did we discover that our experiment was a failure. The almost completed furrow near the sea was filling with rainwater running off the sand dunes, and now this spread inside the course, leaving more water than there would have been if we had not used the plough at all. But it became evident that this could be remedied if the second furrow were cut on the landward side, carrying out our first intention. A message was sent to the tractor, and the driver started back, cutting this second furrow.

I could wait no longer. The surface was firm, although very wet, the car had been tuned up to real speed, and everything was ready for a real attempt on the record. I wanted to miss no opportunity because the weather, bad as it had been, might become still worse. I was determined that we would return to Povey Cross with the record, or with the conviction that 'Blue Bird' could not break it. This none of us would believe, and I wanted to secure it if only for the satisfaction of all those who had worked for so long on the car.

We restarted the engine and I climbed into the cockpit. I could not see the plough, which was now cutting a second furrow, travelling in the same direction as 'Blue Bird' would be moving during the first run. I settled down in the cockpit, with the engine roaring, flames and thin smoke streaking from the exhaust ports. The sound of the motor made speech impossible, and I waved the mechanics away, then sent the car off.

It pitched into a fierce skid an instant after leaving the boards, but I brought the machine straight and put my foot down hard. Soon I picked up the banner which marked the measured mile and, from a glance at the revolution counter, I knew that 'Blue Bird' would go through the distance faster than any machine had ever travelled before. I crossed the timing tape with the throttle wide open, while sand, thrown up by the front wheels and caught by the wind, smothered me. Water shot up in sheets, smashing over the windscreen, but the marking flags were a guide, and when I had cleared the measured distance I knew that, beyond any question of doubt, the existing figure had been beaten by a wide margin on that run.

I had still to return to secure the record, and I drove as far along the beach as I could before bringing the car about then, with the machine headed back, I opened up once again. Some trick of the wind made conditions worse when I neared the mile, travelling at well above 175 mph. Sand and flying water made it impossible for me to see, and I could hardly tell whether I was on the course or off it, and as I went over the tape, I remembered the tractor and the plough.

They were coming towards me. If I approached them only a few feet out of the straight, a collision was inevitable. I could not sight them through the spray and sand which lashed up over the front of the car, and I had to take my foot off the throttle. If I hit the plough, it meant absolute disaster for all concerned, and I could not take that risk. 'Blue Bird' slowed, and I glimpsed the approaching plough. The car was headed towards it, and I had just enough time in which to ease outwards and miss the tractor.

This check spoiled all chance of reaching record speed. When I stopped, the fast-running tide was already washing the edge of the course. We could not run again, and 'Blue Bird' returned to the shed.

The day's work, however, was more than useful. We had learned how best to employ the plough, and knew that a single furrow cut along the landward side of the beach would do all that was necessary. Next morning the weather changed and brought bright sunshine, although some wind remained. As soon as the tide began to go out, the plough started its six-mile journey, cars raced away with the flags, the timing apparatus was made ready and 'Blue Bird' was brought to the sand.

After so many exasperating failures and so much bad luck, we felt that we had to break the record this time, or give up altogether. Yet we had been aware of similar feelings prior to earlier attempts, and when these had failed, we had always kept on trying. But I did hope that this morning would see the acquisition of the record for which mechanics and assistants had worked so very hard and so cheerfully.

Groups of people went along the sands as the water drained away, picking up flotsam and shells. The sun grew stronger and helped to dry the beach, while the furrow which the plough was making did all that we had hoped. At two o'clock in the afternoon, everything was ready but, as a last blow, 'Blue Bird' sulked. It took some time to get the engine going, and the delay nettled me, so that I missed a change on the difficult gearbox immediately after getting away, and was obliged to stop.

Mechanics came to my help, and I restarted from where the car had halted. 'Blue Bird' made up for everything by gathering way very rapidly indeed, showing tremendous acceleration on the firm beach. I was running with the wind, and the car was absolutely steady; I was not much troubled by flying sand or water and the machine gave me a very real impression of high speed, an impression as vivid as anything that I had known up to that time.

The wind had a pressure greater than that of any hurricane. It screamed past my head, and I found it impossible to hear the engine, the roar of which had been so deafening at the start. The sensation of everything rushing to meet the car was greatly heightened, and my most outstanding feeling was one of exhilaration. During part of the dash, 'Blue Bird' was moving at 184 mph, while the speed through the measured kilometre was 179.1 mph.

The car reached more than three miles a minute, but to gain the record I had to return and, this time, 'Blue Bird' was facing the wind. Everything went well during the second run until I was actually in the measured mile, then a bump sent me upwards in the cockpit, so that my head was jerked into the airstream. My goggles were blown completely away, while water and sand slashed over the car, stinging my unprotected eyes, temporarily blinding me.

'Blue Bird' must have been moving at 175 mph in that moment. I had to lift one hand from the wheel, wiping my eyes to clear away the water and sand before I could see. Fortunately, the car remained straight and I finished the measured distance without taking my foot off the throttle pedal.

I felt convinced that we had taken the record, and a minute or two after the car stopped it was officially announced that the average speed through the measured mile, for the two runs, was 174.2 mph; over the kilometre, the speed was 174.8 mph. We had broken the record.

When they heard this, the mechanics paraded around the car, cheering and singing. We had not set up 180 mph, but we had come very near it, and to make the day's success complete, I wanted to try again. The wind had freshened by the time our excitement had abated, and all was ready for another run, but 'Blue Bird' seemed to have lost speed, and the double run which I now made was at a lower figure than the new record.

There was no time to make a third effort, and it seemed wise to leave the figures where they stood, and the day ended with our helpers accepting an invitation to a dance at the local hotel. The party which followed was similar to that which had succeeded our former success at Pendine, then, triumphant after our two and a half years' of work, 'Blue Bird' was taken home.

§6

Before leaving Pendine, we received a letter of congratulations from Parry Thomas and, at the same time, he booked accommodation at the little hotel, which made it plain that he intended to attack the new record almost at once.

He was urged by the fact that Segrave's new car was almost ready, and that it was due to leave for Daytona Beach on March 1st, 1927, hardly four weeks after we came away from the sands. Like myself, Thomas wanted to try and break the record, and gain some recompense for all his work, before the big Sunbeam could make its run and set up figures that were quite beyond the reach of 'Babs'.

'Blue Bird' had been built on more or less orthodox lines, but Segrave's car was revolutionary. It must have been one of the first machines ever to have two engines, and the total capacity of these twelve-cylinder power units was 44,880 c.c., rather more than twice that of our car. The Sunbeam weighed four tons and was over twenty feet in length, but everything had been so cleverly arranged that the top of the fairing behind the driving seat, the highest part of the car, was less than four feet above the ground. The wheels were completely shrouded by the bodywork, and this lent the car a slug-like appearance, although there was nothing sluggish about the machine when it was in action. It was painted red, a colour which added to the impressiveness of this truly enormous car.

Segrave sailed for Daytona, taking the Sunbeam in a crate which was over ten yards in length. The day before he left, Parry Thomas arrived at Pendine with 'Babs'. He had been in bed at his Brooklands bungalow over the weekend, fighting off an attack of influenza, and he was still suffering from its effects. He planned his attempt for Wednesday, March 2nd, but bad weather post-poned it until the next day, and the period of waiting affected him in an unusual way.

Normally, Thomas was always very cool and calm, but now he seemed uneasy. Possibly it was the effect of his illness, or it may have been a reaction from the fact that he intended to try and reach 200 mph, hoping to touch this mark before Segrave could achieve it. He did not think he could lift the actual record to this speed, but a strong wind was blowing down the beach, and he thought this might enable the car to attain the speed in one direction.

It is an odd fact that he was very concerned about the transmission on the Sunbeam, which, as with his own car, had driving chains. Engine power can be conveyed to the rear wheels either by a propeller shaft – as on 'Blue Bird' – or by chains; at that date, knowledge was not so complete as at the present time, and designers were unable to find metals sufficiently reliable to enable the propeller shaft to be used on the Sunbeam. Chains, however, could stand very high stresses.

Thomas believed that chains were safe enough on his machine, because it weighed less than two tons, but the Sunbeam was twice as heavy. He believed that this offered some danger to Segrave because, if a chain were so overstressed that it broke, it would flail around the wheel at tremendous speed and might strike the driver.

When 'Babs' was taken on to the sand, Thomas made four runs, each time with the machine subject to carburettor trouble. He drove tensely, and during halts for adjustments, he was impatient and on edge. He made a fifth run, going through the mile at very high speed. He turned to come back, driving flat out towards the measured distance. The car was moving at 160 mph when it suddenly pitched into a wild skid, flung broadside to the course, and made a complete somersault, landing on its wheels again and skidding in a half-circle before coming to a stop, flames and smoke bursting from the engine.

Spectators rushed to the car, to find the tyre torn from the off-side rear wheel, while the bodywork above it was smashed. The driving chain to the wheel had broken in the way that Thomas had feared might happen on the Sunbeam. It had struck his head, killing him instantaneously, and that broken chain brought a great loss to motor racing. He was carried away, while the incoming tide washed the tragic skid marks from the sands. Later on, the wreckage of 'Babs' was buried at the foot of the dunes.

News of the tragedy came as a shock to me, and it must have

been even greater for Segrave, who was then in mid-Atlantic and who received the information by wireless. Naturally, the driving chains on his Sunbeam were later subjected to the closest possible examination, but it was decided that they would stand up to the work required, and his attempt went forward.

On the very day of Thomas's death, an agreement was signed in Paris between the American Automobile Association and the International Association of Recognized Automobile Clubs. These governing bodies came to an arrangement by which all world's records would be subjected to the Commission Sportive; this meant that if Segrave set up new figures, they would be recognized both in England and in America. It had taken some years to conclude this agreement, which cleared up a difficult situation. If it had not been signed, no records at Daytona would ever have been officially admitted in Europe.

Segrave arrived at Daytona and, after a series of tests, he made an attempt towards the end of March, and raised the record to 203.79 mph, beating 'Blue Bird's' figure by more than twenty miles an hour. It was a magnificent effort, particularly in view of the fact that the car had never been run before it left England. The success was a fine tribute to the men responsible for building the machine, because all their theories were sustained. They had estimated that the Sunbeam could touch 215 mph; in actual performance it reached 207.015 mph during its fastest run – not very much below the theoretical limit of speed.

Segrave received the overwhelming congratulations that he deserved. 'Blue Bird's' successful run at Pendine had received much attention in England, but Segrave's roused the whole world. It stirred America in particular, and the imagination of the people there was caught by the fact that an Englishman had come to their country and had beaten every high-speed record that their own men had set up. American racing drivers began to consider the possibility of building cars which would secure the world's record for the United States.

At home, we found ourselves in a situation which we had fore-seen for a long time. The 1,000 h.p. Sunbeam had completely outclassed 'Blue Bird', and for some time we wondered if the car could be made fast enough to go over to Daytona and attack the new record; no further efforts could be made at Pendine, because the R.A.C. had banned the sands for such attempts, following the death of Parry Thomas.

We calculated that there was a possibility of tuning 'Blue Bird' up to above 200 mph. If the car were given a perfect surface and splendid conditions, we believed that it might break the record, but the chance appeared remote. In the end, we were forced to the conclusion that the record was just beyond the reach of the car.

I could not make up my mind whether to go on with world's record attempts, or to give them up, as the expense already incurred had been very great. I knew that 'Blue Bird' was useless in its present form, and further efforts meant the construction of what was tantamount to a new car. I had a very clear recollection of all the work that we had put into the machine, and it was cer-tain that another effort would bring in its train a repetition of all the worry and endeavour which had so recently concluded. To carry on was equivalent to starting all over again, and I found it difficult to arrive at a decision.

Segrave's return to England was followed by a series of lunch-eons and dinners, at which interested people gathered to do him honour. Some of these I attended, and I soon became aware of the general opinion about the new record; it was said that no one would surpass it for many years to come. This was in the nature of a challenge to myself, although a challenge was never intended, because I felt that the record could still be beaten.

Sitting at a dinner one evening, listening to a repetition of the general belief that 203.7 mph would stand for a very long time, I thought of the American drivers who were rumoured to be planning big cars. It seemed to me that, before another year was out, the record might go to America, but whether the Americans made any attempt or not, I was conscious of a wish to disprove the experts.

Then and there I decided to reconstruct 'Blue Bird', no matter what the expense, to strip the car down and rebuild it with a bigger engine built into a chassis that had been completely redesigned. I decided to do this in time to take the car over to Daytona the following year, there to try and stave off any American challenge and to push the land-speed record still higher.

THE SEVENTH CHAPTER

§ I

OUR PLANS FOR A NEW 'Blue Bird' began to take shape at the start of the 1927 racing season, which opened with a mishap for myself. During the winter, Ettore Bugatti had partly redesigned his racing machines, and I bought one of the earliest of the new models. It was sent across from France in order that I might run it in the opening Brooklands meeting and, during practice, I had the car moving at rather more than 125 mph along the Byfleet banking when the machine hit a bump.

I was jolted upwards in the cockpit. When I landed again my seat broke, so that I crashed through it and dropped upon one of the chassis cross-members. The impact was severe, and I jarred my spine. The car almost went out of control before I was able to slow down, when, in considerable pain, I drove on around to the paddock and pulled up by my workshop.

Villa and another mechanic helped me from the Bugatti, and for half an hour I was stretched out on the garage floor. It was a long while before I fully recovered from this, and there are times when I still feel the effects of that accident. I was, however, well enough to drive in the Brooklands meeting when it became due, particular attention having been paid to the rebuilt seat, and handled the machine in one of the fastest races in which I had ever taken part up to that date.

There were four starters in the last event of the day; these included my new Bugatti and a red-painted Sunbeam driven by Kaye Don. He led at the end of the first lap but, at the start of the second, I drove flat out from the banking behind the Members' Hill, chasing him down the railway straight and taking the lead just before we went through the curve on to the Byfleet banking. Possibly, the speed of the Bugatti took him by surprise, because he opened up, brought his radiator to the French car's tail and remained there for the rest of the lap.

There was hardly a yard between the two machines as they started the third circuit of the track, and we went down the railway straight at over 130 mph. He tried to pass, but could not quite manage it, and again we went around the Byfleet banking nose to tail, the machines riding very close to the upper edge, and each of us running with the throttle pedal down on the floorboards.

Kaye Don pulled out, once more endeavouring to take the lead as we came off the banking to the Fork, but again he was unable to find enough speed, and he gradually fell away as we went on to the finish, the Bugatti winning by two lengths. It was a very close race, thoroughly exciting in spite of its short duration, and winning came as some compensation for the accident of a few days before. Immediately after this meeting, definite work began on the design of 'Blue Bird', and we solved the problem of securing a suitable type of engine.

Napiers, who had built the power unit in the old record car, had evolved a new aero engine for the Schneider Trophy race, which was to be flown at Venice towards the end of September. This engine had twelve cylinders, arranged in three banks of four each, and it gave off about 900 h.p. It was still on the Air Ministry's secret list, but I asked the authorities for permission to instal one of these engines in the new car. This request was granted, but a promise had to be given that mechanical details would not be divulged, and that no one would be permitted to examine the unit.

It was arranged that the chassis of 'Blue Bird' should be

assembled at the Napier works, which were situated at Acton Vale, just outside London, but that they were not to instal the engine until near the date of the Schneider Cup race. When it was eventually built into the car, some parts remained under seal.

Wind tunnel tests were made in order to determine the best design for the body, and it was found that the exposed wheels created about sixty per cent of the total wind resistance; without the wheels, the body formed an almost perfect streamlined shape, in accordance with our knowledge at that time. The resistance provided by the wheels was greatly reduced by building streamlined fairings before and behind them; it was the first time that this had ever been done.

Another innovation was a tail fin, fitted to help stabilize the car while it was travelling at high speed. Two of these fins were made, for use in accordance with whatever wind might be blowing when the car ran, one fin being smaller than the other. In order to remove the resistance normally offered by a radiator at the front of a car, we fitted two radiators, one either side of the tail and placed end on. This arrangement involved running pipes from the radiators to the front of the engine, two being brought under the driving seat, and two more set one at each side. These pipes promised to become uncomfortably warm when the car was in use, so they were bound with rubber as a protection.

The radiators were not altogether successful in practice, because we found that they travelled in a partial vacuum, and although they did all that was necessary during the record attempt which came later, they were afterwards scrapped. As a sidelight upon the expense attached to the building of such a car, it might be mentioned that these radiators, constructed by a well-known aircraft factory, cost nearly four hundred pounds, and were eventually sold as scrap metal for exactly five pounds.

An unusual arrangement was in the location of the gearbox, although this had been similar in the old 'Blue Bird'. It was placed in front of the driving seat, so that I should have to straddle it, with the clutch pedal on the left, the brake and throttle pedals being on the right, while the gear lever came up between my legs. The gearbox, torque tube and rear axle casing, formed one solid unit, so that when the car was in action, the big gear-box would be constantly in motion – 'floating', as it were – in response to the movement of the back axle.

Joseph Maina worked out the fundamentals of the new chassis, incorporating as much as possible of the material which already existed in the first 'Blue Bird'. The clutch was remodelled, and the gearbox was rebuilt, while we employed the same duplicated steering gear, so that each front wheel was directly controlled. The Rudge-Whitworth firm built a set of wheels specially constructed to withstand the great stresses and the impacts which would be occasioned by bumps when the car was moving at speed, while their wheels were balanced with the utmost exactitude.

The Dunlop Rubber Company provided the tyres, as they had done both for Segrave and for my own earlier efforts. These tyres were made with the greatest care and thoroughness; each had a life of about three minutes at 200 mph, and I was advised to change them at the end of each run down the beach. They had no treads at all, because these would have been thrown off at speed; the cord foundation was covered with rubber hardly more than one millimetre in thickness.

During the building of the car, I wondered if it was possible to find in Europe a stretch of sand which had the merits of Daytona Beach, and which could be reached without the expense attendant upon a trip to America. Various inquiries were made, and I went to see sands near Aberdeen, and also surveyed another beach in the Isle of Anglesey, but neither of these were suitable. A fine stretch was discovered on the Belgian coast but, unfortunately, it had many groins and great patches which always remained soft and which made the sands useless for our purpose. In the end I came to the conclusion that Florida was the only place in which the record could be attempted.

All this work was, of course, spread over many months, and our hopes were raised when England won the Schneider Cup at a speed of 281.49 mph. Our own engine was a duplicate of the one used in the seaplane, and the air race at Venice told us that we should have all the power we were likely to need. This was encouraging, because rumours were reaching us from the United States concerning cars which were being built there for an attempt on the record. We knew nothing definite, except that the opposition would probably be very strong.

§2

It was just before the Schneider Cup Trophy was run, and at a time when 'Blue Bird's' engine was being installed, that I raced in the Grand Prix of Boulogne, held over a twenty-three miles' road circuit just outside the town; I had been looking forward to this event, after my experience of the year before. It was run off over rain-soaked roads, and was attended by a certain amount of excitement.

Practice had made it plain that the Bugatti which I had entered stood quite a good chance against the nineteen other cars that lined up; actually, only six of these were in direct rivalry to my own machine. The rest were split up into various classes and were not competing in the Grand Prix itself, but ran in subsidiary events, although all were on the course at the same time.

Rain had been falling since early morning, but this eased temporarily as the machines were brought to the line; the cars against which I was running were all Bugattis, with one exception. I slipped into the cockpit, and Villa cranked up the engine; other machines started up, and it was then that heavy rain came again.

In a minute or so we should be off, and I realized that my gloves would slip on the wet steering wheel. I threw them to Villa, then borrowed the leather jacket which he was wearing. I buttoned this up and, watching the starter, rested my hands on the wheel, only to find that they slipped just as badly as when I had been wearing gloves.

Something had to be done, but there was no time in which to do very much. Suddenly I thought of binding the wheel-rim with insulation tape, which would give a very secure grip; Villa carried this out while, every moment, I expected the flag to fall. The job was hardly finished before all mechanics were cleared from the road, and a few seconds later the race began.

Eyston, who had won the previous year, was driving again, and he took the lead from the start, followed by a driver named Sabipa, distinguishable in a yellow oilskin and a crash helmet. As these two shot away, my Bugatti followed with a bunch of machines roaring behind, and we went down the road with water and mud flying from the wheels, heading for the St Martin hairpin, the cars jumping from the bumps of a level crossing just before reaching the turn.

This corner could not be taken at more than about thirty miles an hour, and even then the cars slid on the slippery pavé. Once around it, there followed a winding road to the woods at La Capelle, beyond which was the straight stretch to Le Wast. The rain was teeming down, and there were no spectators here; a few gendarmes were spaced out along the side of the road, but that was all. There was a damp-looking crowd at Le Wast, after which the course turned along a twisting stretch to Desevres village, where the road was wide and hundreds of people had gathered. Beyond the village were nasty bends, after which the road became fairly straight to the end of the lap.

I had lost sight of Eyston and Sabipa long before the finish of that first circuit; no other cars were in sight and, for all that I could see, I might have had the course to myself. I knew that I was in third place, and only afterwards did I learn that the two men ahead were struggling hard for the lead.

The second lap was much the same as the first except that, having grown accustomed to the wet road, I opened out; twelve laps had to be covered, and I was afraid that the leading machines might get too far ahead. On the third lap, I sighted a Bugatti in front, half-hidden under a cloud of spray from its wheels; I had already overtaken small machines in other classes and I thought this car might be a Grand Prix entrant delayed by trouble. It was moving very fast, but gradually I overtook it, finally coming up with a rush and discovering that Eyston was the driver.

Evidently he had been passed by Sabipa and when I had left him behind, I was running in second place. I started the fourth lap and now, after going through Le Wast, I came upon an extraordinary sight. A Bugatti was almost upside down at the side of the road, and the driver was trying to get it back on its wheels.

I had a glimpse of the car's racing number, No. 46, and knew that it belonged to Prince Ghica, but not until the race was over did I learn what had happened to him. At the end of his second lap, he had pitched into a tremendous skid in front of the grandstand, moving broadside down the road at 90 mph. He corrected the first skid, but oversteered, and for the quarter of a mile the car lurched from side to side before the driver managed to straighten it out. He went on without stopping, only to run completely off the road on the uphill bend where I saw him. He contrived to get his machine back to the course after my Bugatti had passed, only to turn it over again before he reached the grandstands, escaping without serious hurt, but retiring from the race.

The fact that Ghica had left the course in this way gives some indication of the wet and slippery state of the road, and now I began to find trouble.

Insulation tape is sticky and, when wet, it develops abrasive properties; neither Villa nor I had thought of this when we bound it around the wheel rim and the tape began to attack the skin of my hands. It dragged on my palms every time I put the Bugatti through a corner when it was most essential to maintain a very firm grip on the wheel and gradually the skin began to tear away.

At first this was only a minor discomfort, which I ignored in

the effort to overtake Sabipa, then the tape began to attack the
second layer of skin and the pain increased, becoming worse with
every succeeding lap. Before the race was half run I found it ago-
nizing to grip the wheel at all. By the time that I had covered eight
laps I was driving along the straights with only the base of my
palms resting on the wheel-rim, keeping the Bugatti on its proper
course by pressure alone.

On the bends and corners, however, I had to hold the wheel
properly, and when I completed the last lap but one my hands
were raw and bleeding; hardly a square half-inch of skin remained
on the palms or on the inside of my fingers. As I approached the
pits, I saw Villa and the rest of the pit crew leaning out and waving
frantically, every gesture urging me to more speed. Then I saw a
halted car, and recognized the driver by his yellow waterproof. It
was Sabipa; he had pulled up with clutch trouble, and was making
an adjustment. I had a glimpse of him, waving his arms at his
mechanics, shouting demands for some tool which they could not
provide. I passed and, knowing that I was in the lead, eased the
speed a little, trying to drive with the backs of my hands on the
wheel, hating every corner which made me hold the rim properly.

That last lap was the worst of all, and I tried everything of
which I could possibly think to avoid gripping the steering wheel
normally, at times pressing my forearms against the sides, and at
others holding the rim with finger and thumb. My only conso-
lation was that the Bugatti held the lead, and that the rain had
almost stopped. Finally, the car entered the last of the two hundred and seventy miles which formed the race, winning at an
average speed of 67.2 mph. Eyston had overtaken Sabipa, and the
two fought all through their last circuit, Sabipa securing second
place by only two-fifths of a second.

The event had lasted for more than four hours; rain, flying
spray and mud, combined with the discomfort from my hands,
made it the most uncomfortable that I had ever known. All this,
however, was forgotten in the pleasure that victory brought. It

was the first important race that I had ever won, and the fact that it was a road race made success still more pleasing.

Immediately after leaving the car I sought medical attention for my hands, because I had entered for the second British Grand Prix, which was to be run at Brooklands three weeks later.

§3

My hands healed rapidly, and this was fortunate because the British Grand Prix of 1927 promised to be even more interesting than the race of the year before. If all the cars entered had come to the line, the race would probably have made history.

Amongst the machines down to run were three twelve-cylinder Fiats of an entirely new type. These cars were still experimental, but one had been tried out at Monza, and had won easily, proving itself the fastest 1,500 c.c. racing machine ever built. At the time when these cars should have been prepared for the Brooklands event, the Fiat mechanics were overwhelmed with work on engines for the Italian seaplanes entered in the Schneider Cup Trophy; the racing cars could not be made ready in time, and were scratched.

Another entry was a Duesenberg, which was to be driven by George Souders; he had won the five-hundred miles' race at Indianapolis earlier in the year on a machine of this type. Before coming to England, Souders drove in the European Grand Prix at Monza, as a result of which he decided to withdraw from the Brooklands event. The Deusenberg had been built primarily for smooth, boardtrack work, and could not stand up to the hammering of rough concrete, while it was not designed for the cornering necessary on the Grand Prix course, which had again been planned with artificial turns formed by sandbanks.

With Italian and American competition eliminated, the remainder of the entries were formed by three Delage cars which had finished first, second and third in the French Grand Prix three months earlier, half a dozen Bugattis, and three British cars, two Thomas-Specials, which had been built by Parry Thomas before he died, and a front-wheel drive Alvis.

This last car broke a piston during the last day of practice; mechanics worked overnight and on the morning of the race the machine was taken out for a practice run, only for a fragment from the smashed piston to jam the oil-pump drive, damaging the gearing so badly that the car could not come to the line.

On the day of the race, eleven cars rolled out of the paddock and ran down to the starting point, which was set halfway along the railway straight. It seemed most likely that one of the Delage machines would win, and a victory for France was certain; the only British cars were the two Thomas-Specials, but these were unsupercharged, and could not possibly rival the speed of the rest.

Albert Divo, Benoist and Bourlier were on the Delages, and an official Bugatti team was formed by Count Conelli, Louis Chiron and Emilio Materassi. These men were six of the finest drivers that the Continent could produce, and a fourth Bugatti was handled by Prince Ghica, who had recovered from the effect of his crashes at Boulogne. Eyston was also driving a Bugatti, and I had the car which I had driven in the first British Grand Prix. Discounting the efforts of the drivers of the Thomas-Specials, Eyston and myself were the only men representing England, although we were both mounted on French cars.

We drove foreign machines because no British cars were available for us to drive; even the Thomas-Specials were not the product of a factory. They had been built privately in Parry Thomas's workshop. The only English firm down to race was Alvis, but the entry was no more than a patriotic gesture, because the car was a new model, and only extraordinarily good fortune would have enabled it to compete seriously with the French machines. As it was, the car did not start.

It had been raining hard for some time before the machines came out at a little before twelve o'clock, when they were lined up in a row across the railway straight. Bourlier's Delage gave a little trouble when the mechanic tried to rouse the engine; he had to push frantically on the tail of the car, rolling the machine ahead of the starting line before the flag fell. The engine fired then, and Bourlier waited where he was until the flag dropped, allowing all other machines to pass him before he attempted to move; this was a sporting gesture on his part and, although it gave him a bad start, he could not be accused of having tried to jump the flag.

I concentrated upon getting my Bugatti away quickly, knowing that it was necessary to make use of every possible means of gaining ground if the car were to have a chance against the Delages. Yet, splendidly though the car started, Materassi beat me, streaking ahead as we ran towards the Byfleet banking. His rear wheels sent great showers of spray from puddles on the track, and he slid a little as he entered the bend to the banking.

We met a gusty wind beyond the curve, and more rain came in squalls as we gathered speed along the concrete, with Eyston close behind my machine. As we went round, I wondered what had happened to the Delage cars but, near the end of the banking, Bourlier came up, slipping past as we dropped down the slope to the Fork; his Delage was very low, and he was huddled down into the cockpit, as if to take shelter from the rain. These cars had all been fitted with little mudflaps behind the front wheels, so placed that the tyres could not sling water and grit at the drivers. Such protection was worthwhile in a long race. Along the railway straight, at the end of the first lap, the other two Delage cars came up and passed Eyston and myself. Bourlier went into the lead, then Divo passed Materassi and the Bugatti driver clung to Benoist on the third Delage, reluctant to let him go ahead. They hung together until they were halfway round on the next lap, then the three Delage cars seemed to streak ahead as Materassi fell back. Soon he pulled into the pits to change plugs, then I found that Eyston was no longer behind me and that he, too, had stopped. This left me in fourth place, but my brakes proved inadequate on the bends, so that first Chiron and then Count Conelli passed me.

The Delages were well in the lead now. One behind the other, they went round the track, moving fast through the turns and accelerating fiercely out of them. They had everything beaten right from the start, and they must have been very carefully prepared for the race; in fact, a fuel specialist had come over from Paris with the team, to prepare the mixture on which the machines ran. No other car could stay near them, although the official Bugattis did their best.

My control station had been set up at the start of the railway straight, in one of the concrete bays cut out at the side of the track. We had a saloon car, and signals were shown to me from the windows; almost the only signal that I received, as the race wore on, was an insistent command to go faster. I was doing all that I could, but I lost time on the bends because of the indifferent brakes. When I passed the saloon, I tried to explain what it was that cut down my speed, but it proved a little difficult to convey ideas by signalling with one hand at over 100 miles an hour. It was not long before the Thomas-Specials retired, unable to show real speed because they were not supercharged, then I noticed Prince Ghica's Bugatti being rolled away. Other cars paused briefly at their depots, but the race ran on without real incident and what had promised to be an extraordinarily fine event developed into the spectacle of a group of hopelessly outmatched machines vainly pursuing the three Delages.

We fell further and further behind as the race wore on. My Bugatti was going up to 120 mph along the Byfleet banking, but the bend in the finishing straight reduced the average speed considerably. At about half-distance, just over a hundred and fifty miles, I pulled in for fuel, changed the rear tyres, then started off once more.

The rain had eased now, but spray from the track was troublesome, and the second turn, where the course entered the railway straight, had become very slippery. The Delages skidded each time that they took it; several times, when I followed one of the machines through, it seemed to pitch into a four-wheel slide, but the driver always held the car.

It was soon after I had replenished that, racing along the Byfleet banking, I saw Count Conelli's Bugatti close to the inside of the track; he was running beside it, pushing the machine around to the pits. For two or three laps after that I passed him again and, finally, I saw that he had reached his pit, where mechanics were busy refuelling the car. He had run out of petrol, and pushing the machine halfway round the track had so exhausted him that his reserve driver had to take the car on.

His delay enabled me to bring my machine into fifth place, with only Chiron between me and the rearmost Delage. I used full throttle wherever possible now, because there was a chance that, if Chiron slowed or if one of the leading cars failed, my Bugatti might yet be placed. The speed of the car began rapidly to fall away. Soon, the engine started to spit back and I thought at first that this was due to lack of fuel pressure, then it appeared as though a sparking plug had cut out.

I pulled in at the pit, changing the plug and replenishing the petrol tank, but when I started again there was no improvement in the running of the engine. I stopped once more, working with Villa, trying to locate the cause of the trouble. Presently we discovered a badly jammed valve which defied all our efforts to free it, and we were forced to retire.

The race ended about half an hour afterwards. Benoist won with his Delage at an average of 85.59 mph, a speed higher than the fastest lap of the race a year earlier. Bourlier, on another Delage, arrived seven seconds behind him, and Divo, on a similar machine, came third. Chiron brought home the first Bugatti, but he was more than twenty-five minutes behind Divo.

I stood by my pit, watching the Frenchmen receiving congratulations and being showered with bouquets while the rest of the cars came home. I had seen enough of the official Bugatti team to appreciate that these machines were all superior to the car that I had driven, and which I had entered for the Two Hundred Miles race; this was to be run a fortnight later over a similar course, but with the addition of hairpin turns.

Since my machine's brakes had proved inadequate, there was a possibility that it would be outclassed in this later event; if, however, I could acquire one of the official Bugatti machines I should have a much more efficient mount. With this in mind, I offered to buy one of the team cars, and was told that I could have whichever machine I cared to select. My choice fell upon the one that Count Conelli had driven, because this car had not been pressed so hard in the race as the others.

§4

Instead of returning immediately to France, the Bugatti mechanics remained at the track to tune the car, and after three days of hard work it was ready for a test run. I covered two laps and then came in, thoroughly pleased. We changed the plugs, as a matter of routine in deciding those on which the engine ran best, and I took the car out again. After one more lap at high speed, the engine 'blew up', and inspection showed a connecting rod poking through the side of the crankcase.

This was disastrous. Extensive repairs were required and these could not be made in England, but the Bugatti people were equal to the situation. They rushed the car over to France, promising to return it within a week, which involved driving the machine from Molsheim to England, and it arrived at Brooklands on the day before it was due to race.

When a racing car is run over ordinary roads at touring speeds, its tune must suffer. We did what was possible to bring it back to racing trim, and at five o'clock on the Friday afternoon I took the Bugatti around the track, only for the brakes to jam when I went through one of the hairpin turns.

We towed the car to the shed, and freed the brakes; I covered two laps more, after which the track closed for the day. Villa and another mechanic spent all night in making alterations to the brake cables, trying to make sure that there was no risk of another seizure and completing the work at five o'clock in the morning. Looking the car over, Villa had occasion to inspect the gearbox, when he discovered that second and third speeds were almost non-existent, and that they were almost certain to fail completely before the race ended. He judged it better to say nothing of this to me, although, when we were taking the car to the starting line, he did suggest that I should be as careful as possible with the gears when negotiating the corners. I appreciated the significance of his remark later on.

Gearboxes and brakes would be heavily stressed in the race, because of the nature of the course. Cars coming from the Byfleet banking had to go through a hairpin turn at the Fork, then take another hairpin immediately afterwards and enter the old finishing straight, down which there were two more artificial bends before the railway straight was reached.

Some of these turns appeared likely to become congested during the event, because the race was so arranged that all classes of cars started together. Hitherto, the smaller machines had run a race of their own in the morning, but now they were to run in company with the bigger cars and, altogether, twenty-nine machines came to the start.

Two of the front-wheel drive Alvis cars were on the line; the two Thomas-Specials turned out again, and there were four Bugattis, of which only mine and one driven by Eyston were supercharged. Behind these machines were the smaller cars, the most outstanding of which was a team of three supercharged six-cylinder Amilcars; one of these, driven by A. Morel, provided the biggest surprise of the race.

The fall of the flag began a 'dog-fight', and this lasted until we reached the far end of the railway straight. The big cars sorted themselves out, and my Bugatti was very close to the leaders when we came off the Byfleet banking to the first turn. I took the lead after the second lap, but my recollection of the race is not particularly clear, largely because the series of corners came so rapidly one after the other. They required care, and the car seemed hardly to have cleared the last of them before it had covered the outer part of the track and was approaching the first hairpin again.

On so short a lap, there was little time to notice what other competitors were doing, but I recollect that one car smoked so excessively that it had to be flagged off the track, while another pulled off the course near the end of the Byfleet banking, where it burst into flames and burned for a long time. On about my fifth lap I came down the first hairpin and found officials struggling to drag the driver from under an overturned car; luckily, he was not injured.

Everything went well for some time, then, changing down before one of the corners, I found that second speed was ineffective, and, almost immediately afterwards, third speed went out of action. Villa had foreseen this, but, because there had been no time to make a repair, he had not told me; possibly he hoped that, after all, the gears might last out the race. The Bugatti slowed, and Eyston went in front, while I decided to come in to the pit; originally, we had estimated that the car should run through the race without a stop.

I pulled up, and shouted to the mechanics, telling them of the trouble. I did not know just what had gone wrong, but they understood the situation, and told me that I could do nothing except race on. I sent the car off, but now that I could use only bottom and top gears I had no acceleration at all in leaving the bends, and this slowed the Bugatti considerably. I tried to make up for this by driving flat out once I had gathered speed in top gear, holding the pace as long as I dared in the approach to the first hairpin, then braking hard for the turn.

Eyston stopped, and I regained the lead, and it was now that

Morel overtook me with his very fast Amilcar. This machine had an engine only two-thirds the size of the Bugatti's, and the car was running in a lower category, yet Morel handled it so well that he clung to my car for lap after lap. On one occasion, we came down to the first hairpin side by side, neither of us cutting out until the last possible moment, then both overshooting the turn before we could pull up and go through it.

He passed, and for some time he held the lead, but at three-quarter distance I went ahead, although he was never very far behind. His car was a beautiful machine, and he drove it like a man inspired. He knew that I was slow on the corners, and here he always gained ground, only to lose during the dash around the rest of the circuit. Finally, he approached the hairpin too fast, spun completely round, and stopped a few inches from some railings. He got his car going again, but the check put him some distance behind, and after that the Bugatti was never challenged. It ran on to the checkered flag, winning at an average speed of over 76 mph. Morel finished in second place, just three minutes behind; his speed was only about a mile and a half slower than that of my car.

This event formed the second important success which I had secured that year, and it was my last race of the season, so that I was able to turn wholeheartedly to the new 'Blue Bird'. The car was now rapidly taking shape; before many weeks had passed, the chassis was covered with canvas sheeting and towed away from the Napier works at dawn. It went to Barkers, the coachbuilders, who had undertaken to provide the special body.

It was about this time, when more rumours of American challengers were drifting across the Atlantic, that 'Djelmo' reappeared. This was the 400 h.p. car which had been built in Paris, long before we actually commenced work on the first 'Blue Bird'. Its initial trials had not been successful, but Jules Foresti had now taken the car over, with the intention of making an attempt on the record at Pendine Sands. He spent many weeks in tuning the machine, working quite unaided. He found difficulty in making the car travel really fast, and it was in November 1927 that he made his last effort. The sand was then very wet, and when 'Djelmo' was moving at 150 mph, the car got out of control. It skidded and turned completely over.

Foresti was thrown out and, by the greatest of good luck, he was flung towards the tail of the machine, which passed above him as the car rolled back on to its wheels. For some moments, he lay on the sands, while the car slithered in a circle and came to a stop. Foresti rose to his feet and actually walked to meet cinematograph operators who were running to his assistance. The car was badly damaged, one front wheel being almost wrenched off, but Foresti was not very much hurt. 'Djelmo' did not compete for world honours again.

Soon after Foresti's crash, I obtained definite information concerning the opposition we should have to face at Daytona. At one time there had been indications that at least four American machines would compete. With the close of 1927 we knew more or less definitely what cars would appear, and it seemed certain that there would be no more than two.

One of these cars had no less than three Liberty aero engines, giving the machine 1,500 h.p.; one of its engines was set in front of the driver, and the other two were placed side by side behind the cockpit. The engines had a total capacity of almost twice that of the 1,000 h.p. Sunbeam which held the record, and nearly four times that of the Napier-Lion engine we were putting into 'Blue Bird'.

This American car became known as 'Triplex', and without question, it was a leviathan. If power were the only requirement, it appeared as if it must easily beat 203 mph. I heard that 250 mph was expected, but I knew that so much power would demand very careful work in the designing of the car itself, and that the driver might find it impossible to use all the power at his disposal. At the same time, it was certain that the machine would be well handled, because the selected driver was Ray Keech, a very experienced man.

The second car which America produced was an altogether different proposition. It was called the 'Black Hawk' Stutz, and its design had been supervised by young Frank Lockhart, who was to drive the machine; Lockhart was then about twenty-four years of age. In his twentieth year he had been competing on the California coast in dirt-track events; from this he had gone to board-track work, and afterwards he had raced at Indianapolis. He had also set up wonderful class records on a dry lakebed, accomplishing most of his fast work on cars which he himself had tuned.

The body of his machine had the most finished streamline effect ever yet given to any car, and he had also made the same discovery as ourselves concerning the wheels; he completely enclosed them, except for a few inches at the bottom, in streamline fairings. His 'Black Hawk' was a triumph of scientific design and ingenuity, built to reach an estimated speed of 220 mph. This possible speed was remarkable in view of the fact that his sixteen-cylinder engine had a capacity of only 3,000 c.c. 'Triplex' was twenty-seven times as large, and 'Blue Bird's' engine was seven times as big.

When I first heard about Frank Lockhart's machine, I was anxious to see it and to meet him. Obviously, he was a designer-driver, of much the same type as Parry Thomas, and I formed the opinion that his car was even more likely than 'Triplex' to beat anything that 'Blue Bird' was able to do.

The year 1927 came to an end, and in the middle of the following January our car was completed. The mechanics, the makers of the engine, Dunlops, and the builders of the body had all worked hard, and the appearance of the machine was to their credit; anything that it was able to achieve was done only through their fine co-operation.

From the tip of the blunt, rounded nose to the end of the tail fin, the length was over eighteen feet. The body swelled up at the cockpit, incorporating a separate streamlined shape into which a special windscreen had been built; it was a box-section, the upper part sloping steeply downwards. Behind the driving seat was a head fairing which ran down to the tail.

When I looked the car over, seeing it in completed shape, it gave me a feeling of confidence that, whatever we might do at Daytona, we should make a good show.

§ 5

We left England early in February, arriving at Daytona at about one o'clock on the morning of Sunday, February 12th, 1928. I had arranged to stay with friends, and at the first opportunity I went down to look at the beach. My first impression was one of disappointment; the weather was cold, the sea was rough, and the sand was very uneven.

The beach is formed in a very odd way, and is not part of the true coastline. It lies along a narrow spit, which is divided from the mainland by the Halifax River, and stretches for twenty-three miles. Four long bridges link it with the city of Daytona.

Its entire length is not available for record attempts, because a pier cuts the beach in two. The course is set south of this and only a stretch of about ten miles is available. At the north end the pier limits the course, and at the south the Halifax River bends round to the sea.

When the tide is out, it leaves a broad stretch of firm sand, with one side bounded by the Atlantic rollers and the other by soft sand which runs up to the dunes. The beach is very sensitive to weather conditions, demanding a wind from the north-east before it can be left really smooth. If the wind is in the wrong quarter, the sand becomes rough and lumpy, and sometimes strewn with shells. When we arrived, the wind was blowing from the south. We could only make the car ready for its tests, and hope that conditions would improve.

We had brought out our cases of spare parts, and two special gas engines for starting up the power unit. There was a big case containing a spare engine, and ten others held spare wheels and tyres. Two more cases were filled with spare parts for the engine and the gearbox. This made eighteen cases in all, apart from the huge crate which contained the car itself.

I had Villa with me, and another mechanic named George Miller, who had worked on the 'Blue Bird' erected at the K.L.G. factory, and who had afterwards joined Villa and myself. We also had Charlie Coe, a mechanic from Napiers, and Steve MacDonald, from Dunlops, whose particular concern was with the tyres. Any further assistance which became necessary was readily secured on the spot.

I was impatient to test 'Blue Bird', because the machine had never run under its own power; it was not possible to discover how the machine would behave, or what adjustments might be necessary, until it had been tried out. The sooner we could do this, the more time would be available in preparing for official attempts.

The car was ready by Tuesday afternoon, but it was then too late to run, because the state of the tide would not permit it. We hoped to have a chance on Wednesday, but a strong wind was blowing and the sand was very rough. Next day, Thursday, conditions were still bad, and the wind was high, but I could wait no longer. I did not ask to have the course marked out, because I had no intention of trying for the record; I simply wanted to test the car.

The police cleared the beach and, like everyone else at Daytona, they were most friendly, willing to do anything they could to assist us. Visitors to the town left the sands readily; Daytona was crowded with people attracted by the idea of three cars competing in an effort to travel faster than machines had ever run over land before. So far, neither Keech nor Lockhart had brought their machines out, regarding the conditions as unfavourable.

'Blue Bird' was towed down while the beach was still being cleared, but it was not long before everything was ready for the first run. Spectators lined up along the dunes, protected by a broad patch of soft sand which lay between themselves and the course; if a car chanced to get out of hand, the sand would check it before it could dash into the crowd.

While we were waiting, and while the engine was being warmed up, some of the police came over to us, and I soon gathered that the sympathy of the entire force was with myself and my mechanics. Many of the officers had some sort of connection with England, and mentioned towns from which their relatives had come: Birmingham, Lincoln, London, and there were many men from Ireland.

I slipped into the cockpit when word came that all was ready, the engine was restarted and, almost at once, I sent the machine away, driving towards the south end of the course. The car gathered speed, but I made no attempt to use full throttle. I hit one or two bumps before I changed into top gear and then, moving at about 180 mph, the car hit a bad ridge which was immediately followed by another.

The machine jumped, travelling fully thirty feet with all four wheels clear of the sand. It landed with a crash, and I was jerked right out of my seat, while the car started to skid, a great cloud of sand spraying up at one side. As I straightened, slowing down, I heard a clattering from beneath the machine, and knew that some damage had been done, although I had no means of telling what it might be.

I ran on to the far end of the course, knowing that Villa and other mechanics were following. When their car reached the spot where the machine had jumped, they discovered part of the undershield, which had been torn away. We examined the car, and found that half the under-pan had been ripped off and was doubled right back under the tail. Shock absorbers were broken and the rear springs were so much damaged that the rear of the car which should have had a clearance of some five inches was all but touching the ground.

We could only tow 'Blue Bird' back to the garage and begin

repair work, having learned very little from that first test. The mechanics worked all night, changing the rear springs and making new parts for the shock absorbers, while we engaged panel beaters to hammer out a new undershield and repair a damaged section of the body. The work occupied two or three days, with a cold wind blowing all the time, and even when the machine was ready again, the sands were too rough for further attempts.

Although neither 'Triplex' nor the 'Black Hawk' Stutz had been tried out, I had opportunities of seeing both cars, and both drivers paid us friendly visits. Ray Keech was a big, heavily built, red-haired man, and his physical strength seemed in keeping with the power of his machine, which was garaged about four miles away along the beach. His 'Triplex' was an enormous car, and no effort had been made to streamline it, with the exception of a narrow cowling at the front. The twin engines behind the cockpit formed the tail, and it was plain that the designer regarded the machine as being possessed of sufficient brute force to overcome wind resistance and break the record. I believe the engines were built into a frame taken from a lorry, which may help to indicate the weight and the size of the machine.

I found young Frank Lockhart altogether unassuming and friendly, and his car demonstrated his cleverness. It was beautifully built, painted white, streamlined to the last degree, with every projection faired off. The Stutz was obviously the result of much careful work and fine designing. It occupied the same garage as 'Blue Bird', from which it may be understood that such rivalry as existed between Lockhart, Ray Keech and ourselves was of the most cordial nature possible. For all that, our car was never left unattended, and two of the mechanics slept beside it every night, either Villa and George Miller, or Coe and 'Mac of Dunlops'.

The machine was ready for another test on Saturday, but there was heavy rain and a high wind; nothing could be done, except hope that Sunday would bring an improvement. The rain stopped on Sunday morning, and we decided to try the car again; this time, I asked for the beach to be marked out and official times taken. There was no suggestion of making an attempt upon the record, but before we brought the car from its garage I told the mechanics that I would put my foot hard down if there was the least chance of reaching record speed. From a survey made earlier, there was not much promise of a really smooth beach, but it was in better condition than when we had last taken the car out.

More and more visitors had poured into the town. The knowledge that thousands of people were on the scene made it very hard to wait quietly for ideal conditions, because I now felt that everything was right with the car.

When we set out for the beach there were heavy clouds, and a strong crosswind was blowing from the north; this would be behind me during the first run and would help the car, but it would be against 'Blue Bird' on the return journey. By the time we had made all ready, the course had been set out with true American efficiency, and I received word that I could start as soon as I liked. Villa and the other mechanics looked around the car for the last time, when I sent the machine away. When I left the men behind I had no idea that I was about to face the worst experience of my life.

§6

One of the difficulties with 'Blue Bird', and which I had discovered during the first test run, was in changing gear, because it was impossible completely to free the clutch. When I shifted into top gear, at about 150 mph, it was as much as I could do to ram the gear home; the top-gear dogs kept kicking against one another, and the gear lever had to be forced in by sheer strength.

The car went away well, and I changed into top safely, then devoted myself to handling the machine, and that was not easy. As the speed mounted, 'Blue Bird' seemed to become alive, and terribly strong. I had actually to wrestle with the car to maintain a straight course, fighting against a tendency to snake from side to side, clinging to the steering wheel with all my strength.

Struggling to control the enormous power of the car, I had to concentrate everything upon physical effort. There was no chance to consider that what was happening was dangerous. There was no time, no thought for anything, except to use all the strength that I had in fighting the machine. As I neared the start of the mile, I glanced at the revolution counter. It was showing 210 mph and, with my foot hard down on the throttle pedal, I went into the measured distance.

All visibility now became an impression of the beach rushing to meet me, everything else forming a blurred kaleidoscope which raced past me on either side of the car. I could not distinguish anything that I passed, except as merged and hazy shapes of different shades. I kept my eyes focused directly ahead, and the objects which I was able to pick up, seen from the corners of my eyes, became vague as they rushed towards me, merging into the shapeless blur which constantly streamed by.

'Blue Bird's speed rose all the way through the mile, and when I neared the end I looked at the revolution counter again. It now showed 220 mph, and hardly had I seen this when, just clear of the timing tape, the car hit a bump. The impact shot me upwards out of my seat and into the truly tremendous airstream which rushed past the cockpit.

The air felt solid. It tore my goggles from my eyes and forced them down on my face. I was exposed only for the fraction of a second, but the wind seemed as if it would lift me from the car; I believe I should have gone, but for the tenacious grip that I had on the rim of the steering wheel.

I dropped to my seat again, but my foot had lost pressure on the throttle pedal. The engine, which had been pulling at the moment we hit the bump, now exerted a braking effect because the throttle had been partially closed and the machine pitched into a skid, shooting into a great stretch of soft sand. 'Blue Bird' was now all but out of control, caught by the side wind, and skidding in a huge cloud of sand at over 200 mph, while I was half-blinded because my goggles were jammed aslant across my face.

If ever I imagined that my end had come, I believed it in the moments which followed, and it was instinctive action which saved my life. I did not attempt to correct the skid, as I would have done had the surface been hard; instead, I helped the car to work itself out of the soft sand. Had I tried to straighten out deliberately, the chances would have been all in favour of the machine turning over. As it was, it required nearly a mile before I had 'Blue Bird' back on a safe course.

The car was still travelling very fast when I adjusted my goggles and looked for the mechanics who had been sent to the far end of the course. I saw them as the car slowed right down, and in the back of my mind I was working out that my speed through the mile must have been something very close to 215 mph. I had crossed the first tape at 210 mph, and the second at 220 mph, and the average of these two speeds gave me the car's approximate rate of travel through the distance. The record I had to beat stood at 203 mph, so on this run I had surpassed it, but to gain the record I had to return over the course.

The realization that I had to cover the same ground again, that I had to fight 'Blue Bird' once more, was not in the least pleasant. Sitting in the cockpit, using the brakes carefully, I felt exhausted. The muscles of my arms were wrenched, and my whole body felt strained. And I was tired. According to programme, I should have halted to change wheels as a safety measure, but I decided not to do this. I knew that if I stopped and got out of the car, I should never step into the machine again. Near the waiting mechanics, I began to turn, then waved to them and started straight back again.

I put my foot down and 'Blue Bird' gathered speed once more. It was only when I came to change into top gear that I discovered just how much that first run had sapped my strength. I could not get the gear in, and, travelling at 150 mph, I had to take both

Sunbeam 350 hp crosses the finish line at Pendine Sands in 1920.

The palm tree on Cocos island with the previous treasure hunter's initials engraved.

Sir Henry Segrave, Campbell's great land speed record rival in the 1920s.

Travelling at 130 mph at Pendine with Campbell wiping wet sand off the windscreen.

The dramatic lines of the Stutz Black Hawk.

The burned-out wreck of 'Babs' on Pendine Sands.

Parry Thomas in 'Babs' at Brooklands.

Campbell where he was happiest, in the cockpit of 'Blue Bird'.

Campbell's Napier 'Blue Bird' in 1928 at Daytona.

The Napier-Campbell at Pendine Sands in early January 1927. Note the water on the sand.

Frank Lockhart and his Stutz Black Hawk at Daytona.

hands from the wheel, using the last of my remaining strength to force the gear lever home. It went in, and I snatched at the wheel, my foot going down on the throttle pedal.

The wind was against the car now, and this, as the pace rose, tended to make the machine even less tractable than it had been before. I had to fight over every yard, and it was when I sighted the entrance to the measured mile that I remembered the bump and the soft sand that lay near. This was just in front of what was now the start of the measured distance. If I hit the bump, and if there was another skid, I knew that I should not have enough strength to hold 'Blue Bird', while the skid would send the car towards the sand dunes, the spectators, and the machines which were packed in front of them.

The start of the mile flashed nearer, and I held my breath as the car pitched towards it. There was an instant of suspense, then the machine was over the tape, clear of the bump, and racing on with everything rushing past me. I now seemed detached, no part of the blurred world that came to meet the car and vanished behind. I could hear only the rush of the wind, and saw nothing clearly except the far end of the mile.

There were long-drawn moments of suspense before I reached it and cleared the tape, then I began to ease my foot on the throttle pedal, doing this very carefully, while the car travelled more than another two miles before I attempted to use the brakes. 'Blue Bird' slowed, ran to the end of the course, and stopped. I remained in the cockpit while the mechanics hurried over. I felt weak and they helped me out, then came news which was like a tonic.

On my first run, 'Blue Bird' had covered the measured mile at 214.79 mph, and the return had been at a fraction below 200 mph. The mean speed for the two runs was 206.956 mph, which meant that we had broken the world's land-speed record by a clear margin. Leaning against the side of the car, finding it hard to stand, I realized that we had accomplished all that we had hoped.

§7

We believed that 'Blue Bird' could go still faster and there was, in any case, a chance that either Keech or Lockhart might beat my figures. So we stood by ready to make another attempt if the new record should be broken, or, if there was an opportunity, to improve upon our own figures.

Two days later, when the weather had improved, Lockhart's 'Black Hawk' Stutz came to the sand for tests, and conditions were so much better that we decided to run 'Blue Bird' again, after Lockhart had made his attempt.

The sand was good, but there were squalls of rain when the little white car started its trials. We warmed up 'Blue Bird's' engine, and Lockhart started his last test run from where we waited. We watched him vanish from sight, then I climbed into the cockpit.

It was quite impossible for us to see anything which happened down the course, because the start of the measured stretch was four miles away. We waited there for some time, and I was eventually told that I could go. I was about to give the word for the mechanics to start up the engine when a policeman appeared, travelling flat out on his motorcycle. He skidded to a stop beside the car.

'For God's sake, don't start!' he shouted. 'There's been a terrible accident. Lockhart's dead.'

I climbed from the machine, jumped into another car and set off along the beach, to find a big crowd gathered near the mile, where men were wading breast-deep in the sea, dragging out Lockhart's battered car. He had been moving at about 190 mph when a squall of wind caught the car; Lockhart, trying to correct the machine as it skidded, found himself headed for the sea. He was unable to bring the machine straight, and hit the water with a tremendous splash, the car skimming on over the surface in a series of great leaps before it slowed down and sank; some say that the car virtually looped the loop in its wild dash.

The metal fairings over the wheels were broken and battered, and Lockhart was almost unconscious when he was dragged out, but he was not dead. In fact, his injuries were not as bad as they might have been. His arm was broken, the tendons of his wrists were cut, and he suffered very severe shock.

He was hurried to hospital, and I believe it was the next day when Ray Keech made initial test runs with 'Triplex'. A connection to the radiator of the forward engine broke when he was moving very fast, so that a shower of steam and scalding water played over the driver's legs. He held the car somehow, and brought it to a stop, then he, too, was rushed away for medical attention.

These mishaps brought the trials to an end, because it would have taken a long while to repair the 'Black Hawk' Stutz, and it was obvious that some time must elapse before Keech could try again. We began to pack up, but, before leaving, I saw Frank Lockhart. He agreed that his escape had been a narrow one, and I asked him not to be in a hurry to try again, but he told me that as soon as his car was ready he would make another attempt. I could only shake hands and wish him all the luck in the world, and soon after that we left for home.

The new record which 'Blue Bird' had set up was not to stand for very long. Two months later, Ray Keech reappeared with 'Triplex' at Daytona. On Sunday, April 22nd, 1928, he made a first run at a speed of 203.9 mph. On the return trip, with the wind behind his car, he was estimated to have reached 210 mph, but a fault in the timing apparatus left the run unregistered. An hour later he tried again, and this time the wind caught the car, carrying it towards the very edge of the course when he was travelling at his highest speed. Keech held the machine safely, however, and was timed at 201.56 mph. Coming back again with the wind, his pace through the mile was just a fraction below 214 mph.

His average speed worked out at 207.5 mph 'Blue Bird's' record had been 206.9 mph. By travelling one third of a mile an hour faster, Ray Keech had broken our record and had set up a new

one. It was a splendid effort, because he found the car very difficult to hold, while, during his last run, a backfire badly burned
his right forearm.

The following day, Frank Lockhart took his 'Black Hawk' Stutz
out to attack the new figure. He worked up the car's speed on
two trial runs, then made a third dash southward, registering
203.45 mph. After this third run, he turned to come north, and
he was approaching the centre of the course at a speed well above
200 mph when he burst his off-side rear tyre. The car skidded for
nearly five hundred feet, then made a gigantic leap through the air,
jumping for a hundred and forty feet and landing on the timing
tape. The machine then made a second wild leap of a hundred
and twenty feet, and jumped a third time, covering seventy-five
feet before it thudded down on its side. Lockhart was flung out of
the car, which came to rest close against him.

There was no hope for him after such a crash. It brought to an
end a career that had hardly begun.

§8

'Blue Bird' had raised the record, but had in turn been beaten
and the land-speed figures now stood to the credit of America. I
almost wished that we had remained at Daytona, because I felt
that 'Blue Bird' had not travelled at anything near her maximum
speed, and that the car was fully capable of regaining the record.

In the weeks following Ray Keech's success, we discussed 'Blue
Bird', finally deciding to make another attempt early the following year, but I was doubtful about running the car at Daytona.
The days of waiting, before our attempt, had been a strain, and it
was obvious that no one I could ever be certain of when the sands
would be in a safe state for the very high rate of speed which had
been reached.

I wondered if an inland course could be found, one over which
the car could be tested without hurry, where the ground could be

carefully cleared and, if necessary, levelled off. On such a course, arrangements could be made well in advance, obviating all uncertainty and delay.

It seemed certain that a suitable place must exist somewhere, and it might prove to be more conveniently located than Daytona, where the car was several thousands of miles from its base, and where the whole attempt might be endangered if some small thing had been overlooked or forgotten.

Discussion made it evident that there was no need to rebuild 'Blue Bird'. We were convinced that the car could do better than the figure which Keech had set up, although it was possible that an improvement could be made in the streamlining of our machine and that the placing of the radiators required alteration.

News came that Segrave was entering the field again, this time with an entirely new machine of special design. He announced his intention of taking this car to Daytona, where it seemed certain that 'Triplex' would defend the record. Accordingly, I finally decided to make minor alterations to 'Blue Bird', and, when the car was nearing completion, to try and discover another course on which we could run. With this settled, I turned from record work to racing.

THE EIGHTH CHAPTER

§1

THE FIRST IMPORTANT RACE OF the 1928 season, so far as British drivers were concerned, was one of the most sporting events in which I have ever driven. It was known as the Six-Hours Endurance race, and was run off at Brooklands in the middle of May. The event was not for racing machines, but for sports models in touring trim, and the circuit was much the same as that used for the British Grand Prix.

The cars were lined up at the side of the course, drivers and mechanics being stationed opposite. They had to run across the track to their machines at the fall of the flag, erect the hoods, get the engines running, and start off. Ten laps had to be covered with the hoods in position, after which the drivers could pull in at the pits, lower the hoods, and carry on with the race.

These arrangements may seem to be more fitting to a gymkhana than a serious event, but there was a very good reason for them. The hood fittings would be subjected to a rigorous test, while starting up the engines was a test for the batteries and the power unit generally. The whole race was, in any case, designed to prove the roadworthiness of the competing sports cars.

Forty starters appeared, on a sunny Saturday morning, divided into various classes, although all began the race together; I had bought a new Bugatti, and Lord Howe was driving a sister car.

The only saloon model in the event was first off the line, and it was followed by a team of 4-litre Bentleys, with Howe at their tails. Two other machines left before I was able to get away, when I chased the leaders, the rest of the cars roaring in a pack behind,

A big Mercedes followed my Bugatti down the railway straight. The Bentleys had passed the saloon when Howe went in front of them, taking the lead, and I followed, with the Mercedes at the tail of my car. We maintained this order, while the track became filled with machines, many of them in difficulties with their hoods. On one, the hood collapsed completely, enveloping the driver and his mechanic; the back of the hoods blew out upon others, the material giving way under the strain of a 100-mph gale, representing the speed at which these machines were travelling. On about the fifth lap I took the lead from Howe; my Bugatti was now travelling very well, and was first in at the pits when, after ten laps, the hood was lowered. Next time round, slower cars swooped towards their depots, stopping while their crews leaped out and attacked the hoods.

Relieved of these encumbrances, speeds went up, but at the end of another six laps I still held the lead. Then, passing the pits, I saw Howe's car stopped; he had magneto trouble, and the machine was pushed away to the dead car' park just as we met trouble. Part of the tread from the near-side rear tyre suddenly broke away. The rubber, flying off with tremendous force, hit the wing guarding the wheel, bending its supports and smashing it against the body, so that the lower part of the metal rubbed against the tyre. I slowed and ran in to the pits, where difficulties with a jack brought a long delay before we could change the wheel, repair the wing and dash off again.

Every car in the race was now being driven hard, and there was some particularly fierce cornering on the bends. In front of the Bugatti, as we came to the second turn, one machine chipped the end of the sandbank, throwing up a great cloud of sand, which shot like a curtain across the course. The machine continued at speed and, when we burst through the sand, we saw the car skidding across our path; the driver straightened out and put his foot down once more.

Machines were constantly diving in at the pits and coming away again, while, on the Bugatti, we were beginning to make up the ground we had lost, when the gearbox gave trouble. This reduced our speed on the corners and then, to make matters worse, the fuel pressure began to drop. We limped in to the pit with the engine spluttering, and upon investigation it was found that the neck bearing the tank filler cap had broken away. It was impossible to maintain pressure in the petrol tank, repairs were impossible, and the Bugatti retired.

Just after the Endurance race, I heard that the famous team of Delage cars were for sale; these were the machines which had finished first, second and third in the French Grand Prix, and had repeated the performance in the British Grand Prix of 1927. The cars were in Paris and, accompanied by Villa, I went over to see them; we tried each of the machines in turn, then selected the Delage which had been driven by Benoist.

We rushed it back to England, and it was my intention to run it in the race for the Brooklands Gold Vase at the Whitsun Bank Holiday meeting; this was to be in the nature of a preliminary test. The machine performed perfectly during practice on Friday and Saturday; on the Sunday some small matters required attention, but when we tried the car we found it immovable, although it had been in good order when we left it. At first we thought that the engine had seized, but examination traced the trouble to the gearbox. Here we found one of the pinions broken; a segment had fallen completely out, wedging in the box and locking everything. Apparently, the pinion had been broken for some time, and it had stopped in just the right position for the sector to drop away. We had to cancel the entry for the Gold Vase, which meant that the first race in which I could run the car would be the Two Hundred.

When repairs had been effected and I was able to take the

Delage out for practice, the car ran like a thoroughbred, and we began to plan our tactics for the race. These were very simple, because we judged that the machine could carry enough fuel to run right through the event; this meant that, if all went well, I should drive non-stop. Villa and his companions were to watch my tyres closely, and signal me in for a wheel change if they showed signs of failing.

On the day of the race twenty-six cars lined up. The sun was brilliant, and planes from the aerodrome in the centre of the track were zooming above the concrete as we watched the big red and white semaphore arm which replaced the starter's flag. At two-thirty it dropped, and a maroon was shot into the sky, exploding with a report which I could hear above the sound of exhausts as I sent the Delage from the line.

The car took the lead from the start, and was unchallenged after the first half-mile. It was well in front by the time that I came to the first hairpin turn; the course was the same as that employed for the previous race. Next time round, I saw that a car had skidded into the fencing by the first bend, but no one appeared to have been hurt, and this was almost the only unto-ward happening throughout the race. The Delage lapped at very little below 80 mph, increasing its lead all the time then, about halfway through the race, an official who stood by the banking at the start of the railway straight began signalling to me.

Each time that I passed, he waved excitedly and pointed to the front of the Delage. I craned out of the cockpit, but I could not see anything wrong. He persisted in his signals, and at last I pulled in at the pits, where the mechanics looked the machine over but could discover nothing faulty. Even then the official con-tinued his signals for some time, and it was not until after the race that we guessed the reason for his action.

The exhaust pipe of the Delage was near the carburettor and, in taking the bend to the straight, when the car ran partly up the banking, a little petrol was thrown from the carburettor on to the pipe. This flared up, and to the watching man it must have seemed that the machine was catching fire.

After this incident, the Delage travelled steadily on, setting a pace which brought it first to the finishing flag at an average speed of 78.3 mph, the car coming home nearly a quarter of an hour in front of the machine in second position.

This victory made me the only private owner ever to have won the event on two occasions. Segrave had actually won it three times, but he had been backed by a manufacturer and had been a member of an official team.

§2

We were now in the middle of the racing season, and the plans concerning 'Blue Bird' had taken definite shape. A new body had been designed, and this was to be built at the Arrol-Aster works, in Dundee. Instead of radiators placed beside the tail, one was to be positioned in front of the car, covered with a special cowling. Everything else was to be left as it had been at Daytona.

The car was standing in the shed at Brooklands, and Villa was working on it alone. We had plenty of time for its preparation, and the work went slowly forward while I ran in two more events. One was the Tourist Trophy race, which was being revived on a circuit outside Belfast, and the other was at Boulogne. The French event was due during the first week in September, and the TT was dated for mid-August; when these races were over, I intended to devote myself entirely to 'Blue Bird', and to the search for a new course.

The TT race was, at that time, run under regulations similar to those of the Six-Hours Endurance event, but the TT was altogether more rigorous, because it was being held over a true road circuit. The length of the course was 13.66 miles, and this had to be covered thirty times, making a total distance of 410 miles.

No Tourist Trophy race had been held for six years, and earlier events had always roused great interest; the revival created some excitement, and it attracted a very large entry. Forty-four cars came to the line, France, Germany, Austria, America, Italy and England being represented.

I entered the Bugatti which we had run in the Endurance race, and practice laps showed that the car was very fast, although we had some trouble before the brakes were satisfactory. I had never previously engaged in a race which created so much excitement, and preliminary work on the course was very keen. As far as I can remember, we made the fastest lap times in practice, and that augured well for our chances. The car was in good trim when Villa and I turned out for the event, running through the stream of traffic still making for the circuit.

People had been pouring out of Belfast since the first hint of daylight, and the course was lined with spectators hours before the cars were due to start. Once again, drivers and mechanics lined up opposite their machines and waited for the flag to fall. It was noticeable that the crowd became completely silent, and when the signal came the only sound which broke the quiet was that made by the men who ran across the road. There followed the noise of starter motors, and it seemed to me that nearly every machine got away at the same time, after hoods had been erected; two laps had to be covered with these in position.

The Bugatti was trapped in a bunch of machines when we raced for the first corner, and we ran wheel to wheel with cars on either side as we went up the hill around the turn. The press did not begin to clear until we were dropping down to Newtownards, a town set at one corner of the course. A Bentley was leading then, with Birkin at the wheel, and he was still in front when the first lap ended. I was not sure of our own position in the race and, in any case, I regarded the two opening laps as useful for warming the car up thoroughly; after that, and when we had lowered the hood, I intended to put my foot hard down.

We covered the second lap rapidly, but the fuel pressure began to fall, and I knew we were in for trouble. Actually, one of the seams of the tank had burst as we hit a bump in the road, and petrol spilled on the exhaust pipe. The tank containing thirty-two gallons of fuel caught alight but, owing to our speed, the flames were swept backwards. The moment we slowed down to come into the pits, the car became a roaring furnace and Villa and I only just managed to get out in time. We both dived at the pit counter for fire extinguishers, and sent streams of chemicals at the tail of the car. Officials raced up, boy scouts on duty at the pits came to help, but the extinguishers were useless.

Great clouds of smoke rolled out, half-hiding the flames. The hood caught alight, and the bodywork became smothered with the yellow-white chemical we were using. The smoke, drifting across the road, obscured the course, forming a danger to other machines and, with the car burning, it was rolled forward and off the course. There we attacked it again, but it was quite hopeless. The fire could not be checked and the car was soon reduced to debris. In a little while, what had been a fine and fast machine was changed to a smoking shape, its metal twisted, the skeleton steel supports of the hood showing above the wreck; even the lead ballast which we had to carry flowed in molten form on to the road.

It was very bad luck, and the car was totally uninsured. The mechanics who had worked hard to prepare the machine never had the pleasure of watching it run, and all that could be done was to look forward to the next event, at Boulogne.

For many reasons, I was even more keen about the French event than I had been over the Tourist Trophy race. I had entered the burnt-out machine for the Georges Boillot Cup, which was to be held on Saturday, September 8th, and I intended to run the Delage from the Two Hundred Miles in another event, known as the Trophée Nationale, the following day.

I now lacked a car for the Boillot Cup, but managed to secure a 1,500 c.c. Bugatti in time for the event. This was a perfectly normal car, and we worked frantically to get it ready in time, because the opposition in the race was led by a driver named Dutilleux, who had a supercharged straight eight Bugatti.

Before we crossed to France, I bought another of the Grand Prix Delages, this machine being that which Bourlier had driven; we took both these cars, as well as the Bugatti, to Boulogne, and it was as well that we did so. The Delage which I intended to use in the race gave trouble, but we overcame this by taking both engines down, using the best parts from each for the car I intended to race. The Delage still persistently oiled up its plugs, but we hoped that, once the machine got going, it would present no further difficulties.

The Bugatti was in good condition when, at nine o'clock on the Saturday morning, the machines lined up. My only doubt about the car lay in its steel brake-drums; there was a chance that these might prove too small, because the twisting sections of the course make braking an important matter.

I was racing against three Alfa-Romeos – these Italian cars were then rapidly achieving distinction on the Continent – two Bugattis, one of which was handled by Dutilleux, and a front-wheel drive Alvis, with C. M. Harvey at the wheel. Another Alvis, a Frazer-Nash, and a Tracta completed the list of machines, and, when the flag dropped, Harvey's Alvis leaped into the lead.

The Alfa-Romeos challenged myself and Dutilleux in the rush for the hairpin turn at St Martin, all of us chasing Harvey. We continued to chase him around the circuit, while Dutilleux slipped ahead of my Bugatti; when the first lap ended I was nearly a quarter of a mile behind him, while he clung to Harvey's tail. The Alfa-Romeos were then out of sight in rear, and leadership was a fight between the British car and the two Bugattis.

On the second lap, Dutilleux passed Harvey along the straight between the wood at La Capelle and Le Wast, and I closed in. Then, on the third lap, as we came to La Capelle again, I saw a crowd at the side of the course. Bits of wreckage were scattered about, and I had a glimpse of the machine jammed against a tree, with one side of its frame torn outwards.

It was on this lap that I broke the record for 1,500 c.c. machines, averaging 72 mph. I had to drive flat out all the time, but, getting the feel of the corners, managed to travel even faster next time, clipping another ten seconds off the record, and passing both Harvey and Dutilleux. My four-cylinder machine was not so fast as the eight-cylinder Bugatti and, although I could beat the Frenchman on the corners, I lost ground along the straights. For two laps I held him off, then he called at the pits for fuel.

Only by overdriving my machine could I now keep in front. All this time my pit staff were urging me to go faster, but this was impossible, as I was straining the car and using every available ounce of power. I cut every bend and every turn, and this brought trouble. Along the winding stretch beyond Le Wast, the car's brakes suddenly lost their power, and I was unable to slow enough to take a bend. The machine ran off the road and hit the bottom of a bank. It jumped into the air, coming down with a tremendous crash, but I held it through the curve, and continued on my course.

The front axle appeared to be bent, and I knew that the brakes were bad, but there was little more than three laps to be covered, and I continued, driving hard, changing down and using the gears instead of the brakes in slowing for corners. At the end of the next lap, I went fast into the St Martin hairpin, a little too fast. I changed down, and ran through the turn, but the gearbox would not stand such treatment, and the car stopped just around the corner. I swung it on to the footpath and, realizing that it was impossible to continue, abandoned the machine and walked back to the pits on my last lap.

Dutilleux was now in the lead, but his luck was no better than my own. He was far ahead of any challengers on his last lap when one of his wheels collapsed, putting him out of the race, after which one of the Alfa-Romeo team went on to win. Dutilleux had no opportunity of seeking recompense for his misfortune, since he was not driving in the National Trophy race the following day.

This event was over the same distance as that of the Boillot Cup, and the race was due to start at the same time in the morning.

The flag was very late in falling, because the race could not begin until a railway train had traversed lines which ran over part of the circuits, and it was half an hour before the train was reported as having passed. My Delage took the lead from the start, leaving in a cloud of smoke and, at the end of the first lap, it was almost a mile in front of the next machine. The car was not as easy to handle as the Bugatti had been the day before, but it was much faster along the straights and averaged 72 mph on its first lap, almost equalling the record lap in the Boillot Cup event.

The race was not exciting, because the Delage remained in front all the time. About mid-morning, a service began at the church built inside the hairpin turn by St Martin's and, when I cut out for the corner, I could hear organ music sounding above the whine of the brake shoes as the car took the bend.

The speed of the Delage rose with each succeeding lap, and the car broke the record for the race on its seventh circuit with 78.1 mph, which was very high for such a course. Three laps later, the engine began to misfire, then stopped altogether. I thought that the machine had run out of petrol, and switched on the reserve tank, cranking the engine without result. I spent three or four minutes in looking the car over, then suddenly suspected the magneto switch. As a test, I tore off the earth wire, then cranked again, and at once the engine fired. I slipped into the cockpit just as the Bugatti which held second place appeared from a bend behind. It passed me with a rush, and was still in front at the end of that lap, but I caught it just beyond St Martin's, regaining the lead, and when the Delage ran home at the end of the last lap my car was fully seven minutes in front of the next machine.

This success brought to an end a racing season in which I had met with a mixture of bad luck and very good fortune. After returning from France, I drove in one or two meetings at Brooklands, and then settled down to consider the question of finding a suitable course on which 'Blue Bird' could again try to break the land-speed record.

§3

Much earlier in the year, I had given up an opportunity to drive in the twenty-four hours race at Le Mans in order to go to Denmark where, I was informed, a wonderful beach was set on the north coast. The reports were incorrect, however, and the stretch of sand proved unsuitable.

Following this, a search was made on the Continent, and a friend examined the new autostradas in Italy. It was reported that these motor roads were dead straight for many miles, but they proved too narrow for 200-mph speeds; in any case, they were nearly all built on low embankments above the surrounding fields, and the drop from the road edge would give a car no chance of escape if the machine left its course. Reports from Belgium and Spain were also followed up, but they proved fruitless, and it was then suggested that a suitable spot might be discovered in country which was sparsely inhabited.

I heard of a level stretch in the Syrian desert, and had begun to make preparations to fly over and inspect it, when the tribesmen there began to give trouble. It was certain that their reception would be anything but friendly, and local co-operation was vital if ever we took the car out, so we abandoned the expedition.

Following this came information of a great plateau, with an absolutely level surface, which existed in the Sahara. Details concerning it were sparse, but the reports seemed worth investigation and, early in November, I started from Croydon in a Gipsy Moth, accompanied by Squadron Leader Don, an old friend of war-time days.

We crossed the Straits of Gibraltar, and followed the coast to Oran. The flight was very rough and bumpy, and the North African coast looked very inhospitable, because the Atlas Mountains here come straight down to the sea, forming a rugged coastline; the mountains are inhabited only by turbulent Riff tribesmen who, at that time, were giving trouble to the Spanish authorities. We reached Oran, where certain formalities had to be completed and permission secured to continue the flight, which was now over French territory. We then headed south to Colomb Beshar, crossing the Atlas Mountains on the way. These heights were most impressive, and appeared to us as enormous masses of sheer rock; here was no visible sign of life, with the exception of a Riffian village, which appeared as a cluster of open courtyards set amongst a few trees.

From Colomb Beshar we flew above the French fort at Beni Abbes, set right in the desert. Here compact buildings were ranged inside an encircling wall, the fortress forming an open square, with massive keeps at each corner. We landed finally beside the fort at Reggan, and were now in the heart of the Sahara and about six hundred miles north of Timbuktu. Don was unwell when we arrived, and he remained at the fort while I borrowed a car and spent two days in the desert, locating the place of which we had been told.

It was a great plateau, as level as a billiards table and stretching for miles. The surface was gritty, and covered with small pebbles; when these were swept away, perfectly smooth, level ground was disclosed. Unquestionably, the plateau was ideal, and its only real defect was formed by mirages; I secured a photograph of one in which it seemed that, barely a mile away, waves were breaking on a sandy shore.

Unfortunately, the plateau was hopelessly remote. It lay at least four hundred miles from any railway line, and it would have been impossible to transport, over this distance, the car and equipment, mechanics, timekeepers, necessary kit, and labourers required to clear the ground. I collected samples of the surface and of the pebbles, then drove back to Reggan; Don had recovered, and we started the return flight to Oran. To all appearances, the enterprise had been a failure. As matters turned out, however, things were now to happen which, quite indirectly, brought about discovery of the course we sought.

On reaching Oran, it was our intention to follow the shore line, recrossing the Mediterranean at Gibraltar. Before leaving, we were warned that a certain stretch of the coast was exceedingly dangerous, because of the presence of hostile Riff tribesmen. The place was indicated to us on a map – it lay some seventy-eight miles short of Tetuan, opposite Gibraltar – and at this point the mountains were particularly rugged and came sheer down to the sea, forming great cliffs which made any sort of landing impossible; we were not, in any case, likely to descend there.

We began the flight from Oran at about six-thirty in the morning. Aboard the plane we had a small bottle of Vichy water, a flask of brandy, and two packets of chocolate, those being our sole preparations for emergencies. We followed the coast, and had been two hours in the air when we found ourselves level with the territory against which we had been warned.

Shortly afterwards, when we were fifteen hundred feet up and about a mile out to sea, there came a blowback from the engine, followed by such vibration that it seemed as if the power unit would shake itself loose; an inlet valve had jammed, and it was only by good fortune that fire did not follow.

With the engine dead, the machine was turned in towards the coast, while Don and I searched anxiously for a landing place. We had insufficient height to glide inland and hope to find a valley and, as the plane had to come down, our only chance was to discover a level stretch on the edge of the shore. We saw nothing but rocks and cliffs falling directly to the water until, with the plane now very low, we cleared a headland and, beyond this, discovered a small bay with a narrow, shingle beach. It was the only possible landing place, and the craft came down just on the edge of the beach, partly in the sea.

It was rocking on the water as we climbed out, jumping in

up to our necks, grabbing the tail as the machine slewed round. There was a very strong undertow, and we were almost dragged off our feet. We knew that if we lost the machine, our chances of escape from that inhospitable country were very small, while there was a possibility that, if we got the plane clear of the water, we might be able to make a repair and find some way of taking off again.

We had been struggling for two or three minutes, floundering in the water, clinging to the tail of the machine and just holding our own, when I glanced over my shoulder. When we landed, there had not been a living thing in sight. Now I saw, grouped on the beach, forty or fifty of the most outlandish men I had ever seen.

They were Riff tribesmen, wearing dingy skirts, and every man was armed. I stared at them, remembering the stories I had heard of their way of holding prisoners to ransom. These Riffs are warlike, recognizing no masters of their inaccessible country and I remember thinking, as I clung to the machine, that we were literally between the devil and the deep sea.

We were up to our chests in water and completely helpless, but I realized that a bold course might be the safest and we shouted to the Riffs to help. They did not understand, but they could see our plight, and a dozen of them waded grabbing at the machine, shouting amongst themselves and hauling until the plane was standing safely on the little beach.

A few of them looked it over curiously, and the rest gave their attention to Don and myself. They were a bearded, dirty, evil-smelling crew, and it was not long before they began to jostle us roughly, obviously looking for an excuse to start trouble. We pretended to take this as a joke, while I spoke to them first in English, then in French, and afterwards in German, all the time doing my utmost to make them realize that we were not Spaniards.

It was the most fortunate thing in the world that they did not understand me. The only reason we were not immediately taken prisoner was because they imagined us to be Spanish airmen; they were afraid that, if they mishandled us, bombers might arrive later on a punitive expedition.

Unable to talk to them, I singled out one who appeared to be their leader, and offered him a couple of five-peseta pieces, some of which I chanced to possess. These are big coins, and they pleased him; the rest crowded around and I distributed more coins, then indicated that they had received all the money I had. Since there was nothing more to be gained, the Riffs finally let us go, vanishing into the rocks beyond the bay, abandoning us and the disabled machine.

It was a relief to find ourselves clear of the tribesmen, but Don and I were left in a difficult situation. We now saw that even if we managed to get the engine going, it was impossible to take off from the beach, and in any case, we dared not remain there. We agreed that the one essential thing was to cover as great a distance as possible before darkness fell. We knew that the nearest town was Tetuan, with no kind of civilization between ourselves and that city, and the only thing to do was to make for it, following the coastline as well as we were able. We collected the Vichy water, brandy and chocolate and started off.

When we began, we realized that we were attempting something which appeared impossible. We could not hope to cover more than seventy miles of inhospitable country on the Vichy water and choc-olate which we carried, particularly over such rugged terrain, and we were unarmed. But the only thing to do was to attempt it, and the trek during the rest of that day was the hardest that I have ever attempted. The going was very rough, most of the time being spent in clambering over rocks, and we often found our way barred by jutting cliffs, around which we were obliged to swim. What had originally been a simple search for a new high-speed course was turning into an adventure which had elements of very real danger.

We carried on until we were forced to rest, and both of us then believed that we should not get through. We made an agreement that, if either of us met with a mishap, or found that he could go no further, he should be left and his companion should struggle on. After making this agreement, we continued, and we were dead beat by the time that darkness fell.

We decided to keep moving for as long as we were able, and we now turned inland a little, blundering slowly forward until we heard dogs yapping in the gloom and realized that we had reached some sort of village. We pulled up, wondering what kind of reception we should get if we ventured nearer. We were wet through, tired and desperate; it was past midnight, and we had been on our feet for nearly twelve hours. As we stood there, one of the biggest men I have ever seen appeared from the darkness. He must have been at least six feet six inches in height, and after we had tried to talk to him, he beckoned us forward, leading us into a kind of courtyard.

Cattle were tied up around a midden; I saw goats and chickens in the darkness, and at one side was a structure built against the wall. In the lower part lived the wives of the local chief, and we were taken up a ladder to the floor above, the ladder consisting of two poles with notches cut in them. We found half a dozen Riffs squatting on the mud floor at the top; the place had no windows and no ventilation other than that provided by the little door; the atmosphere was terrible and the sole illumination was a candle.

The chief proved to be friendly, and he extended some sort of welcome. Presently a basket was hauled up from below containing a bowl of rancid butter and some loaves of harsh, sour bread, and we were invited to share the meal. The Riffs broke off pieces of bread, dipping them into the butter, and I imitated them, but my first taste of the butter was nauseating, and it was hard enough to swallow even a few morsels. Don was affected in much the same way, and both of us looked hopefully towards a bucket which was presently hauled up. This was passed from hand to hand, and when it reached me I saw that it contained water that was almost black. I could not bring myself to drink it, and the bucket passed on.

This concluded the meal. The single candle in the room was extinguished, the Riffs stretched themselves out on the floor, while the chief sprawled across the doorway, a knife lying on his thighs. In spite of the conditions and the discomfort, Don and I managed to get a little sleep, but all the time the Riffs around us were twitching and muttering, very like dogs in uneasy slumber.

At six o'clock in the morning, the basket and the bucket came up again. I was ravenously hungry and extremely thirsty, but my first effort to eat the sour bread almost brought a fit of sickness, and I was glad that I had not touched the water when I saw the Riffs wash themselves in it after drinking. The bucket was then passed down, the water being reserved for the next meal.

Stumbling on to this village as we had done was very fortunate for Don and myself, because we had been able to rest, but we were anxious to get away. We knew the treacherous nature of Riff tribesmen, and preferred the open air to remaining in that two-storied hut. We made our departure after I had given the old chief most of the belongings in my haversack, resuming our tramp along the difficult coast, growing less and less hopeful of reaching civilization as the hours passed.

We swam around points and climbed across rocky headlands, with the sun beating down all the time, while we hardly ever found a level stretch. We were constantly either climbing or scrambling down rough slopes and, during that morning, I slipped on one of these, falling heavily and landing awkwardly. I found myself unable to move, and I thought I had fractured my hip; my leg was quite numb, and I believed that I should be unable to go on.

I reminded Don of our compact, but he insisted upon staying with me. We tried to ascertain what injury I had sustained and, after a while, I found the numbness passing and I was able to move my leg. My hip and thigh were badly bruised, but nothing was broken and presently we were able to continue, although I was now limping and in great pain.

At the end of six hours of tramping, Don had lost the sole

of one shoe, and at noon we shared the bottle of Vichy water. We had had nothing to drink since leaving Oran thirty hours before, and the mineral water now served only to make our thirst more intense. We plodded slowly on and presently came to great stretches of rusted barbed wire, marking an area over which fighting between the Spaniards and the Riffs had recently taken place. We scratched and tore ourselves in getting through these defences.

By mid-afternoon, it proved impossible to continue without another halt, and Don dozed for a time under the shadow of some rocks. We could not guess how far we had travelled, nor how much distance we had still to cover and, as our shoes were giving out, it was impossible that we could go very much farther.

Sitting against a rock on that desolate North African coast, familiar scenes at Brooklands and at home seemed very remote, and I was thinking of this when I drifted to sleep. I roused after a while, and when I sat up almost the first thing that I saw was the silhouette of a man on a ridge. He was fully four miles away, standing against the sky, but even at that distance I saw that he wore trousers; this indicated that he was not one of the Riffs, and that Europeans must be nearby.

I wakened Don, and we started forward, scrambling through more barbed wire, eventually coming up with the man and discovering that he formed a part of a Spanish outpost. We were taken to the commandant, and never have I drunk water which tasted as good as that which he gave us. The Spaniards could not understand how we came to be there, but they produced a sergeant who could speak French and I was able to explain. We remained overnight and were treated with great courtesy, eventually travelling on to Ceuta. A guard was sent down to look after the plane, and the Spanish authorities followed this with a cruiser and a lighter. The plane was loaded on the lighter and brought back to Ceuta, eventually being shipped across to British territory at Gibraltar.

When we returned to England, we found that the story of our unexpected adventures had received a good deal of attention, and news of our search for a high-speed course reached South Africa. A few weeks later, I was told of a dry lake which was called Verneuk Pan, which lay about four hundred miles north of Cape Town.

There was a little village named Brandvlei, about fifty miles from the lake, and here lived a Dr Marin. He had chanced to see a notice concerning our search and wrote to the *Cape Times*, suggesting that someone should inspect Verneuk Pan. He said that the lakebed offered a stretch of level, hard surface, twenty miles long, and ten miles wide.

The newspapers sent an assistant editor to the Pan, and he reported that the dry lake was everything which Dr Marin had said. The smoothness of the surface was proved by the fact that he had driven a car for some miles at over 70 mph without touching the steering wheel. While he was preparing a full report and photographs, the Cape Times sent a cable to me, and this arrived three weeks after our return from the Sahara. It was followed by further particulars, and at the end of December I sent out a representative to secure still more details. As a result of his report I decided to take 'Blue Bird' to South Africa, and try to break the record there.

We left England in the middle of January, and about a fortnight later Segrave started for Daytona with his new machine, which had been called the 'Golden Arrow'. Both of us were to try and break the record, Segrave on the sands of Daytona Beach, and 'Blue Bird' on the dried mud of a South African lake.

§4

When 'Blue Bird' was shipped to South Africa, the chassis had been completely overhauled, and the engine had been tuned to give increased power; the only alterations to the car were the position of the radiator and the new bodywork. We retained wheel fairings, and the fin became part of the tail; owing to the shape of the body, the driving position, immediately above the propeller shaft, appeared high. This position gave a very good view forward from the cockpit, but it detracted from the streamlining of the machine.

At one time, we had considered the possibility of placing the driving seat behind the back axle, which would have given us perfect streamlining, but this proved impracticable, and it would probably have resulted in a very uncomfortable ride for myself. We took with us fifty-six cases of spare parts, including R.A.C. timing gear, thirty-six tyres, eight hundred gallons of special fuel, five hundred sparking plugs, and my aeroplane, which had, in the interim, been completely overhauled.

Segrave's car was powered with an engine similar to 'Blue Bird's, but of a little later type. Theoretically, his machine was capable of over 240 mph, and, aware of this, we had so tuned 'Blue Bird' that we felt the car to be capable of matching anything that the 'Golden Arrow' might do. Even if Segrave's machine were actually faster, conditions at Daytona might prove a handicap, whereas I hoped to prepare everything carefully at Verneuk Pan, making my attack only when all was exactly right for achieving 'Blue Bird's' utmost speed.

The Pan had certain defects which were evident from the start. It lay eighty miles from the nearest railhead, and was fifty miles from Brandvlei, which formed the nearest link with civilization. It would be necessary to form a camp on the lakebed, and make sure that we took all supplies and equipment likely to be needed.

Long before we landed at Cape Town, South Africans who were interested in the effort did all they could do complete preliminary arrangements, while plans were made to enable people to watch the record attempt. The railway company reduced its rates to Zak River, the railhead; the postal authorities arranged an office, and a wireless station on the Pan, while aeroplanes were chartered to carry spectators over four hundred miles from Cape Town.

While we were on the way out from England, the work of preparing the track was pushed forward, because the whole affair had developed into something of a race between Segrave and myself for the honour of being the first to attempt to regain the record from America. It was only when actual operations on the course were commenced that Verneuk Pan presented its first difficulties.

There were deposits of black pebbles on the lakebed, and in some places, these had built up into long ridges, but it was not expected that they would be hard to clear away, while the thin bushes which grew in patches on the surface of the Pan could easily be removed by hand. It had been calculated that about four hundred natives would be required to make the course perfect but, right at the start, it was found that very few were available in that remote district. When native labour was sent up from Cape Town, the discovery was made that conditions at the Pan did not agree with these men; many fell sick, while scores deserted.

Examination of the ridges of pebbles showed that they covered outcrops of shale, which could be levelled only by mechanical means and this, disturbing the surrounding surface, made additional work necessary. Over and above everything else, there was a natural scarcity of water; it had not rained in that region for five years.

We were due to arrive in South Africa on February 2nd, 1929, by which time the course should have been cleared and almost ready for 'Blue Bird's' first trial; I expected to attempt the record about a month later. As a result of the difficulties presented by the Pan, things were considerably delayed although, when we landed, it still seemed possible to have everything prepared by the first week in March.

Having come so far, my immediate anxiety was to see the course, and we started by car the following day. For about a hundred miles the road was good, then it deteriorated, and there followed about a hundred and fifty miles of desert, where not so much as a blade of grass was growing. We stopped at the little town of Calvina, and again at the tiny village of Brandvlei; in each place the whole population turned out to wish us luck, then we drove on to the Pan.

The countryside through which we now travelled was arid, with low, flat-topped hills here and there. We climbed steadily all the time, because the Pan lies at an altitude of 3,000 feet, and at the top of a last slope our destination came suddenly into view. We saw a great, flat space, with cliffs dimly visible at the far side. The lakebed was formed by sun-baked mud, the surface was so smooth that even at high speed there was little perceptible movement of the car as we drove out to where the ground had been cleared. The moment the car stopped, I alighted and examined the actual surface of the Pan, at once making a very unpleasant discovery. Embedded in the mud were little particles of shale; they were sharp-edged and small, but were enough to tear 'Blue Bird's' tyres to pieces at speed. I examined other sections of the lakebed, but everywhere the fragments of shale persisted, and I realized that the car could not be run over such a surface.

'Blue Bird' and the mechanics were waiting in Cape Town, with all our equipment and spares, ready to come up to the Pan. We had travelled a long way from England, and it was now impossible to go on to Daytona, and it looked as though the whole venture was a failure. During the discussion which followed, it became plain that, if the car were to run at all, every one of those particles of shale would have to be picked up along the twelve-mile stretch which was to be used for the record, and this would be an endless task.

Naturally, I had no intention of returning to England without running 'Blue Bird', and we tried to find some way in which the surface could be made satisfactory. In the end, the whole question was referred to the chief of the Provincial Roads Department at the Cape. He came up to the Pan, and left the finest of his assistants to advise and help us. This road engineer, Mr Nesbitt, decided that the only way to prepare the course was to cover the central fifty feet of the cleared area with a mixture of mud and water, taking the mud from the lakebed itself. In other words, he intended to scrape the surface free of shale and to lay an entirely new surface over the whole length of twelve miles and this, when completed, would be absolutely smooth, flat and free from all pebbles, shale outcrops or fragments of razor-edged stone. Work on this enormous task began without delay, all water being brought from a source five miles away, while a water-diviner tried to find a spring nearer the Pan.

This resurfacing involved recruiting a large number of labourers, and repeated journeys were necessary between the Pan and Cape Town, while the work was going on. Invariably, I travelled by air, using the plane which I had brought out with the car. Everything went well until the course was almost ready and then, during a flight on a borrowed machine, while my own was being over-hauled, I became involved in an accident at Calvina, the plane smashing its undercarriage and propeller. I was knocked about rather badly, losing some of my teeth, sustaining a deep cut across the mouth, and part of my nose was severed; this gash had to be stitched immediately, and the scar still remains. I was not piloting the machine myself, but was merely the luckless passenger sitting in the front seat.

Another plane came out to take me on to Cape Town, where, in landing, a gust of wind turned this machine completely over, reo-pening the cuts I had suffered in the first smash. A month passed before I recovered sufficiently to enable me to get about again.

Nearly five weeks had now passed, and still our arrangements were not complete. At any moment, we expected news that Segrave had tried for the record, but there still seemed a possibility that we might yet be ahead of him. The resurfacing of the course had been almost completed, when something occurred which was the equivalent to a local miracle.

A shower of rain fell at the Pan, and a storm broke next evening. A wind swept across the open space with the force of a tornado, and the five-years' drought was broken by a torrential downpour which lasted all night, and which came just in time to wreck the plans we were making for our actual attempt.

Tents were blown down, and the shelters protecting the labourers were demolished. When dawn broke, the lakebed lay under water six inches deep; the cars and lorries were hopelessly bogged, and the mud formed a slime on which it was difficult to stand.

Rain was still falling, and the whole of the Pan was flooded. Storms were raging over the country outside, all roads were blocked and dry watercourses had changed to torrents. We were cut off from the world, except for the contact maintained by wireless. No stores could come through and no one could reach us, while we were unable to move any vehicles because of the mud. We were marooned for a week, and, towards the end, we lived on tinned salmon, brackish water and native bread which had a peculiar aniseed taste.

The storms passed, and, as the ground dried, supplies came through and work was resumed. Shortly afterwards, I flew to Cape Town to celebrate my birthday, and in the evening something arrived which, as a birthday gift, I could receive only with very mixed feelings. It took the form of a message advising me that, during the afternoon, Segrave had broken the world's record. He had raised it from 207 mph to 231.36 mph.

What this meant may be appreciated from the fact that, with the engine turning over at maximum revolutions, 'Blue Bird' was capable of a theoretical speed of 231.8 mph, making no allowance for wheel-slip or for the loss of power occasioned by the fact that, on the Pan, the car would be running at a high altitude.

'Blue Bird' could not possibly beat Segrave's speed. We were defeated, and after being on the course for six weeks, we had not yet had a chance to run our car.

§5

We had gone so far, so much time and money had been spent, that there could be no question of returning to England without giving the 'Blue Bird' a chance to show what she could do. I still wanted to try for the land-speed record, although I was sure that we could not break the new figures; in any case, we could attempt world's long-distance records and, perhaps, set up new speeds over five miles. Success in this might offer some recompense to those who had worked, and were still working on the course. We continued almost as if nothing had happened, and help came from every hand. We were all imbued by a hope that, somehow, 'Blue Bird' might yet beat 231 mph; I knew that this was a technical impossibility, yet we intended to try.

A dyke was constructed around the cleared stretch on the Pan, designed to prevent further flooding, and at the end of another month Mr Nesbitt completed the course and began to mark a broad, white line down the centre. The resurfaced track was only fifty feet wide and, at speed, it would not be distinguishable from the ground at either side; the line would serve as a guide and would help me to keep the car straight.

In Cape Town, 'Blue Bird' was packed in the great case in which the machine had come from England, and everything was in readiness when it was found that no lorry was available to take the car over the four hundred miles' journey to the Pan; the one originally chartered had been converted into an omnibus during the long period of waiting. We succeeded eventually in securing the loan of a four-wheel drive machine, just when news came through that more rain was expected.

If this fell, it would make the roads impassable for so heavy a vehicle as the lorry, with its five-ton load. We made arrangements for an immediate start, only to find that the weight of the case containing 'Blue Bird' was too great for the springs of the lorry; the car was removed, loaded on to the lorry without the protecting case, sheeted over with tarpaulins, and then the journey began.

The car arrived at Verneuk Pan in the afternoon of Thursday, April 18th. As we had no apparatus for unloading it, a pit was dug, the lorry was backed into this so that its floor was level with the surrounding ground; then 'Blue Bird' was run off. A camp was now set up at one end of the course, the car being in a marquee.

About a quarter of a mile away was the start of the cleared stretch across the dry lakebed, with the white line streaking towards the horizon. Newspaper men and photographers appeared, and Dutch farmers arrived to watch the first tests of the car, which were to begin next day. I was to drive for records on Saturday.

Late that night it was discovered that part of the apparatus necessary for changing the wheels on 'Blue Bird' had been left at Zak River railway station. The car could not run until its racing wheels had been fitted, and Dr Marin, the man who 'discovered' the Pan, volunteered to fetch them, making an all-night run over the lonely veldt and returning at dawn.

Owing to the presence of mirages on the Pan, it was necessary to make our tests as soon after daylight as possible. We breakfasted hastily, then the machine was pushed down to the starting point; a crowd of spectators had gathered, having apparently come from nowhere during the night. The engine was warmed up and I slipped into the cockpit, while the car was pushed forward until it straddled the white line. Very soon after that, I sent 'Blue Bird' away on her first run.

I did not start with the intention of doing more than test the car, but the machine accelerated in the most amazing way on that even surface, and the revolution counter had shown 215 mph before I pulled up at the far end of the line. I discovered one or two bumps, and was troubled by engine fumes, but the test was most satisfactory, and our enthusiasm rose once again, because the trial gave prospects of a good finish to all our efforts.

We had planned to run next day with the car officially timed, but a wind sprang up over the Pan and it seemed better to wait until this died down. It vanished on Saturday night, but came more strongly than ever after dawn on Sunday, when we were warned that there were indications of more rain within the next few days. When the wind eased, early on Sunday afternoon, we decided to make our attempt upon Segrave's record, and the car was rolled from the marquee to the starting point.

It was my intention to open right out. I did not think that I could beat the 'Golden Arrow's' speed, but nothing could be lost by trying to do so. The machine was made ready, I settled down in the cockpit, and soon 'Blue Bird' was accelerating down the broad white line, gathering speed just as splendidly as she had done before.

The line slid under the nose of the machine and was swallowed up, and I found it a splendid guide as the car ran towards the start of the measured mile. I had the throttle fully open then, and it was not easy to hold the car. Once I had crossed the timing tape, the bumps seemed worse, but the machine behaved very well. I glanced at the revolution counter while I was in the measured distance, and saw it showing rather more than 230 mph.

My hopes were high when I reached the end of the course and turned. A great cloud of dust had been raised by the car, and this hung above the track, drifting slowly away on the wind. I wondered what speed had been registered, and there seemed just a chance that I might yet break the record, although only by a very narrow margin, if the return run was as fast as the first one. I restarted, and my experience was much the same as on the outward journey, except that I could feel that the machine was not so fast. The mud surface was friable, and had been cut up by the earlier runs, and this slowed the car. When I stopped, I found that the recorded speed on the first trip had been 225.5 mph, and on the return run 'Blue Bird' had reached 212.5 mph, giving an average speed of 219 mph for the mile a long way below Segrave's figure.

I had expected that, and it had been too much to hope for more. The car had run wonderfully, and now we made arrangements to try for the five-miles' record, which stood at 140.6 mph, and for the five kilometres; Segrave had taken the latter during his run at Daytona with 202.7 mph. I felt sure that 'Blue Bird' could pass both speeds, although I had been warned by Dunlops that my tyres were intended only for the mile – and had not been built for a sustained effort over five times that distance. I decided to risk it.

The timing tapes were so arranged that I had about three miles in which to get up speed before the car entered the measured five miles, then came another three miles in which to slow down and stop from over 200 mph.

During the next few days the wind became stronger, and dust storms swept the Pan. We found that the wind died at night, and that it did not come again until about half an hour after dawn. We judged that, if we had the car ready, the attempts on the five-miles' record could be made in the still air immediately after dawn. This would have to be done before sunrise, because the track was set from east to west; if the car ran after the sun came up, I should be driving straight into its rays.

We brought the car out an hour before dawn. The course was examined and found to be clear, the engine was warmed up and switched off, then I waited in the cockpit until there should be sufficient light by which to drive.

The time passed slowly. When I could see well, I asked the mechanics to start up the engine. It sulked, but finally they got it going and the men gathered at the tail to push the car away and relieve the load on the clutch. I sent the machine off, but it stopped after a hundred yards or so. They raced after it and restarted the engine; this time, 'Blue Bird' went away excellently, roaring down the white line.

I used all 'Blue Bird's' power of acceleration, but the machine was still short of maximum speed when I crossed the first timing tape. The car gathered pace as it roared on, covering the whole five miles at well above 210 mph. I slowed without difficulty, and turned round, then stopped close to the mechanics who waited there. They looked the car over and changed the wheels, the tyres being so badly cut that no tread remained. Then I started back.

The wheels spun as 'Blue Bird' got away, and this stripped the thin rubber tread from the near-side rear tyre. For the whole of the return journey, the car was running on the canvas of that tyre, and the fact that it did not burst is a tribute to the men who made it.

The average speed over five kilometres proved to be 216.03 mph, beating Segrave's record for this distance and the pace over the five miles was 211 mph, 70 mph faster than the existing record.

With this success we had to be content; we had used all the tyres we had brought out, and no more were available. We packed up and began the journey home. My last memory of Verneuk Pan is of the long white line gleaming in the sunshine, and the cleared space of the course stretching like a scar across the lakebed. This, and 'Blue Bird' rolling slowly away on the big lorry.

That deserted and desolate scene helped to bring home the fact that the car had reached the highest speed of which it was capable. It could have no hope of beating the new record of 231 mph. Once again we were faced with a situation which had arisen before; we had a machine which had been outclassed, just as the original 'Blue Bird' had been two years before. We had started for Verneuk Pan with the hope of beating 207.5 mph; this we had done, but, in the meantime, the record had been raised still higher. Once more I had to decide whether I would abandon these record attempts, or whether we should build a new car and try again.

THE NINTH CHAPTER

§1

WE RETURNED FROM VERNEUK PAN towards the end of May, 1929. Great crowds came to see us off from Cape Town, and the friendly South Africans appreciated that luck had been against us; the fine send-off was their way of showing sympathy. On all sides, we heard hopes expressed that we would come back to the Pan and try again, while almost the first thing I was asked, after we reached England, concerned the possibility of our making another attempt.

I had made up my mind about this during the voyage, and at an official luncheon given by the R.A.C., soon after our arrival, I said that we certainly should try again. Another guest at the reception was Segrave, who had been knighted after his return from Daytona, and I tried to make it clear that any future effort with 'Blue Bird' would not be made from rivalry to himself. It would arise partly from the pleasure existing in achievement, and partly from the fact that the Americans were said to be planning another car.

'Triplex' had been wrecked just after Segrave had broken the record, but if the United States produced another machine, designed to beat 231 mph, they might succeed; they had already taken the record once. The only sure way of retaining the record for England was by building a car which would raise the speed higher still, while, apart from this, holding the record maintained the prestige of our motor industry. These were worthwhile objectives, and were quite aside from any personal enthusiasm on the part of the actual driver.

At this time, 'Blue Bird' was still on the way home from South Africa, and before the machine actually arrived we were considering whether the car should be scrapped completely and a new one built, or whether the machine should be redesigned and reconstructed. I was in favour of the latter, because I did not want to see the entire elimination of the old 'Blue Bird' with which we had first broken the record.

No decision could be reached immediately, because there were many technical details to be determined. We needed more power, and we discussed a plan for using two aero engines of the type already fitted to the car. A difficulty existed that this might make the machine too heavy, and it was not easy to determine whether two such engines should be fitted in tandem style, with the driver between them as in the 1,000 h.p. Sunbeam, or whether both should be at the front of the car.

We were still in the midst of these considerations when 'Blue Bird' came home; the car went on exhibition for some time and, during November, formed part of the procession in the Lord Mayor's traditional show. Thus, even at the end of the year, nothing active had been done about rebuilding the car, and our plans were still nebulous.

In the interim, I drove a three-litre Sunbeam in the first Irish Grand Prix, held over a road circuit in Phoenix Park, Dublin. The course was about four and a quarter miles in length, and was unusual in shape; there was a fine two-miles straight, and the rest of the circuit curved so that its plan formed a flattened letter 'D'.

The first turn was called Mountjoy Corner, and was very deceptive after the long straight. From this, the road curved on a down-grade past zoological gardens back to Gough Corner, and the start of the straight again. This last corner was not easy to take, since it was actually formed by two bends.

The Sunbeam was entered by Mr A. Nolan, a member of a Dublin firm, and this added local interest in the car, which appeared to be a first favourite with those who watched the machines at practice. It was, in fact, very fast, lapping at well over 80 mph, and touching 120 mph on some parts of the course. It appeared to have a very good chance in the race, even against a most representative entry. Several Bentleys, Alfa-Romeos and Bugattis were running, as well as Lagondas, Austro-Daimlers and Italian O.M. cars, while the fastest machine of all appeared to be a big Mercedes.

My car was carefully prepared, and, in order to give the machine the best opportunity, I was loaned a Sunbeam mechanic named Perkins, who had acted for Segrave and Lee Guinness. He was most efficient and keen, and travelled with me on the car during the race. The event was run on Saturday, July 13th, 1929, having been preceded the day before by an event for smaller cars; these two races were combined to form the actual Grand Prix.

Eighteen machines were on the line when the flag dropped, but luck was not with me, and the rest left before I got the car away; it gave indications of a clutch trouble which was to become more pronounced later, and most of the others had vanished around Mountjoy Corner before I started. The speed was high from the outset, with the Mercedes in the lead and a group of Bentleys behind, setting so high a pace that other drivers took chances on the wide corners in their efforts to keep up with the leaders. Twice I came upon skidding machines on the turns, then I ran into trouble myself at Mountjoy Corner.

My brakes seized in the heart of the turn, and the car skidded broadside, partly blocking the course. Officials and helpers ran out to haul the car, with its locked wheels, from the road, while other machines raced past, then Eyston appeared on his Bugatti. Smoke was trailing from his machine, and there were flames near the cockpit as he stood on the brakes and pulled up behind the Sunbeam, just as it was hauled to the side of the road.

Eyston's Bugatti was the car which I had driven in the last TT race, and which had been burnt out. We had taken the wreck back to Brooklands, and had begun rebuilding the machine when Eyston offered to buy it. He had completed the work, but it now appeared that this car was fated to catch fire. There was a rush towards him with extinguishers, while Perkins and I investigated our own troubles. We had to knock our brake toggles free with a hammer, and we readjusted the brakes as officials put out the fire on Eyston's machine; we restarted just before he got going again. I saw him halted at the pits later on; the bodywork of his car was stained from the fire-extinguishing chemicals and, soon afterwards, he retired from the race.

We now tried to make up time with the Sunbeam, while more and more skid marks appeared on the grass outside the Mountjoy turn, left by drivers who had run off the road. After a few laps, an Alfa-Romeo, driven by Boris Ivanowski came to the tail of my machine and remained there for several laps, despite all that I could do to shake Ivanowski off.

We parted only when the Sunbeam's brakes seized again at Mountjoy Corner, and this almost brought us both to disaster. Ivanowski locked his steering over and took to the grass, just missing the skidding Sunbeam's tail, then he carried on and had vanished from sight long before I could free the brakes once more and follow.

A few laps later the Sunbeam was again in difficulties, again at Mountjoy. This time it was the clutch, and we found that repairs were impossible, with the result that the car had to retire, being rolled off the road by the men who had come to our assistance when the car had stopped dead in the early stages of the race. In all, I had covered twenty-nine laps, which meant that I had travelled farther than during the TT race, but it seemed as though Irish road circuits were unlucky for myself. It was a pity that the car should have been so unfortunate, because it was very fast, and might have finished well in the race.

§2

I did not drive again that season in any important event, but returned to consideration of what should be done about 'Blue Bird', and it was soon after the Irish Grand Prix that I became interested in a project to provide England with a course suitable for attacking world's records.

The scheme was a daring one, and the idea was to build a sea wall along one side of the Wash, below Skegness, reclaiming a great strip of useless foreshore. The recovered land was to be used in building a dead-straight road, one hundred feet wide and fifteen miles long, designed for record attempts, with a course on the inside for road-racing, overlooked by grandstands which would accommodate about a quarter of a million spectators. There were to be feeder roads to the course, a flying field and a drainage canal. It was estimated that some eight thousand acres of waste foreshore would be put to good use, and that the operations would provide three thousand men with work for more than a year.

Such a course would have been ideal, but negotiations and arrangements dragged on until, at last, all active interest vanished and the Wash Speedway never came into existence.

It was while we were surveying plans for the Wash project that considerable speculation arose concerning the fate of the 'Golden Arrow'. There was no prospect of Segrave using the car again, because he had given his attention to the water-speed record. There was talk of H. R. S. Birkin buying the car, but nothing developed from this and it finally became a museum piece.

Just about this time a definite competitor for world's record honours was announced. This took the form of a new Sunbeam of 4,000 h.p., which was to be driven at Daytona by Kaye Don. The car eventually became known as the 'Silver Bullet', and it had two twelve-cylinder engines, each of 2,000 h.p., set one behind the other, making the car one enormous mass of machinery.

Work had been going forward on this car for almost a year, but its details were not revealed until November, 1929, and even then it was a couple of months before the machine was actually seen by anyone other than those who were working on it. It proved to be thirty-one feet in length, with a blank, rounded nose, twin stabilizing fins at the tail, and fairings behind the wheels. When Kaye Don was in the cockpit, he had about twenty feet of bonnet in front of him.

The 'Silver Bullet' must have been the highest-powered car ever built, because it had more horsepower even than 'Triplex', great as this American machine had been. Kaye Don took the car to Daytona in March, 1930, and remained there for some weeks. Adverse conditions delayed his attempts on the record, and when he did get the car going he was unable to register much more than 180 mph. He abandoned his efforts and the 'Silver Bullet' came home to stand derelict and idle.

While Kaye Don was at Daytona, plans for a new 'Blue Bird' were completed. We had decided to build a new car, but to use as much of the old one as possible, although it was evident that not a great deal of the original machine could be employed. The work of reconstruction was put in hand, and continued all through the 1930 racing season, which proved to be a very unsettled period, marked by a series of disappointments and unhappy occurrences.

I entered my Delage for the Brooklands Easter meeting, but we had engine trouble and the car could not run. I then bought a Mercedes for the Double-Twelve race, also run at Brooklands, but the machine was not ready in time and could not start, although I took part in the event as co-driver to Lord Howe. It was a very hard race, and was marred by a tragic accident, when two cars collided, one dashing through the railings into the crowd.

Five weeks later, Sir Henry Segrave was killed on Lake Windermere during attempts on the water-speed record with *Miss England II*. He was attacking the American record of 96.25 mph, and made two runs, registering a mean speed of 98.76 mph, and breaking the record. Endeavouring to improve on this, he made a third run when, at high speed, the craft swerved and dived. It came to the surface again, but Segrave died soon after he had been dragged clear.

He was a fine driver, and he had had a wonderful career, and was only thirty-four when he died. His passing left only myself of all the men who had attained high speeds in attacks on the world's land-speed record, after Segrave had first lifted it to above 200 mph. Frank Lockhart had gone, and Ray Keech had been killed in 1929, during a crash involving seven cars at Altoona Speedway, Pennsylvania. Another driver named Lee Bible had crashed with 'Triplex' while the 'Golden Arrow' was at Daytona. And now Segrave had gone.

There was no luck at all in 1930.

I drove in the Irish Grand Prix again, a month after Segrave's death, using the new Mercedes. The car broke the lap record on three successive days before the race began, and the event had hardly started when a thunderstorm swept the course, bringing torrential rain, making every corner slippery so that it was very hard to prevent the big car skidding. Clutch slip developed, and we dosed this with fire extinguisher; I was able to keep the car going, but it stood no chance in the race, and the best that we could do was to achieve fifth position, owing to the time which we had lost in rectifying the trouble. Following this came the only satisfactory event of the whole year, so far as I was concerned. This was the 1930 Tourist Trophy race, again run off over the road circuit outside Belfast. Even here, the start was preceded by considerable trouble.

§3

I was responsible for the entry of a team of three Mercedes-Benz cars, one of which was to be driven by Rudolf Caracciola, then recognized as Germany's finest road-racing driver; another was to be handled by Lord Howe, while I was on the third machine. We had no sooner got on the circuit for practice than I became puzzled by the performance of my own car, because it simply could not match Caracciola's for speed, as it should have done.

When we were out on the circuit, his Mercedes showed much greater pace, and I could not get near the lap times which he was able to put up. Villa and the mechanics worked all night after our first practice, trying to gain more speed, but when I took the car out next morning, it was still so much slower than Caracciola's that we grew desperate. I drove as hard as I was able, but the car was always many seconds behind the German driver's times.

Again we worked all night on the car, but there was no improvement when I turned out next morning, starting the last day of practice. After one lap, I came in and picked up Villa; I wanted him to come round with me and watch the behaviour of the machine. This time, I drove just as fast as I knew how to send the car over the circuit and, for the only time that I can remember, I deliberately took risks.

While I knew that Caracciola had greater experience in road racing, I could not believe that his ability was as superior as his lap speeds suggested. When I started with Villa, it was with the intention of proving either that the German driver was altogether more skilful, or that my machine was not so fast as the one he was using.

After that ride, Villa admitted that he had been badly scared, for the first time that he had ever travelled with me. When we came in, the speed we had recorded was still nowhere near Caracciola's, so I asked him to take me round the course in my car. This he willingly did and, sitting beside him, it seemed that his driving methods were very like my own.

He assured me that the car was satisfactory, but suggested that its performance might be improved if a lower gear were fitted, and we carried out his suggestion; this would not allow the machine to reach such high maximum speed, but it would give the car better acceleration.

On Friday, the machines went before the officials for

scrutineering and only then did the mystery become solved. All three Mercedes in the team were supercharged and the scrutineers found that by some error, the German driver's machine had a larger blower. A supercharger of this size was not fitted to other Mercedes cars, and the regulations under which the TT was run did not permit one of this size on Caracciola's machine. There were many lengthy arguments amongst the stewards and, finally, his blower was barred; it was found impossible to fit the smaller type in time for the start, so that Caracciola had to withdraw from the race.

This was very bad luck for him, and was a blow to our team, because the opposition was very strong indeed. Our immediate opponents were three supercharged 4½-litre Bentleys, one of which was being driven by H. R. S. Birkin, and there were three big Alfa-Romeos handled by Achille Varzi, G. Campari, and Tazio Nuvolari, easily the greatest team of drivers in Europe. Other machines were Alvis, Lea-Francis, O.M., Triumphs, Rileys and Austins – thirty-six starters in all; every car had a chance of winning, because the race was run under a handicap.

The sky was cloudy when we brought the cars to the course, and it seemed as if rain would fall before the race was done. The crowds were enormous, and there was an atmosphere of excitement as the machines were lined up in front of the iron-roofed grandstand. This year, the pits had been given roofs, and were not open to the sky as they had been during the previous race. The cars were parked aslant in front of their pits, and the opening laps had not to be made with hoods raised, so that machines, which started in groups, according to their handicap, would be able to get into their stride right from the fall of the flag.

The first group was sent away, and others followed at intervals, until only our two Mercedes were left on the line with a couple of Rileys which, although starting at the same time as Lord Howe and myself, actually had a lead of three laps; it was assumed that they had covered these before they left.

The starter's arm dropped and my Mercedes slipped ahead of Howe's. We shot around Quarry Corner, just beyond the pits, climbing the winding hill, then roaring through the bends of Bradshaw's Brae, running downhill to Newtownards, with the Mercedes picking up speed all the time. There was a nasty corner here, with the side of the Town Hall waiting to receive any driver who failed to get through the turn, beyond which was an open square. The Mercedes raced across this, diving between sandbags into a narrow street, after which came a long straight beside Strangford Lough.

The car was warming up nicely now. It went neatly through the bends beyond the straight, charged over a level crossing, then ran into the narrow streets of Comber village. There was a harsh right-angle turn here, after which came a long, winding run through Ballystockart and under a railway bridge to the Dundonald hairpin. Around this the end of the circuit lay about a mile distant.

We had overtaken a handful of cars on that first lap, and picked up others during the second circuit. We were halfway around the third when we saw excitement amongst the crowd beside the course near Ballystockart. I eased the throttle as we swung into a bend, and saw a car upside down on the footpath at the side of the road. Debris lay near it, and a driving seat was by the kerb, while the nose of the machine was rammed into a hedge, the car itself pointing the wrong way of the course. The car was Captain Waite's Austin, and he was then being rushed to hospital; he had intended that this TT should be his last race, and even when he regained consciousness, he was unable to say how the crash occurred. He was badly hurt, his jaw being fractured and his nose broken, but it was not very long before he was about again.

Next time round, the scene of his smash had been tidied up, and now the Mercedes was lapping at well above 75 mph, but the car was undergeared, and this entailed over-revving the engine, which was dangerous. On this circuit, I had to pull over to let Howe go by as we covered the straight from Newtownards, as I realized that I must keep my 'revs' down. He was able to take advantage of the fact that we had given our car a lower gear, and he must then have been moving at many miles an hour faster than myself.

As the race went on, I gradually dropped farther and farther behind him. He was three-quarters of a minute ahead after we had been racing for two hours, and then rain fell. It came down very hard just at the time when we were driving as nearly flat out as we dared, striving to make up our handicap. The Alfa-Romeos had gone into the lead, and every car in the race was pursuing them. Rain favoured the Italian cars which, being lighter, were easier to handle on a wet surface than the much bigger Mercedes. The German machines weighed nearly two tons, but the Italian cars had hardly half this weight.

The corners grew very slippery, too, making caution necessary, and the rain changed from a drizzle to a downpour. I was near the scene of Waite's crash, and was holding the Mercedes into a bend, when I saw a warning flag ahead and sighted a cloud of smoke. Then, as the road bent, I saw a machine completely upside down, half in the road and half on the footpath. Flames were spurting from it, and the driver was just being dragged from under the car. As we burst through the smoke, I sighted the number of the machine and recognized it as Kaye Don's.

I learned afterwards that he had skidded in the bend but, the road being narrow, he had no room to straighten out his car. The petrol tank had split, the fuel igniting from the exhaust pipe. His crash was the more unfortunate, because he had just set up a class lap record in the race; he sustained four broken ribs and a broken shoulder blade, but he was out of hospital within a couple of weeks.

The race ran on and, opening up, I went in front of Lord Howe. For a long time nothing more happened, but, from what I could see of the scoreboard, it appeared impossible that I could ever bring my car sufficiently near the leaders to be placed when the TT ended. I continued to drive as hard as conditions would permit, and it was when the race was two-thirds run that we came upon a third smash.

This had occurred near the same spot as the two others. Birkin's Bentley skidded and shed a tyre, the car charging straight for the crowd. Birkin, struggling to avoid them, put the machine into a second skid, when the Bentley rammed its nose against a stone wall, which forced the car's retirement. We passed shortly after the smash, in time to see the driver and his mechanic inspecting the damage.

No one could catch the Alfa-Romeos, which now lay far ahead. The race ran out and, when we came to the finish, a crowd was cheering a red machine. Tazio Nuvolari had won, Compari was second, and Varzi was third. The best that my Mercedes could do was to run home in tenth place although, in point of fact, the car had averaged 71.5 mph. This was the fastest average speed in the race as a whole, but since the event was run under handicap and we were on the scratch mark, this could not bring the car amongst the leaders.

§4

The TT race ended my competitive efforts for 1930, with the exception of a Brooklands meeting, and 'Blue Bird' was now within measurable distance of completion. The chief difference in the new machine lay with the transmission and the body.

On the earlier cars, I had always sat above the propeller shaft, which came down the centre of the frame, and this made the driving position very high. In small machines built for very fast work, the transmission was sometimes so arranged that the propeller shaft was set at one side, and the driver was placed on a level with it. This brought him altogether lower in the car, and we had decided to adopt the same plan for 'Blue Bird', because it increased stability and enabled us to obtain still better streamlining.

Until this time, in building a car, we had first designed the chassis, and the driving position had been a secondary consideration. Now, however, we arranged mechanism solely to accommodate the driver, which meant that we were considering the man equally with the machine. Placing the propeller shaft at one side involved a great amount of technical work and made necessary special investigation into metals and design, but we knew that it would materially aid the efficiency of the machine.

The arrangement brought the actual drive to one side of the rear axle, instead of in the centre. This had proved satisfactory with small cars, but there were people ready to tell us that, in so big a machine, this would cause the car to turn in great circles, making it impossible to keep 'Blue Bird' on a straight course. Such forecasts were given greater weight when it was seen that the tail fin, being directly behind the cockpit, was offset and was not in the middle of the tail, as it had been before.

Actually, so long as the fin was quite vertical, it did not much matter where it was placed in relation to the tail, since it did not operate unless the car turned from the straight. The possibility of the unusual transmission making the car hard to hold was one overcome in the design of the chassis itself.

Hitherto, we had used wire wheels, covered with discs, but it was felt that such wheels might no longer meet the stresses set up by the very high speeds at which we hoped 'Blue Bird would run. For this reason, we employed wheels which had no spokes at all, and which were stamped from steel.

We planned to carry ballast on the car, in order to keep the rear wheels on the ground and, in all, we carried between twelve and fourteen hundredweight of lead.

The original power-unit was discarded, and we secured one of the latest Napier engines which, in a Gloster-Napier seaplane had set up a speed of 336 mph. This engine gave us 1,450 h.p. at 3,600 rpm, which promised sufficient power for the speed I wanted to reach. My object was to lift the record to four miles a minute, 240 mph, and the car gave me a chance to reach a higher rate of travel if it ran under really good conditions.

As the weeks went past, and 'Blue Bird' took on final shape, we were still undecided whether to go to Daytona, back to Verneuk Pan, or to try still another course. A site was suggested near Cordoba, in the Argentine, where dried salt lakes existed. The surface was formed by caked salt, but I did not investigate this because salt can play havoc with unprotected metal, and reports about the course were not very promising.

Another suggestion was that I should go to Ninety Mile Beach, in New Zealand, where a contender for the land speed record had appeared. This was Norman Smith, nicknamed 'Wizard' Smith, who had built a big car and had already tried it out. His machine was the subject of many modifications before he seriously attacked the record.

Ninety Mile Beach was some two hundred and fifty miles north of Auckland, and it included a dead-level, perfectly straight stretch of some seventeen miles which, according to all reports, was ideal for high speed. The spot was desolate, and it would be necessary to form a camp on the shore, but it appeared to hold advantages over Daytona – and many disadvantages as well. It was a very long way from England, and a month would be occupied in reaching it, while Daytona was hardly more than a week away, and here the American authorities had everything available and thoroughly organized. We could go to Daytona, make our attempt and be home again almost as soon as we could reach New Zealand. In the end, we decided to try Daytona Beach again. It was much more accessible than either Ninety Mile Beach or Verneuk Pan, the advantages of the latter being outweighed by the difficulties which this South African course could present. The attempt was planned for early in February, 1931, and by the first week in January of that year 'Blue Bird' was finished.

The appearance of the machine was such that it completely outdated the former 'Blue Bird', and the body was a beautiful piece of work. Gurney Nutting and Company, who built it, used over six hundred square feet of aluminium panelling, covering this with ten coats of cellulose, the final application being carefully polished to reduce skin friction.

The car was as different externally as it was in design, and only those who had seen the machine in course of construction could appreciate how carefully it had been erected. Thompson and Taylor had carried out this work, following the design of Reid A. Railton, who had supervised the car from the start, and was responsible even for the plasticine model which had been made prior to the first wind-tunnel tests that decided the lines of the body.

The finished 'Blue Bird' had several unusual features. One rear spring was stronger than the other, so that the car was tilted slightly to one side. This was arranged in order to absorb the torque which, in the old 350 h.p. Sunbeam, used to send the car 'crabwise' at speed; the effect would now be to bring the car back on an even keel.

The radiator was separate from the rest of the car. It was carried on an extension of the frame, and the bonnet over the engine was brought closely down behind it; thus, air passing through the radiator would not enter the car at all, but would escape behind the cowling and be sent over the smooth surface of the engine cover.

There was a special ventilator in the cockpit, designed to cope with any fumes from the engine, and to deal with backdraught at speed; if provision were not made for this, the suction of the draught would tend to drag the driver out of the car.

We had fairings behind both wheels and in front of the rear ones. These fitted very closely to the tyres, and would be still nearer when the car was moving, because tyres attain a greater diameter at speed. If one should burst, it was liable to foul the fairings and make matters more difficult for myself; accordingly, part of the fairing was made of very thin aluminium, which would crumple up if struck by a burst tyre, thus offering no resistance and not complicating matters when I tried to keep 'Blue Bird' under control.

The total length of the car was some twenty-five feet, and its very size presented certain difficulties, particularly with the wheels. Each of these, when complete with tyres, weighed two hundredweight, and three men were needed to change one wheel, an operation which took some time. We foresaw that it might not be possible to change wheels between runs at Daytona where, according to the regulations, a second run must be made within half an hour of the completion of the first, if the registered speeds are to count for the record. In view of this, and because it was doubtful if a wheel-change could be effected in the half-hour allowed, I decided to make each set of tyres do for a double run on the course.

'Blue Bird' was packed away, the cases of spare parts and equipment were arranged, and plans were made for departure. On this venture I was accompanied by Leo Villa, Charlie Coe, Steve MacDonald, another man from Dunlops, and Harry Leech, this being his first trip to Daytona. Everything had been settled when, at the last moment, there came a hitch.

Apparently, there was some political dispute at Daytona, and there was some doubt about my being given permission to use the beach. Although I was advised not to go, I went ahead with our arrangements; we were actually on the boat, with the car aboard and the liner due to sail, when I received a cable. It informed me that no agreement had been reached by the authorities at Daytona, and that I should be unwise to leave England.

There was very little time in which to do anything. I cabled a reply, which intimated that we were on the point of sailing, and that if there were any difficulties when we reached New York, we should proceed immediately to Ninety Mile Beach, New Zealand. I had not the slightest idea of how I could get to New Zealand from New York, but I guessed we should find some way of accomplishing it.

During the voyage matters were straightened out, and our reception in America was as friendly as could possibly be imagined. We received many telegrams on arrival in New York, and one of these read: *Florida National Guard welcomes you to Daytona Beach. Special ringside section reserved for yourself and party for every fight staged in local Armoury during your visit. May we expect you at Armoury fights next Monday night? I prepared Beach for your trials here in 1928, under Mayor Armstrong. Yours to command if I or National Guard can be of service in any way. Captain John O. McNamara.*

Other telegrams were: *On behalf of Racing Association I extend you a very hearty welcome. This organization will aid you in every possible way. A. P. Underhill, Secretary, Daytona Beach, Voluspa County Racing Association.* And there was another *Daytona Beach Chamber of Commerce welcomes you to our country, our state and our city. If we can be of service, you have but to command us.* With this message arrived one from the Mayor of Daytona: *City of Daytona extends you a most cordial welcome and best wishes for your success.* These, and very many others, were backed by a telegram from Dick Le Sesne, the official photographer to the American Automobile Association, who made a wonderful pictorial record of the attempt: *Welcome to America, Daytona Beach, and a long string of records.*

Such greetings as these served to banish any last doubt which might have remained after the earlier difficulties, and there was one more telegram detailing arrangements concerning the trials. It came from the Racing Association: *Final proposition as follows: City police beach, unload and reload car, furnish garage and watch-men. Service car to beach. Timing wires and telephone service on beach. Time limit for trials fifteen days.* This message indicated that the last details had been settled satisfactorily, and that everything should now go forward smoothly.

The car was disembarked at New York, and sent down to Daytona with its twenty-one cases of spare parts and equipment. I went ahead of the machine, which reached the beach on Thursday, January 29th, 1931.

§5

The weather was very warm at Daytona and, although the beach was in good condition, visibility was bad. The air was hazy, and even though this mist was not heavy enough to be noticeable in the ordinary way, it made a great difference at speed. Until the air cleared, I could make no attempt on the record, but I could try the car at a pace high enough to be sure that everything was in good order.

We were ready by the Saturday following 'Blue Bird's' arrival, and we asked for the beach to be cleared. I had no doubt about the machine, but I was anxious to try it out, because it had not been tested in any way before leaving England. One of the great difficulties on these record attempts is the impossibility of learning anything about how the machine will behave, until it is actually on the course. I knew that everything humanly possible had been done to bring 'Blue Bird' to perfection, but the stability and control of the car could be determined only under test.

Another difficulty, and one which, fortunately, never has arisen is that if, by some mischance, the car should prove ineffective, or dangerous to drive, it would produce an awkward situation. After spending so long in building the machine, and after travelling so many thousands of miles, it would hardly be possible to abandon the attempt; the people on the spot could not be expected to appreciate the true reasons behind the withdrawal. Short of the machine being quite impossible, one is under some compulsion to make the effort; otherwise visitors to Daytona would be disappointed, and some reflection would be certain to fall upon those responsible for the car.

Thus, a variety of considerations exist which inevitably cause some anxiety until the car has been driven and its performance ascertained. It will be understood that I was very keen to get under way although, when the car was rolled down to the beach, the air was so misty that we were able to see little more than the quarter of a mile ahead. The machine was halted near the pier and, while we were making ready, crowds of spectators gathered on the beach behind, standing between us and the pier. Most of them drove down in automobiles, parking them on the sand; there was considerable congestion behind 'Blue Bird', but the beach ahead was kept quite clear by the police.

The engine started up without trouble, and soon I was off. I found the sand very smooth and 'Blue Bird' travelled well, although I went up to only about 120 mph on the first run. I turned the car and started back without stopping, returning at much higher speed and giving attention to the way the machine handled. Everything was most satisfactory, and 'Blue Bird' roared along at rather more than 200 mph until I judged that it was time I began to ease the throttle.

I could not tell where I was, or how far down the course I had come. There are no landmarks along the beach to serve as a guide, and only a few scattered houses stand behind the sand dunes. 'Blue Bird' had slowed to about 190 mph when I suddenly remembered the people who were lined up across the beach, behind the point from which the car had started, and next moment, I saw the spectators stretched solidly in front of me.

Instantly, I literally stood on the brakes. They worked for a moment, then their retarding effect completely faded out, while blue smoke came from the drums. Using the brakes at over three miles a minute generated so much heat that grease in the bearings melted and, running in to the brake linings, made them ineffective.

I could see the people clearly now, and I hoped they would disperse, then I remembered the cars parked solidly behind the spectators; even if the people ran, I should crash into the standing machines. My only hope of stopping 'Blue Bird' was to change into second gear. I did this, then switched off the engine, pulling the car out, ready to head into the sea if it proved impossible to stop. For long seconds the machine ran on, but it was slowing all the time and, finally, pulled up only fifty yards short of the crowd. After that experience, I always asked for the beach to be cleared completely at either end of the course, so that I always had a safety margin in which to check the car.

Various minor adjustments were required, and we worked on 'Blue Bird' over the weekend, then made another trial run on Monday, February 2nd. This time, I put my foot down over a four-mile stretch, the car travelling at approximately 240 mph along this distance. As a result of this very satisfactory test, I told the officials that we would make an attempt on the record next day, if weather permitted.

A gale rose during the night, and a 45-mph wind was blowing down the course at dawn. This died somewhat during the day and, although the beach could have been in better condition, I decided to carry on with the effort, fearing that the weather might grow worse if I waited. Visibility was not at all good, and the wind was still very strong; it blew towards the south, the direction in which I always make the first run.

When we took the car down to the sands, great crowds had appeared along the dunes. I received word that the beach was clear, and that everything was ready, then sent 'Blue Bird' away. As this was the real record attempt, I used the throttle to some purpose, and I was amazed at the acceleration of the machine. The response of the car was really tremendous, bringing with it all that strange exhilaration which I had experienced on former occasions.

I watched for the square red panel which officials had placed at either end of the measured mile, as a guide for the machine, and my foot was hard down when I picked it up out of the haze. It was then rather less than half a mile distant, and I glanced at my revolution counter; it showed the equivalent of 260 mph, nearly 30 mph faster than the existing record. I realized that I was travelling nearly flat out and, not wishing to overstress the engine, which had already passed the safety limit, I eased the throttle pedal slightly. At once clouds of smoke came from under

With his son Donald in January 1933 next to the Railton-engined 'Blue Bird'.

The three point hydroplane 'Blue Bird' K4 on Lake Coniston in August 1939 when he took the Water Speed Record to 141.74 mph – Ajax News – Feature Service: Alamy Stock Photo.

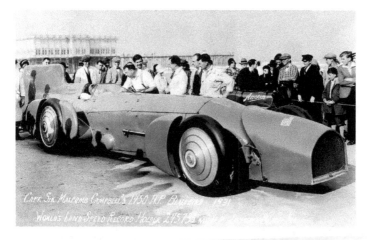

1931 'Blue Bird' that took Campbell to 245.733 mph on Daytona Beach in 1931.

Young Donald Campbell looks out of the cockpit of 'Blue Bird' in 1933.

The new 'Blue Bird' nears completion in 1932.

Campbell in the Austin Special at Daytona in early 1932 – PA Photo: Alamy Stock Photo.

Water speed record boat 'Blue Bird' K3.

Sir Malcolm Campbell's Campbell-Napier-Railton 'Blue Bird' car, the holder of the World Land Speed Record, at Brooklands – PA Images: Alamy Stock Photo.

the bonnet, and streamers of flame shot from the exhaust pipes, while the needle of the revolution counter swung right around the dial, which meant that the engine had raced up to the absolute limit of its revolutions.

Just for a moment I wondered what had happened, then realized that the gear lever had jumped out of mesh; when I had eased the throttle, the load on the pinions in the gearbox had been removed, allowing the lever to slip back. At the same time, now that the engine was not driving the rear wheels, it had increased its revolutions, and it was a miracle that the engine did not 'blow up' altogether.

It was impossible to re-engage gear at that speed and, in any case, all my attention was concentrated on keeping the car straight. I coasted on through the mile, realizing that the attempt had been spoiled, and very much afraid that some damage might have been done to the engine. I ran on to the far end of the course, then brought the machine about and made the return trip very carefully, not daring to go really fast. It would have been unwise to make use of throttle until we were sure that the engine was not harmed.

I pulled up near the pier and told the mechanics what had occurred, explaining that the car had been doing 260 mph when the gear lever jumped out; but for this, the record would have been certain. Even they found it hard to believe that the car had been so fast, and agreed that it was necessary to check everything over before making another attempt. We advised the officials of this, then 'Blue Bird' was towed back to the garage.

We spent all that night and the whole of the next day in an examination of the engine, finding nothing broken. There was a chance that its tune had been spoiled, but this could be learned only at speed. We had brought out a spare engine, and considered fitting this, but changing over the power units would take several days, and there was no need for the work if the existing engine was still in good condition, as it appeared to be. Leech made a special catch for the gearbox lever, which would ensure that it could not slip out of mesh again, then I asked the authorities to make arrangements for us to try again on Thursday, February 5th.

We brought 'Blue Bird' to the beach at about three o'clock in the afternoon; the sand was smooth, but there were great stretches where it was very wet. The car was warmed up, and I climbed into the cockpit, awaiting the word to go, the machine standing at the zero mark. As on the attempt two days earlier, the entry to the measured distance was marked by a red panel set high above the sand; on the seaward side, the course was edged by short flag posts placed one hundred yards apart, designed to act as a guide and help me to keep the car on a straight course. There were no flags on the other side; I had found, at Pendine, that two lines of flags are confusing. The course was arranged to give me a distance of four miles on either side of the measured mile.

My feelings as I waited were solely of impatience to get started. Although I intended to drive 'Blue Bird' just as fast as the car could be made to travel, there was no idea that I should be in danger, no worry or sense of fear, simply an urge to get the whole thing over.

At ten minutes to four, I received the word to go. The engine was started up, my mechanics pushed me off and, right from the start, I missed the terrific acceleration of two days before. I realized that, as we had feared, the engine had suffered when the gear lever slipped, but 'Blue Bird' was still very fast. At 90 mph I changed into second gear, shifting into top speed when the car was mid-way through the second mile, by which time the crowds on the sand dunes were losing definiteness, becoming a blurred dark ribbon at one side.

On the left of the car, the spaced-out flags seemed to draw closer and closer together as they whipped by. When I entered the fourth mile, they were more like a fence than separate standards, showing as a dark guiding line at the side of the machine, only dimly seen as I watched for the mark that was set above the entrance to the measured distance. I picked it up and, with my foot rammed hard down on the throttle, crossed the timing tapes.

It seemed an age before I saw the mark at the far end, and I had no chance to glance at the revolution counter. I concentrated on holding 'Blue Bird' straight, and I could hear nothing at all except the noise of the wind. At times it was a shrill whine, then it would change abruptly to a whistle, and sometimes, as gusts caught the car, the wind came with a deep, coughing roar. This, while travelling at a speed which I afterwards learned was above 245 mph, was all I heard when I picked up the second mark then, clear of the mile, eased my foot on the throttle pedal. It was much more than another two miles before I dared allow the throttle to close completely. The car had slowed to 150 mph before I used the brakes; it was not wise to apply them when the machine was moving at much above this speed.

I reached the end of the course and turned the machine without stopping, having previously advised the officials that I should start the return run without a halt. Once again 'Blue Bird' picked up speed, while I stared through the haze which, however, seemed heavier as I headed north. I could not see much more than three hundred yards in front, and as the car was soon covering the ground at the rate of a hundred and twenty yards every second, this meant that visibility was reduced to little more than two seconds ahead.

It was, therefore, vital to keep the car straight, and I must have done nearly three miles of the return journey when I was dismayed to see something approaching me, directly on my course. I could see it but dimly as a small, dark, blurred shape which suddenly shot off at right angles. It was, I learned later, a motorcyclist policeman who was following the car's tracks, not realizing that I should return immediately; seeing 'Blue Bird' approach, he sent his machine into the soft sand and, I believe, turned over.

I saw nothing more of him after he had gone, but watched for the red panel, while the drone of the wind increased. Then, suddenly, I saw the mark, and discovered that the car was not headed towards it, but was pointing in the direction of the dunes.

There were only two things that I could do; I could swing 'Blue Bird' back into position at speed, without lifting my foot from the throttle pedal and trust that I should be able to hold the car or, alternatively, I could do this and lift my foot at the same time, playing for safety.

The latter meant that I should lose speed, so I chose the former course and the car responded splendidly; it got into a bad swing, but I held it safely and brought 'Blue Bird' squarely across the timing tape, exactly beneath the red mark. Again there followed that long-drawn dash through the mile; actually, it occupied less than fifteen seconds, but it seemed far longer. Once clear, there came the quite delicate business of easing the throttle pedal, then I applied the brakes and 'Blue Bird' came to a stop at the northern depot, where my mechanics waited.

They rushed to meet me and I learned that the speed over my first run had been 246.575 mph, and that the return had been made at 244.897 mph, giving a speed for the record of 245.736 mph.

We had raised the record by over 14 mph from Segrave's old figure of 231.3 mph, and 'Blue Bird' secured the honour of being the first land-speed machine ever to achieve a speed of four miles a minute.

The car might have been faster, but for the wet sand on the beach, which had formed a drag on the wheels, and it would certainly have set the record higher but for the earlier mishap with the gear lever which had robbed the engine of its best tune.

§6

Although 'Blue Bird' had done so well, I still felt that the car could travel very much faster. In fact, it had actually done so during the first official attempt. We had seen, however, that the limit had been reached with the engine that was then in the chassis, and the only way we could attain higher speed was by changing the engine for the spare one we had brought out. This work could hardly have been accomplished before the date set for the closure of the speed trials, so it was no use attempting it and, therefore, we decided to come home.

American newspaper comment on the record run was interesting, and at times amusing. Before the effort, one paper carried a headline which read: *Campbell Again to Ram Danger's Shield*, while another worked out that, at four miles a minute, 'Blue Bird' would, if driven up a runway set at forty-five degrees, jump over the highest skyscraper in New York, with nearly seven hundred feet to spare. Also, that the car could leap clear across the Hudson River, from New York to New Jersey.

After the record run, a paper appeared with a comment under *Senseless Speed Records*. 'If there are people in this country who wish to travel at the rate of 240 mph, they will hail Captain Campbell as a benefactor of the race. Most of those who have had that sort of itch in the past, however, are today resting under headstones… We have seen no predictions from any quarter that a speed of 240 mph by a motor driven machine will ever be of the slightest use to anybody… In the air, speed is of practical use in shortening distances and saving time. On land super-speed machines like that driven by Captain Campbell are of interest only as providing the swiftest known means of travelling from good health to the graveyard.'

Comment of that nature was bound to arise; I had seen similar observations years before, when four miles a minute had appeared quite out of reach. The man who wrote those words had not appreciated certain viewpoints. Breaking the record was an achievement, taken by itself alone; it was the result of an effort as personal as that of an athlete trying to run a mile in shorter time than anyone has ever done. Everyone applauds the runner and, if he is successful, congratulates him upon setting a new mark; any strain, or any physical risk he may run is his own affair, just as it would have been my own misfortune if anything had gone wrong at 240 mph.

The athlete, however, cannot be said to contribute very largely to the world's work, but breaking the world's land speed record actually does benefit a large number of people. The country responsible for the car gains in prestige, it proves the ability of its craftsmen in the production of material and workmanship which is unsurpassed. The very great amount of research work necessary to create the machine obliges scientists to make quite detailed investigations in metallurgy and streamlining, and to overcome problems of transmission and braking. These problems would not otherwise be set, and the knowledge which their solution brings can be applied to everyday machines; this, in its turn, brings improvements in design and helps to make more stable and roadworthy the cars which are driven on the streets in the ordinary way.

The newspaper was, of course, at liberty to express its point of view, and to call the record attempts 'senseless'. At the same time, such an outlook seems very restricted, and I doubt if it is general. In fact, the overwhelming congratulations which I received at Daytona, after the run, showed the opinion of America as a whole. I was fêted to an embarrassing extent, and it was the more difficult to accept these congratulations since I appreciated that the success was not due to myself alone. Behind me were the engineers and the scientists, the designers and the workmen who had constructed the car, while I owed more than it is possible to express to the loyal work of Villa and Leech, and the rest of my mechanics; it would have been impossible to find a keener and more efficient little group of men.

We stayed a few days at Daytona, then started for home, travelling from New York on the *Mauretania*. At the end of the voyage a tug met the liner, and a Government official came aboard. He brought a message from the Premier, Mr Ramsay MacDonald, which read: *I am glad to inform you that His Majesty has been pleased to approve that the honour of a knighthood be conferred upon you.*

This was altogether unexpected, and it was followed by an official reception in London when I arrived next day, Then, the day after, I was received at Buckingham Palace by His Majesty, when the accolade of knighthood was conferred. It would be difficult indeed to express my feelings at that time, and such an honour could never have come but for the loyal support of all those who were behind the record attempt, and whose assistance helped so materially to bring success.

THE TENTH CHAPTER

§1

'BLUE BIRD' DID NOT RETURN directly to England after Daytona run. The car was sent to the British Empire Exhibition at Buenos Aires where it remained for some three weeks. During this time Norman Smith, in New Zealand, was actively preparing for an attack on the new figure of 246 mph.

After first trials, his car had been modified; it now had some frontal resemblance to the 'Golden Arrow', and was fitted with twin stabilizing fins, while its engine formed almost a duplicate of that employed in 'Blue Bird'. The machine had been designed to reach 300 mph, and this was so wide a margin above the record that there was a possibility of Smith achieving success, although it seemed hardly likely that he would break the record on his first attempt.

It is easy to understand the fact that we wanted to keep the record in England, but I did not, at this time, intend to make another effort unless the record were broken. It was necessary, however, to be prepared for this eventuality, and it was decided that Railton, who had been responsible for 'Blue Bird' in modern form, should take the car over on its return from South America, and do all that was required to make the machine capable of replying to any speed which might be set up at Ninety Mile Beach.

Matters were left like this, and I entered a Bugatti at Brooklands in a meeting held during the first week in April. During one of the Mountain races, when approaching the hairpin turn at the Fork, the track rod came adrift; I had just applied the brakes, and the machine was moving at very little short of 120 mph. The broken rod tore most of the spokes from the off-side front wheel, but the wheel did not collapse, and I was able to bring the car safely to a stop.

Brooklands was again the setting for another uncomfortable experience a few weeks later. 'Blue Bird' had returned by this time and, before handing the car over to Railton for attention, I promised to give an exhibition run on the track. It was impossible to travel at more than about 130 mph with the machine, and the result was a very rough ride for myself. The car bumped badly under its hard springs on the rough track, and I was jarred unmercifully in my seat; there were times when I thought I should be thrown out of the car.

Following this, 'Blue Bird' went into retirement at Thomp and Taylor's, and I began to prepare for the first important race in which I ran that year. This was the Irish Grand Prix, again run over the road circuit in Phoenix Park, Dublin.

On this occasion, I had a team of three Riley cars, the other drivers being C. R. Whitcroft and W. P. Noble. It poured with rain all morning before the race, and when we came to the start, everything was soaked. Spectators at Mountjoy corner were almost hidden under shining umbrellas and, everywhere around the circuit, people were clad in dripping waterproofs.

The surface of the course had been very carefully prepared and was almost completely non-skid, which promised that the race would be fast but, here and there, the road was covered with shallow sheets of water, which held every indication of making things uncomfortable for drivers. The event started at three o'clock in the afternoon, the cars getting away in showers of spray, and my recollection of the race is that it was run off with water flying continually from the road and, at the same time, descending from the sky. A puddle soon formed in my seat, and additional discomfort was provided by the fact that one of the floorboards was loose on the car. Every time the machine dashed through a puddle, spray shot up through the gap, getting underneath the visor which I was wearing and making it impossible to see clearly.

In addition, the car was not fast. We had been troubled with faulty carburation during the last day of practice, and the machine had hesitated at the actual start. The sulkiness of the engine affected the car all through the race, so that I was quite unable to back up the efforts of my team mates, who soon drew well ahead. The event was unexciting, everything seeming to be damped by the saturated atmosphere, and the best that I could do was to run home in ninth place, at an average of 73.2 mph. The other two cars in the team finished fourth and fifth.

§2

It was about six weeks after the Irish Grand Prix that I took delivery of an altogether different 'Blue Bird'. This was a 52-foot yacht, with engines giving off 100 h.p. It was launched at Hampton, in the middle of July, and in less than a month it was instrumental in bringing about an adventure which might have ended very unhappily.

I had sailed round to the Solent then, in the face of a fierce wind, headed back to Bracklesham Bay, just beyond Portsmouth. The yacht was anchored off shore, and I used a small dinghy, about eleven feet in length, to join a luncheon party in a house overlooking the beach. There was a six-knot tide running, the bay held dangerous currents, and rowing the boat ashore was no easy matter. While we were at lunch, we heard screams on the beach and I ran outside accompanied by two friends: Captain Davies, V.C., and Captain Milward, of the Royal Air Force Club.

We saw two men standing in a boat over a mile out to sea, signalling for help, while people were running up and down the beach, trying to find some way of going to their assistance; the boat had been caught in an offshore current, and was fast being swept out to sea. We made a rush for the little dinghy, launched it, and began to row to the men, who proved to be two holidaymakers, clad in bathing suits. They had only a couple of canoe paddles in the boat, and these were quite useless.

We managed to get one of the men into our dinghy, then started to tow the other boat, the man in it helping as well as he could with his paddle. The sea was very rough and the force of a wave snapped the tow rope, sweeping the second boat away. We put about, and were almost swamped when we came up with the boat again, taking the second man aboard and abandoning the craft.

There were now five of us crowded in the little dinghy: Davies, Milward, the two rescued men and myself. We were so cramped that it was not possible to row properly, while the gunwale was so low that the waves constantly broke over it, swamping us. At any moment, we were liable to founder, and we began bailing as well as we were able, removing our sea-boots and using them for this purpose. I expected the dinghy to sink at any moment, because we could get no way on the craft, and as fast as we bailed the water out, more came in.

By the greatest of good luck a girl on shore saw our plight and realized that we were now in serious difficulty. She decided to swim out to the yacht and warn the men aboard; the crew were in the forecastle having lunch and, therefore, had no knowledge of what was happening. She plunged into the heavy seas, and was halfway to 'Blue Bird' when she discovered that a young man had followed her. They reached the yacht together and helped to get up the anchor, when the vessel was brought to our assistance.

We were all in an exhausted condition when we were helped aboard, as we had been rowing hard for more than an hour, but eventually reached shore without further mishap. The girl and the young man left without giving anyone an opportunity to express adequate thanks but, later, I learned that the girl was

Miss Helen Cowie. She was a splendid swimmer and, but for her, it is certain that all five of us would not have come alive from that experience.

The yacht engaged my attention for almost all the rest of that summer, then came the last event of the season: the Five Hundred Miles Race, organized by the British Racing Drivers' Club, and held at Brooklands in the beginning of October. For this I again entered a Riley, and I looked forward with some anticipation to the race, which was the fastest long-distance event in the world, surpassing even the five hundred miles race held annually at Indianapolis. Coming at the end of the season, it attracted an entry of the fastest available cars, with drivers ready to use full throttle for as long as possible, since they had not to save their machines for following events. If a car did 'blow up', the whole winter was available in which to make repairs.

My car was painted red, and had been beautifully streamlined. During practice it lapped at over 116 mph, and this made it a favourite for the race, which was run under a handicap. My driving partner was C. S. Staniland and he handled the car at the start. He travelled half a dozen laps, covering the course at 104 mph and with plenty of power in hand; then he coasted into the pits with engine trouble, which put the machine out of the race. This was very unfortunate for both of us, and I had not even driven the car during the event.

While I was experiencing this bad luck, fortune was not smiling upon Norman Smith, who now had his big car ready for the record attempt at Ninety Mile Beach. He intended making full use of the beach, taking a run of nearly eight miles in which to get up speed before entering the measured distance. I expected, from day to day, to hear that he had been successful, but his efforts failed.

Work had been going forward during the whole of the summer on 'Blue Bird', and the car was almost ready to attempt to raise the record. Although Smith had been unsuccessful, he intended to try again, and I knew that an American racing driver had got out designs for a car to run at Daytona. It seemed that 'Blue Bird's' figures might soon be attacked.

Originally, I had not intended to run again unless the record were broken. This had not been accomplished but, with 'Blue Bird' ready, there was no reason why the car should stand idle. Also, there was a new mark at which to aim, although it stood only a little distance beyond the figures I had already set up. Years before, I had reached 146 mph and had then become ambitious to be the first man to do 150 mph. Now I had achieved 246 mph, and 250 mph lay only a little distance away. It seemed worth while trying to reach this speed.

When I was still in a state of indecision, I received a cable; it came soon after New Year's Day, 1932, and was from the Mayor of Daytona: *The City of Daytona Beach invites you and offers every co-operation to further your attempt to create a new world record.*

This decided me. I accepted the invitation, and thus committed myself to at least one more attempt.

§3

'Blue Bird' had not been greatly altered in appearance except that the radiator had been given a slightly longer cowling, and wind resistance had been further reduced. Tail fin, wheel fairings, bodywork and chassis remained the same, but we had changed the engine for the one which had previously been taken to Daytona as a spare. Minor modifications to the power unit were expected to give the car about fifty more horsepower, while the Daytona authorities made every effort to provide the machine with a good chance of showing what it could do. They agreed to a proposal to increase the length of the course by making use of the sands at the north side of the pier.

The existence of this structure limited the distance available in which to get up speed before entering the measured mile. The piles of the pier were set about fifty feet apart, and the plan was to start the car some distance north of this and drive under the pier at about 140 mph 'Blue Bird' would thus be travelling at this speed when the car reached the spot from which earlier attempts had been started. After sanction to this scheme had been received 'Blue Bird' went once again into her huge crate, and was slung aboard the *Aquitania* on January 26th, 1932. The mechanics went with the car, and had instructions to take it straight down to Daytona; I followed on the *Berengaria* a few days later. This arrangement would save a good deal of time when I arrived at Daytona, because the machine would be all ready for its first tests.

It had been arranged that the beach was to be available for February 14th, and I arrived in New York on the 9th, travelling on to Daytona. A huge crowd was at the railway depot when the train pulled in at midnight, providing a very friendly welcome. My first inquiry concerned the state of the sand, and I was informed that there was not much hope of the beach being favourable for some time, as a very high wind was blowing in the wrong direction.

I went down to the beach early the next morning, and saw at once that conditions were quite impossible. The weather was ideal from the viewpoint of visitors, with hot and continuous sunshine, but the wind had been blowing from the south, piling up waves which had an unusual effect upon the sand. Instead of being flat, it now came down in a curve from highwater mark to the sea. It was not feasible to drive very fast over a cambered beach, while the surface was very uneven.

Nothing at all could be done until the wind changed to the north-east; this would produce rough seas which, pounding on the sand, would level it out. It was unlikely that the direction of the wind would alter for at least four or five days.

I surveyed the beach carefully, and saw that the extension beyond the pier would enable us to do more than attack the mile record only. At Verneuk Pan, we had set up new figures for the five kilometres and the five miles; by taking advantage of the longer run at Daytona, it would be possible for 'Blue Bird' to attack these records. In effect, we could attempt no less than five records during the one effort; these were the one kilometre, one mile, five kilometres, five miles and ten kilometres. The speed for the last record stood at about 152 mph, but all the others were above 210 mph.

On the Monday following our arrival, we took 'Blue Bird' down to the beach, but the weather made it impossible to run the car. Its appearance enabled press photographers to take pictures, and did something to satisfy the crowds, after which we towed the machine back to its garage.

Days slipped past, and there was still no improvement in the weather. I began to grow very impatient, turning out early each morning in the hope of finding the beach smooth, eventually reaching the state of mind when I felt that I could wait no longer. Finally, on Saturday, February 20th, the wind veered round and conditions became a little better. 'Blue Bird' was towed to the beach, although there could be no question of making a really fast test. But I did want to assure myself that the machine handled as well as it had done before; once we knew this, both the mechanics and myself would be easier in mind.

The sand was rough, and a strong wind was blowing in from the sea, and when the machine was pushed off I started on the worst ride I have ever known, from the viewpoint of comfort. The beach was altogether too bumpy for speed, and when I had only 170 mph showing on the revolution counter, I was forced to ease the throttle, because the rough surface threatened to throw the car out of control.

Knowing that the beach was bad, I had strapped myself in, and but for this I should probably have been jerked out of the car. I felt absolutely fit when I began the run, but I was very bruised and tired when I brought 'Blue Bird' back to her starting point, my best speed through the mile having been recorded as well below 140 mph. The test, rough though it was, told me that there was nothing wrong with the car, and I felt happier, except for the bruising when we took 'Blue Bird' back.

The weather continued to improve over the weekend and officials inspected the beach with me at midnight, on Monday. It was then decided to have the car on the beach the next day, ready for low tide at three-thirty in the afternoon. More rain and bad visibility made this quite impossible, and we were forced to wait until Wednesday, when the weather completely changed. The rain vanished, and it grew warmer, although a wind existed when we brought the car down.

'Blue Bird' was on the beach an hour and a half before we were due to start, and preparations were made for what was meant to be another test run. I intended, however, to try for the records if it proved possible, although I knew that the beach was not as smooth as it might have been. We were ready long before the sand was cleared and the timing tapes set. I remained waiting in the cockpit for what seemed an age before we received the word to start, then the car was pushed off, and I sent it towards the dark outline of the pier. It rushed to meet me as 'Blue Bird' accelerated, then I shot between the piles and the open beach showed ahead. A side wind seemed to increase in force as the speed mounted, while, with my foot hard down on the accelerator pedal, I watched for the first timing strip.

Before I picked this up, and when the car was doing about 230 mph, the wheels ran into a patch of water, which rose over the front in a shower of spray and smashed against my goggles. I was completely blinded as the car raced on and, for some moments, my heart seemed to stand still because, at such speed, the machine could leave the course in the fraction of time. Then, after a lapse of about two seconds, I was able to see again, and discovered that 'Blue Bird' had already begun to swerve towards the sea. I straightened out and sighted the red panel, heading for it with the throttle pedal rammed flat.

Because of the roughness of the beach, it required all my

strength to hold the wheel, which was kicking under my hands all the time and this blistered my palms badly. When I was half-way through the mile I glanced at the revolution counter, which showed 3,800 revolutions per minute, equivalent to a road speed of 273 mph. I knew that the car must actually be travelling more slowly than this, owing to wheel slip.

I cleared the mile and continued flat out until 'Blue Bird' was beyond the end of the ten kilometres before I began to slow down. I was able to reduce speed without difficulty, and stopped at the end of the course. I halted only long enough to wipe my goggles and, not waiting to change tyres, began the return run. The wind was now against the machine, and I could feel its effect as the speed rose. Gusts caught the car constantly, and again I was troubled by flying water while I could feel that the machine was appreciably slower. I cleared the timing tapes, picked up the pier again and ran between the piles at about 150 mph; this proved to be quite easy and did not present much difficulty.

Within a very short time, I knew the registered speeds. On the first run, the car had gone through the mile at 267.4 mph, and the run north, against the wind, had been accomplished at 241.7 mph, which gave me a mean speed over the mile of 253.9 mph, eight miles an hour faster than the old record.

The speed through the kilometre had worked out at 251.3 mph. We had also broken the five kilometres record with 241.5 mph but, unhappily, the timing equipment controlling the five miles and ten kilometres distances had broken down and the speeds had not been taken.

This was disappointing but, in any case, I felt that 'Blue Bird' could go much faster if there were no hampering wind. We decided to try again next day, partly because I wanted to lift the mile record still higher, and also because I wanted to register a new record for five miles and ten kilometres. We could not attack the ten miles record because the beach was too short.

We had everything ready the following day, and the sand was

excellent, but it was raining and the Mayor of Daytona refused to allow us to make the attempt. It had to be postponed until the next day, Friday, February 26th. The morning was very bright, and the wind was a little reduced, but the beach was covered with ripples and was very wet. It looked as if I might be in for a rough ride, and this proved to be the case after 'Blue Bird' had started.

I was bumped about a good deal on the approach to the measured mile, but crossed the timing tapes with the car absolutely all out. I saw 4,000 rpm on the revolution counter, which was equal to 287 mph but, at times, the uneven sand was kicking the back wheels off the ground, causing wheel-spin and, actually, the car was much slower through the mile than it had been two days before. No new record was set up over this distance, but 'Blue Bird' succeeded in creating fresh figures for the longer stretches.

The car's pace over five kilometres was now 247.9 mph, more than thirty miles an hour faster than the record made at Verneuk Pan. The five miles were covered at 242.7 mph, also over thirty miles an hour faster. And the speed over the ten kilometres, equivalent to six and a quarter miles, was 238.6 mph, an improvement by some 75 mph on the existing record.

I would have tried again, because I was convinced that 'Blue Bird' could do still better through the mile, but the attempts had to end on that day. However, we had lifted the land-speed record to 253.9 mph, which was well above 250 mph we had hoped to reach, while the car had actually recorded 267 mph on one run. In all, we had secured five world's records, despite the fact that the car had visited the beach only three times.

§4

In actual time, 'Blue Bird's' fastest run in 1932 had involved travelling through the measured mile in only one and one-fifth seconds less than the car's best performance the year before, yet this represented the difference in speed between 246.5 mph and

267.4 mph. Had the car been one and a half seconds faster still, it would have travelled at 300 mph.

From this it will be appreciated that record-breaking at such speeds is largely a matter of gaining mere fractions of time. The least deviation from a straight course, wheel slip, faint ripples in the sand, any one of a number of almost infinitesimal factors can rob the machine of success.

Everything is so enormously multiplied. A hummock of sand only an inch in height can send the car off the beach in a great jump. If attention is relaxed only for a moment, the machine can run off its course. With each second that is gained in speed, still greater demands are made upon the car, and the driver's nervous system is still more stressed.

In these efforts, machine and man must be tuned to a very high pitch of efficiency, if they are to reach beyond the limit that has previously been attained. All the effort which has already been made must be made again, with just a little more effort added.

Although travelling at 267 mph occupied only 13.46 seconds, and although 300 mph means only 12 seconds, the difference between these two times, just 1.46 seconds, demands a great deal. This difference seems very small, and the difficulty in reducing it lies almost wholly in the fact that all which has been achieved before must be gone over again. Even at the risk of repetition, it seems as well to stress this, because it lies behind the reasons why I made up my mind to try and lift the record to 300 mph, after the Daytona effort in 1932.

I had been the first man to do three miles a minute, the first to reach four miles a minute, and it promised much in personal achievement if I could be the first to reach five miles a minute on land. I wanted to do it because I felt that once the goal of 300 mph had been reached, there was a possibility that the record might stand for England for some time to come. It would then be a mark of the excellence of British engineering.

I felt, also, that I had been given quite unique opportunities of making such an attempt. Quite by chance, I had gained more experience of very high-speed work than most men, and it seemed advisable to put this to good use, although I had now gone far past the age when a man may expect, normally, to endure the strain which would be entailed. I began my forty-eighth year shortly after we left Daytona, but I still felt capable of meeting the physical and mental stress of future record effort.

It was plain, from what I already knew, that 300 mph could not be achieved in one single effort. The record had been pushed up only in gradual stages. In survey, the figures showed as: 150–152– 169–171–174–203–206–207–231–246– and, now, 253 mph. Although I had reached 267 mph in actual speed, this did not stand for the record; to attain 300 mph, the official figure had to be lifted by almost another 50 mph. That increase had never been made in one effort, and now that the fraction of time necessary had become still more difficult to win, it was obvious that five miles a minute would be fully as difficult to reach as anything which had been done before; I judged that it would require at least two more attempts. If the mark was gained after only one intermediate effort, it would be only by good luck.

Whatever might be involved, I resolved to try, and this decision was in my mind when we reached England, where a marvellous reception awaited us. There were people ready to suggest that enough had been done, but I felt that our work was unfinished.

There had been a time when 146 mph had looked an odd figure, and I had wanted to lift the record speed to 150 mph; now, 253 mph looked an odd figure, and I wanted to raise it to 300 mph. This speed formed a possible seal on all that had already been done, although I knew that it could be beaten, because five miles a minute does not form the limit of land speed. Given the right surface, a long enough run, and a car designed for the work, a man may reach four hundred, or even 500 mph. The limiting factor to ultimate speed seems determined by the difficulty of finding a course, not by the human element or the car.

There had been a time when 180 mph appeared so far away that it seemed phenomenal. When Segrave took the record for the first time at Daytona, newspaper placards appeared with the simple legend: *203 mph*. The announcement needed no qualifications; in fact, even newspaper men found it difficult to discover words which would adequately express the amazement aroused by Segrave's feat.

Since then, 'Blue Bird' had reached such speeds that 200 mph was regarded only as a reasonable pace for an initial test run. In view of this, it would be unwise to suggest that any new record could not be beaten, or that land-speed would rise to a particular figure and then remain stationary.

So far as 'Blue Bird' was concerned, I did not think we could reach out beyond 300 mph, and if we did attain this speed, we should have done well. In the months following our return we began work on the car, with the definite intention of travelling to Daytona for the speed trials in 1933. When the machine reached England, I drove it during an exhibition run at Brooklands, when wheel-spin tore the rear tyres to shreds, then 'Blue Bird's' reconstruction was started without delay.

§5

I now bought two Sunbeam racing machines, one being the original four-litre car with which Segrave had taken the world's record at 152 mph, driving over Southport Sands. One of these machines was rebuilt at Thompson and Taylor's Brooklands works, and I entered it for the international races held on the Avus track, outside Berlin, on Sunday, May 21st, 1933.

This course is a peculiar one, consisting of two parallel roads, each nearly six miles in length, linked at the ends by two abrupt turns. Cars reach very high speeds along the straights, but the end curves slow them down to about fifty miles an hour. In spite of this, cars were lapping the course during practice at above 120 mph.

A week before the race, mechanics were still working on the Sunbeam, and not until Monday, six days before the event was due, was the car completed. It was rushed to the coast by lorry, then Villa and the lorry driver drove in turns, travelling overland to Berlin and arriving late on Wednesday. I had not driven the car at all, and decided to try it out at once, although the racing tyres had not arrived, and the machine was shod with an old set.

Villa travelled with me for a couple of laps, and we had an opportunity of testing the machine's speed against that of a Bugatti which was out for practice. The Sunbeam passed the French car in the most satisfactory way, after which it appeared better to bring the machine in, as the old tyres were showing signs of stress.

We knew that the Avus race would be run off at extremely high speed, and that even a brief stop for replenishment would jeopardize the Sunbeam's chances. The petrol tank fitted to the car was too small to allow the machine to run non-stop through the race, and we had another one made on the spot. In any case, the small tank had burst under pressure before the car left England; it had been patched up, but the split seams had started leaking again. We changed the rear axle ratio, which appeared too high, then tried the car out with the old tank in position, when we found that the original ratio was better, and put this back. This work occupied so much time that I was only able to do two more practice laps, on the day before the race, but the Sunbeam then proved itself to be quite as fast as anything else in the event.

An enormous crowd gathered on the Sunday afternoon, and I was introduced to the ex-Crown Prince of Germany just as the cars were lining up. The race had aroused a great deal of interest in Germany, and it would have been hard to discover a more experienced set of Continental drivers.

Rudolf Caracciola was driving a new Alfa-Romeo; Hans von Stuck had a Mercedes; another machine of this *marque* had been very carefully streamlined, a clever young driver named von Brauchitsch being at the wheel. A really dashing Italian named

Luigi Fagioli was on a Maserati, and there were two exceed-ingly fast 4½-litre Bugattis in the hands of Albert Divo and Guy Bouriat, all these in addition to a number of other machines, one being a Bugatti driven by Prince Lobkowicz, of Czechoslovakia.

I had not drawn a good position at the start and, after the flag fell, I found myself caught behind a group of five cars, with another group streaking away ahead, and still another bunch coming up behind. Every driver in the race put his foot hard down from the start, the machines stringing out during the rush down the road to the south curve, all approaching this at about 130 mph.

Before entering the curve, there was a slight bend to the right, on the inside of which stood a small building. The leading group of machines was already in this curve, all close together and all struggling for the lead. The second group, with which I was riding, might have been about a hundred yards behind the rearmost of these machines ahead, and all five of us bunched as we came to the bend.

Hans von Stuck was in front, immediately behind him was a Bugatti and my Sunbeam was at this car's tail. We three were in line, and on the outside was another Bugatti, and Prince Lobkowicz was behind it, his radiator level with the Sunbeam's rear wheels. I was easing the throttle when he shot past me, obvi-ously with the intention of trying to snatch the lead before we entered the south curve.

He had to pull wide to get by the French car and, as he did so, I saw his near-side wheels touching the grass which divided the two parallel straights. When a car moving at two miles a minute runs on to the edge of the track, there is always the possibility of the driver finding himself in difficulties and, realizing that there would be trouble, I took my foot off the throttle pedal.

In that moment, the Czechoslovakian's car appeared to bounce back from the grass, and it touched the machine which it was trying to pass. This happened instantaneously and, immediately, everything was obscured by a great cloud of dust and smoke. I drew level with this, and suddenly saw Lobkowicz's car leaping across the grass strip. It was moving at an almost complete right angle to its former direction, travelling broadside about ten feet up in the air, turning over. There was a glimpse of the driver falling out, cushions flying from his cockpit and, at the same time, the car which he had been passing became visible, also on the grass and skidding across it.

As the Sunbeam roared past, I thought of the race leaders coming through the curve. The two cars were pitching towards the return road, and I had time to realize that there was every chance of a tremendous pile-up because it seemed certain that they would hit the crashing machines then I had to concentrate upon controlling my own car.

In watching what happened to Lobkowicz and the other Bugatti my attention had been diverted, although only for a few moments, and I entered the bend so fast that I passed the machines ahead and was soon halfway into the south curve. I came out of the curve to see that the Bugatti had skidded on to the return road, but that the driver had wrenched it back to the grass just in time to avoid the machines which led the race.

The car which Lobkowicz had been driving had jumped sheer across the track, and was rammed against an earth bank on the far side, smoke and flames rising from it. The leaders had gone safely by, and I now passed without touching the debris which lay on the course. When I came round on the next lap, the fire had been extinguished, but I could not see what had happened to the two drivers then, on the third lap, one of the Sunbeam's sparking plugs cut out and another followed. They failed one after the other until I was running on only six cylinders; I pulled into the pits, to find that one of the oil pumps had failed, smothering everything with lubricant. We could not effect a repair in time, and were obliged to withdraw. It was then that I learned that Lobkowicz had been killed, but the driver of the other machine had not been greatly hurt.

The event at Avus was my first experience of a Continental track race, and we had to leave Germany immediately in order to take part in a Thousand Miles race, which was being run at Brooklands on June 4th, 1932. I had entered a Mercedes, and trouble with the car necessitated all-night work before the event, fitting new pistons. The result was that the Mercedes had to be handled carefully when the race began, my co-driver being C. S. Staniland. He took the car away at the start, driving cautiously. After a couple of hours, I took over the machine, and for a long while the Mercedes lapped at 95 mph, then the clutch controlling the supercharger seized up and, following this, a rear tyre burst. This got so hot during the run to the pits, as a result of friction between the wheelrim and the concrete, that the tyre was smouldering when the car stopped. The wheel was changed, when the tyre was removed and flung behind the pits; it then burst into flames and burned for some hours. In the closing stages of the long race, transmission trouble forced us to retire.

Staniland and I had much better luck later in the year, when we drove a Riley in the Five Hundred Miles event. Twelve months before, we had covered only half a dozen laps, but this time we ran right through the race, and finished fifth. The event was marred by a tragedy when Clive Dunfee crashed fatally, his car going over the banking around the Members' Hill.

His big Bentley was lapping at 125 mph when, apparently in placing his machine to pass another, one wheel went beyond the upper edge of the banking. He tried to hold the car, struggling to bring it back, but the wheel caught the trunk of a small fir tree. This made the car leap, so that it rolled half over before it dived beyond the banking, Clive Dunfee falling out on to the track, while the tree which had been struck tumbled to the concrete and remained there in the path of following machines.

There was no hope for the driver when he was picked up, all cars slowing down while the track was cleared. As a result of the crash, a low palisade was afterwards placed along the top of the banking, while the road at the other side, and on to which the car had fallen, was closed, a new entrance being provided to the track.

§6

During 1932, 'Wizard' Smith had tried again with his car at Ninety Mile Beach, but he had not been successful and, as the year drew near its end, it appeared that he had abandoned his attempts. The racing season produced a crop of rumours concerning possible contenders at Daytona, but none of the projected cars had materialized by the time that reconstruction of 'Blue Bird's' chassis had been completed, enabling us definitely to plan for another effort which, I hoped, would be a step towards 300 mph.

Reid A. Railton, at Thompson and Taylor's, was again responsible for the alteration and modifications which had been carried out, and we had now given the car a new engine. This was a Schneider Trophy-type Rolls-Royce of 2,500 horsepower, nearly half as powerful again as the power unit we had last used for the record. Its incorporation had necessitated extensive alterations, and the appearance of the car was much changed.

The radiator was covered by a cowling in which an air-scoop was set to feed the supercharger. Instead of allowing air to rush through the radiator and find its way through an opening behind, the top of the cowling now formed part of the engine cover, and the air emerged through apertures at the sides.

Our greatest problem was to make use of all the power available and, to accomplish this, it was virtually necessary to maintain wheel adhesion; unless the wheels were kept on the ground, speed would be lost and we could not snatch the seconds we wanted to gain. We could not rely upon the tyres to maintain a grip on the sand, because their treads were quite smooth and were very thin, and we had considered the possibility of building a machine in which all four wheels were driven, but this construction would have been most costly.

The very fact that the new attempt was to reach out a little beyond anything that had been done before imposed certain restrictions on the car itself; in other words, there were definite limits to the stress that its mechanism could withstand. If, for instance, any attempt were made to run the machine at full speed for more than ninety seconds, the gearbox and the back axle might fail under the strain; this was not likely to occur, because Daytona Beach was not long enough to permit such a high speed to be sustained for a minute and a half.

Theoretically, it was possible to do 100 mph on first gear, 200 mph on second gear, and well over 300 mph in top speed, but we estimated that to reach five miles a minute a run of seven miles would be necessary before entering the measured mile, while an absolutely smooth beach would also be required. Daytona lacked the necessary length, and we could not expect perfect conditions. In fact, before the car was shipped to America, we anticipated setting new figures at somewhere between 270 mph and 280 mph; this would be an extremely satisfactory step towards the 300 mph which might be attained at some later date.

The tyres were again made by Dunlops, after very careful tests and were tried out on a machine capable of giving the equivalent of 310 mph. The manufacturers considered them to be the finest tyres they had constructed up to that date, and their care is demonstrated by the fact that they used a special Egyptian fibre in the cord; this fibre flexed easily, and helped to keep the tyres cool. A special rubber was used for the treads, compounded to make it more effective in reducing the rasping effect of the Daytona sand. The tyres were designed to run at a pressure of 125 pounds, but even then they would expand an inch in diameter at speed.

The car was twenty-seven feet long, and the bodywork was again constructed by Gurney Nutting. The increased length lent a more graceful appearance, and did much to help make it the most impressive of all the 'Blue Birds' which had so far been built.

Everything was made ready for departure, and 'Blue Bird' left with her mechanics about a week before I sailed. During this interval, I was attacked by influenza, and still had a temperature of a hundred and three when, on the 25th of January, 1933, I boarded the Aquitania, hoping that the voyage would bring me back to normal fitness. I ran a high temperature for the first two or three days, but after that began to recover quickly. When I reached New York I was altogether better, and knew that a few days of sunshine in Florida should make me ready to drive.

THE ELEVENTH CHAPTER

§1

THE CITY OF DAYTONA SURPASSED itself by its welcome when I stepped off the train on February 2nd, 1933. There was an enormous crowd waiting at the station, headed by police, city officials, and members of the Racing Association, accompanied by a band. This band marched at the head of a procession to the hotel, where I found my room filled with flowers sent by friends that I had made in America.

The long journey from New York had been something of a strain and I was still suffering from the effects of influenza. For this reason, I was not so disappointed as I might have been when I was told that it would be several days before 'Blue Bird' could use the beach. Bad storms had struck the coast a little time earlier, but it was not until I went down to the sands that I appreciated that conditions were much worse than ever I had known.

The storms had actually removed some parts of the dunes, while the grandstand and the timing tower opposite the measured mile had been damaged. In places, holes had been pounded in the beach, and at the southern end the sand had been carried away, shortening the course by nearly two miles. In other parts, curves had been cut in the shore line and, for the time being, it was impossible to mark out a straight course.

Nothing could be done until the wind changed, and the sea

levelled and straightened the beach again. The car was ready to run, but we had to remain inactive and, during this time, I threw off all effect of the influenza. Day after day now dragged by, then the wind shifted to the northeast and the sand began to smooth out, heavy seas packing the beach and easing off the curves.

After I had been at Daytona for a week, we decided to make our first test run on Friday, February 10th, but overnight the weather changed. Rain fell heavily, and the wind veered until it was due east. We could only wait on. We inspected the beach each day, and the weekend passed with still no chance of running the car. That morning, the garage in which 'Blue Bird' was housed caught fire, through the upsetting of a petrol stove but, luckily, we were able to extinguish the blaze before any real harm was done.

Each day the wind shifted, and affected the beach, which at times became covered with shells, while the sand built into low hummocks over which no car could be driven at much more than forty miles an hour.

Not until February 14th, nearly a fortnight after my arrival, were we able to take 'Blue Bird' out for a test, and a band of the American Legion, wearing blue tunics and orange trousers, marched ahead of the machine. The beach was far from good, and officials advised me not to attempt to do more than about 150 mph. I wanted to try the car, however, and could learn nothing at such low speed and, while the engine was warming up, I determined to put my foot down, if it was at all possible. It was a little before five o'clock in the afternoon when I received word that all was ready and, at last, 'Blue Bird' went away under her own power.

Right from the start, I was in trouble. The sand was so rough that it was hard to steer a straight course, and real difficulties arose when I tried to change into top gear. This was never easy and, in forcing the lever home, I strained the tendons of my left hand, wrenching muscles and tendons all the way up my forearm.

The surface became worse when I entered the measured mile and here, because of the pain in my left arm, I drove almost one-handed, and this did not make the car easier to handle. Again and again 'Blue Bird' edged off the course, once swerving dangerously near to the sea. To make matters worse, fumes came into the cockpit, but I did my best to keep the car travelling at reasonable speed.

In spite of everything, 'Blue Bird' registered 227 mph over the mile, and averaged about 180 mph along a five-mile stretch, which accomplished all that I had set out to do, and I learned enough about the car to decide that the gear ratio should be lowered, while the clutch needed some adjustment.

I did not make a return run. My hand was too painful, and I felt a little sick as a result of the fumes; some means of preventing these getting into the cockpit had to be found before I attempted the record. 'Blue Bird' was towed back to the garage, where Villa and Leech and the rest of the mechanics began work at once. After so much waiting, they were glad to have something to do, and while they were making the car ready again a doctor came to attend my arm, on which I was obliged to wear bandages.

By Tuesday, the 21st, 'Blue Bird' was ready again, but not until the following day could we take the car out. Even then, there were shells on the beach, and the sand was still rough; I should have made no more than a test run, but for the fact that we had been waiting so long. We took 'Blue Bird' down to the sand about two hours before we could possibly start. We changed wheels, and mechanics went to the far end of the course with a lorry; I told them that, owing to the state of the beach, I should have to change tyres after the first run, because they were certain to be cut about by the shells.

The men disappeared while the beach was still being cleared, then the engine was warmed up, after which there was nothing more to do. Villa and the mechanics who remained with me were full of nerves, and the crowd seemed restless as we awaited the word to start. Close behind the machine stood an aeroplane, and this was to bring Villa along the course after the car had gone away. We had adopted the same plan during a previous effort; if anything went wrong during the outward run, the plane would bring him to the far end of the course soon after I reached it. I liked to know that he would be near me, in case of trouble. He always waited until 'Blue Bird' had actually got away, then he ran back to the plane, jumped in and followed.

I sat in the cockpit of the car, chaffing against the delay. Visibility was not very good, and I was afraid that it might grow worse; I could see stretches of water here and there on the sand, and this was a sign that the beach was anything but smooth.

Finally, we received the word to go, and the crowd near the car silenced as they watched the engine started. Flames shot from the exhaust, smoke rolled behind, then 'Blue Bird' went away to a good start but, as the car gathered speed, it seemed to skate on the wet sand, and I could feel the rear wheels kicking from the bumps long before I changed into top gear.

I had to work hard to hold the machine straight, and I was so shaken and jarred in the cockpit that it was not easy to keep my foot on the accelerator pedal as I sent the car into the measured mile. I had crossed the timing tape when I looked at the revolution counter and, according to the position of the needle, 'Blue Bird' was travelling at 328 mph.

I knew that wheel-slip was reducing the actual speed, but I knew that I was moving very fast indeed, and it felt very dangerous. The pace held until I had cleared the mile, then I began to ease up, watching for the lorry and the mechanics at the far end. When I halted near them, they ran to the machine at once and began the work of changing the wheels, finding the tyres badly cut about by shells, as we had anticipated.

While I stopped, a man massaged my left arm, which felt very strained, and while he was working I was informed that my speed during that run had been 273.556 mph. This was much higher than the record we had set up a year earlier, but it was over fifty miles an hour below the speed which my revolution counter had shown during the run through the mile.

Obviously, the difference was due entirely to wheelspin. The sand was too rough to permit the use of full throttle; the probability was that the car would be just as fast, and possibly faster, at a lesser throttle opening on the return run.

My left arm was very painful and I felt all in; after a halt of almost twenty minutes, 'Blue Bird' began the second run. At once, the weakness of my left hand became evident, while, for some reason, the car 'snaked' more than before. Again and again the machine swung out of the straight as speed mounted, so that I had to fight for control.

One vicious swerve carried me within a yard of the marking flags along the course, just as I came in sight of the measured mile. I pulled the car back, then glanced at my revolution counter and saw it showing what should have been a road-speed of over 300 mph. I eased my foot, so that the throttle pedal was depressed to only about three-quarters of its full travel; this meant that not so much power was being given to the engine, yet when 'Blue Bird' entered the mile, the needle still showed 300 mph.

Somehow, I managed to keep my foot steady, working all the while to maintain a straight course then, clearing the far end of the mile I began to slow, realizing that the effort was over and that I could hardly fail to have broken the record. I ran to the depot by the pier and pulled up, to be informed, within a minute or so, that 'Blue Bird's speed over the second run had been 270.676 mph.

This gave me an average of 272.1 mph. We had raised the land-speed record by nearly twenty miles an hour and, incidentally, we had set up a new five-kilometre record with 257.2 mph, ten miles an hour faster than the speed of the year before.

§2

On the first run I had travelled with the throttle pedal pushed absolutely flat, so that the engine was giving out all the power of which it was capable, but wheel-spin had reduced the car's speed.

On the return, I used three-quarter throttle, when wheel-slip had been lessened, but the car had been less than 3 mph slower.

This illustrates the effect which the rough beach had on the machine. If the surface had been smooth, enabling full throttle to be usefully employed, the record figure must have been set very much higher than was actually the case. I was so convinced of this, that I wanted to try again. I had a feeling that, even with the beach in its present condition, the speed could be raised, if the throttle control were employed more carefully than I had been able to do on the second run. Unfortunately, I was completely tired out, and it really was not possible to attempt another effort that day; in any case, the ligaments of my left arm had suffered so much that it was painful to hold anything in my left hand, and I could not have gripped the steering wheel properly.

I considered going out again next day, but the doctor who examined my arm forbade this. He warned me that further strain might result in permanent injury. As it was, the weather did not improve and, finally, we decided to return home on the *Aquitania*, which docked at Southampton on March 8th. As we came down Southampton Water we received an unusual welcome; it took the form of fifteen speedboats racing out to meet the liner, and a big crowd waited on the quayside to receive us.

The first real step towards 300 mph had been taken, and almost the first question I was asked, following congratulations concerned the possibility of my going on and, if so, where I should make the attempt. I intended to continue but, at so early a date, it was impossible to guess whether the effort would be made at Daytona or elsewhere. In any case, nothing could be done for some time, because we had learned enough to be able still further to improve the car and bring five miles a minute within definite reach.

There followed luncheons and dinners and banquets, in which the feat at Daytona was much praised but, during all of them, I always felt that my mechanics, the engineers and the experts whose work had made the speed possible should have been with me to share the congratulations and the applause. I tried to express my gratitude to them and, particularly, to the men who had made the tyres which had been subjected to such appalling conditions during the run. Without the least exaggeration, my life had depended directly upon their work.

Gradually the round of functions became less pressing and we were able to consider the future, although without reaching any definite conclusions except that whatever happened, we decided again to use the splendid Rolls Royce engine which had lifted the record so high. There, for the time being, matters were left.

I entered one of my two Sunbeam cars in the International Trophy race at Brooklands, which was held at the beginning of May, but engine trouble put us out of the event when we had run three-quarters of the distance, and while I was leading. This was the only big race in which I drove that year, although I ran several times at Brooklands meetings and an event towards the end of the season provided a narrow escape.

It was a race for the 'Mountain' Championship, and I was handling a Sunbeam against eight very fast cars which, at the fall of the flag, got away in a bunch, struggling for the lead in the first turn. As we entered the corner, a Bugatti, just ahead of the Sunbeam, skidded and shot up the banking. I was close behind this machine and, thinking that the car would run down on the banking, I pulled the Sunbeam wide, following the Bugatti up the slope.

The car, however, turned completely round, skidding to meet me so that the two machines struck broadside on, bounced apart, then slithered to a stop with other cars roaring past. Neither of us were hurt, but the Sunbeam was badly knocked about, the back axle being damaged, springs and shackle-pins suffering heavily. The track officials waved blue warning flags immediately the crash occurred, but the cars were left on the course until the event was over.

The racing season ended and, soon afterwards, an opportunity came to plan an expedition which had long been in my mind. It was not a treasure hunt, but it involved seeking a gold reef in South Africa. Information concerning it had come to me after our return from Cocos Island; on the reef, solid gold outcropped to the surface and could be picked up with the hands.

It was situated in Namaqualand, in what had once been a stretch of country inhabited by the Gainin Bushmen, although they had long since gone from it, for very good reasons. The area had become one of the most inhospitable regions in the world, and no one knew very much about it. Mountains stood about fifty miles inland, and the space between them and the coast had once been green and fertile but, for some reason, the prevailing wind had changed and now blew with tremendous force from the heights straight down to the sea. The incessant gales had frittered away the rocky peaks, covering the whole region with sand dunes, which were rarely less than four hundred feet high. In some cases, the sand had built up until it completely hid rocky heights which had once been three thousand feet above sea level. In this desolate waste, a few reefs and rock stretches remained visible, and one of these held the outcrop of gold.

Attempts on the world's record had prevented me following up the clues that I had been given. Various matters made it impossible to prepare 'Blue Bird' for another effort during the spring of 1934, while other circumstances combined to make it feasible for me to go to South Africa at a time when, otherwise, I might have been travelling to Daytona.

I had often thought out the method by which such an expedition might be arranged. My idea had been to charter a small yacht, anchor off shore and use rafts to land tractors. These could convey the party over the sand without difficulty and, by quartering the countryside, we should have a reasonable chance of locating the gold. Everything necessary in the way of supplies would have to be taken, because the locality was said to be almost completely waterless and devoid of all life, except leopards and lions.

An opportunity arose to discuss this with Sir Alan Cobham, and he pointed out that the quickest and safest way of locating the reef would be from the air. He had flown over the country, and he was so much attracted by the scheme that he agreed to come. We made rough plans but, when they were near fruition, he was unable to join me, although I decided to go through with the trip, following Cobham's suggestion and using a plane.

I sailed for Cape Town in the middle of February, and the party consisted of Dr Bleeck, a geologist; Eddie Fulford, a pilot; and Ogden, who was a ground mechanic as well as a pilot. On arriving in Cape Town, early in March I discovered that the territory which we wanted to explore was prohibited, because diamonds had been found there. I explained to the authorities the object of the quest, and received permission to continue, while we were given an inspector of police as a guardian.

Not long after that, we reached Luderitz, which we had chosen as a base and which lay some five hundred miles north of Cape Town. It took Fulford and myself about six hours to fly up there, our supplies and the remainder of the party following by train a journey which occupied three days and nights.

Before we came down, Fulford and I saw enough of the country ahead to realize that one plane was quite useless. I had planned to use the machine to inspect the desert, landing and searching likely places, then flying on; but we now saw that suitable landing places were few, and most of them dangerous. With two machines, one could remain in the air while the other went to earth and, if it found trouble, the plane which had remained aloft could fly back to the base camp and bring assistance.

I made arrangements for a second machine to be brought over from Johannesburg, seven hundred miles distant, the pilot being given instructions to land at Cape Town, and then to proceed base at Luderitz.

The rest of the party arrived and, impatient to get to work, Fulford and I decided to make a reconnaissance flight. Our intention was to be away only three or four hours, and our object was simply to get a true appreciation of what lay ahead. We started just at dawn, and soon we were flying over the strangest country that I have ever seen. Following the shore line, we had the sea on one side, and on the other was a vast area which stretched as far as our sight could reach and which had the appearance of being a second sea, but immobile and moulded from sand.

The sand showed in waves which came right down to the coast. Here and there, outcrops of rock appeared, and nowhere existed the least sign of life. Everything was utterly desolate and empty. Valleys and rivers, hills and trees, grass and wild animals had once existed there; now there was nothing but sand which stretched away to the dim blur of the distant mountains.

§3

Eddie Fulford and I flew about a hundred and fifty miles up country, watching for a mountain which was said to hold the gold reef. This was supposed to be located about a mile inland, and was actually a rocky hill rather than a mountain. We realized, at once, that it would be impossible to be sure of it, even if we did locate it, because the sand, blowing down from the distant heights, had driven back the sea. Instead of being only a mile from the shore, the mountain might now be standing two or even three miles inland. In addition, the summit would show as little more than a reef of rock, outcropping from surrounding desert.

At the end of a hundred and fifty miles we turned inland, the plane sweeping in great circles until we located what appeared to be a likely reef. We decided to land and inspect it, and the plane was headed for a level stretch near the peak. Not until the landing wheels actually touched did we discover the surface to be soft. In a moment the wheels had sunk, and the machine stopped with a crash, ramming its nose deep in the sand, the tail sticking up into the sky.

Fortunately, we were not hurt. Nothing was broken, but it was obvious that the propeller had been damaged, although we could not examine it until we had righted the machine. The only way to achieve this was to bring weight to bear on the tail, and Fulford considered climbing up the fuselage, until he reached the rudder. The tail would then be certain to drop, but under his weight the fuselage of the plane might break.

We solved the difficulty by tying an apple to the end of a piece of cord, and after a few casts managed to get this over the tail-skid; by pulling on the cord, we brought the machine on to an even keel. We found that the engine was quite undamaged, but the propeller was bent nearly six inches out of truth. Fortunately, I profited from my previous experiences in 1929 and had particularly made a point of having our machine fitted with an all-metal propeller, and this had not shattered as it must have done had it been constructed from wood. The fact that it was bent was bad enough, however.

We were a hundred and fifty miles from the base, with very little chance of being found even if the second plane, due from Johannesburg, came to look for us, because no one knew where we were. We discussed the situation and finally decided that Fulford should try and fly the machine back, while I awaited his return. He was more skilled than myself, and he had a chance of getting through alone; with a damaged propeller, the plane might not even get off the ground if two of us were aboard.

We managed to manoeuvre the machine to firmer sand, and it took off safely enough. I watched until it disappeared from sight, then looked around. Deep sand lay everywhere except on the rocks, which reared some three hundred feet at one side. It was absolutely silent, with no indication of any life. I did not worry, because I knew that it should not take long to straighten out the propeller and the machine ought to be back by the evening.

I was wearing shorts and a singlet, and had a light Burberry. I also had two water bottles, a tin of biscuits, another of bully beef, an electric torch and a 32 Colt revolver. I left all these things in a pile while I selected a landing ground ready for the machine's return.

I marked out the area, and this was hard work. I had to dig a trench in the sand all round the site, and then find white stones with which to make an arrow to indicate the direction of steady wind. This took some time and, afterwards, I decided to prospect along the reef.

Walking over the sand was exhausting. My feet sank almost to the ankles at every step, and climbing over the rocks was not much better. Between walking and climbing, I must have covered more than twenty miles before I returned to the landing ground late in the afternoon. I had found no gold, and the plane had not come back. I decided not to touch my food until hunger absolutely compelled it, because I did not know how this emergency might develop.

I was so tired that I dozed off between a couple of huge rocks at the foot of the reef. I cannot tell what it was that roused me, but I wakened suddenly and discovered the freshly made spoor of some animal which had passed while I was asleep. Remembering the lions and leopards of which I had been warned, I wondered why I had not been attacked and, at the same time, realized that the revolver with which I was armed would be of little use.

It was growing late, and I judged it best to find some safe place in which I could spend the night, if that became necessary. I searched higher amongst the rocks, finally climbing to the top of a steep slope. A boulder on either side provided inadequate protection from the wind, but I could be attacked only by an animal leaping down from a ledge behind.

I remained there while the sun dropped towards the horizon, all the time listening for the first sound of the returning machine. The wind began to blow more and more strongly, and darkness was falling when I looked southward for the last time. I did not see the plane, and I decided to make a last survey of the ground around my shelter before nightfall. It was then that I discovered another spoor of the same species of animal on the ledge behind, which suggested that it was only awaiting darkness before making an attack.

In spite of this warning, I decided to take a chance and stay where I was, and I remained there until darkness came. It fell abruptly and completely, and it was like a signal. Pandemonium wakened in that place which had seemed so devoid of life. In the most incredible way, the night became noisy with a wild roaring and baying as animals emerged from their hiding-places in the rocks. After that, I could conceive only one place which offered security, and that was on the topmost peak of the reef. I scrambled up the great mass of rock, and crawled between boulders on the summit, trying to find shelter, while the wind increased, whistling round me. In a little while, a sixty miles an hour gale was raging, as it does every night in that region, bringing more and more sand from the mountains.

It became bitterly cold as I huddled there, and the howling of the animals made it plain that I must keep awake and watchful. I had my revolver and torch handy, but these seemed likely to prove very inadequate if I should be attacked. I kept looking at my watch, but the hands appeared hardly to move across the dial and, after some long while, I tried to force my attention from the situation.

Deliberately scheming to make the time pass quickly, I thought about home, about Brooklands and Daytona Beach, and when I imagined I had occupied myself in this way for at least an hour I looked at my watch again, to find that barely ten minutes had gone. Again and again I tried this; the time dragged in a way which is unbelievable unless one has known a similar experience. In the end, when it was past midnight, I decided that I had to sleep, whatever the risk. I did not know what the next day might bring, and it was essential that I should keep myself fit and ready for emergencies.

I dozed off, to be roused by a sudden noise and, leaping to my feet, I switched on the torch, to find a pair of green eyes shining from the darkness, not ten feet away. I did not shoot, because the bullet might only have wounded the animal, which I could see indistinctly; in that case, it might have made an attack. The eyes vanished and the animal disappeared, and I knew that I must not sleep again. I saw the eyes several times after that, but always some distance away, although whether they belonged to the same animal, I could not tell.

Morning came at last, and I climbed down from the top of the reef, feeling very cold. As I had expected, all trace of the marks I had set about the landing ground had been wiped out by the wind, and I had to make them all over again. I waited for a time in expectation of seeing the plane; when it did not arrive, I began to search the other side of the reef.

I spent until the middle of the afternoon engaged in this, finding no trace of gold, and, very tired now, I went back to the landing ground; I had eaten nothing in the meantime as I decided that it was wise to conserve my limited rations. It was then that, suddenly, I made a guess at why the machine had not come back. Eddie Fulford must have crashed on his way to the camp.

If he had reached it safely, he would have returned long since, because it could have taken only a few hours to straighten out the propeller. If he had got to the camp, he would not have left me there; at the worst he would, somehow, have communicated with the other machine, which by that time must have arrived at Port Nolloth.

I was convinced that Fulford must be somewhere between the reef and the camp, down amongst the sand dunes, and in a plight which was even worse than my own.

I sat down and thought it all out. I had not yet touched any of the water and food which he had left, and I resolved not to eat or drink until the next day. I calculated that I should be able to live for a week on what I had with me, and then I considered

Front view of the large frontal area of the Railton Blue Bird.

Enjoying the thrill of breaking the record. Campbell with H. Leech and L. Villa.

Blue Bird crossing the timing tapes at Daytona Beach at a speed of 246.086 mph in 1931.

US Vice President Dawes presents Campbell with silver trophy in recognition of the new land speed record of 205.9 mph on the steps of the Capitol in Washington.

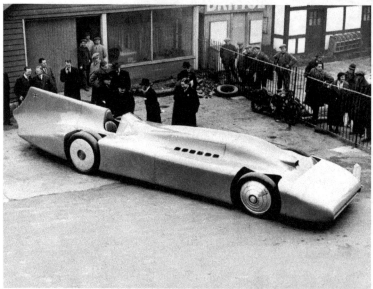

The impressive lines of Campbell's 1935 Railton, V12 Rolls-Royce engined Blue Bird. His final land speed record car.

Blue Bird on a trial run over the sands at Daytona Beach where he would shortly attempt to lower his record for the measured mile.

Campbell with Barney Oldfield, another successful speed record-breaker in 1932.

Blue Bird draws an audience at Brooklands.

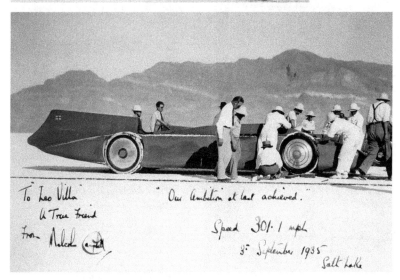

To Leo Villa
A True Friend
From Malcolm Campbell

"Our Ambition at last achieved."

Speed 301·1 mph
3ʳᵈ September 1935
Salt Lake

The final land speed record attempt for Blue Bird is successful.

WHEN A WOMAN MAKES HER WILL: *Page 7*

WIRELESS on PAGE 20

DAILY SKETCH

No. 7,445. [Registered as a newspaper.]   THURSDAY, MARCH 2, 1933.   ONE PENNY.

CAMPBELL PASSES THE POST

Bluebird's Record Dash
That Thrilled the World

The gamble with death won—that glorious first cigarette.

THE SWELLING ROAR OF BLUE BIRD drowning the noise of the waves as Sir Malcolm Campbell hurtled across Daytona Beach, past the timing stand.

These photographs are the first to reach England of Sir Malcolm Campbell when he broke his own world land speed record by 19.14 m.p.h. with an average speed of 272.108 m.p.h. Sir Malcolm, who is on his way home, speaking to members of the Empire Club, Toronto, predicted that at least 330 m.p.h. will be attained.

1933 Daily Sketch front page reporting Sir Malcolm Campbell speed record in 'Blue Bird' at Daytona Beach – John Frost Newspapers: Alamy Stock Photo.

Campbell with his son Donald and George Eyston.

the possibility of trekking the hundred and fifty miles to the camp. I realized at once, however, that this was quite out of the question. Walking over the soft sand was altogether too difficult, and it would have been impossible to cover the distance in seven days; when I grew weak, as must be inevitable, I should certainly wander off my course. Also, there was the hope that a plane might eventually come in search of me, and the chances of my being seen amongst the dunes would be very small indeed. So far as could judge, the wisest thing seemed to be to remain where I was and wait.

Four o'clock came, and the hour which followed was the longest I have ever known. I sat on a rock, realizing how extraordinary it was that I should so suddenly have been taken from racing cars and all the things with which I was familiar, and dumped down in this isolated and remote spot.

The solitude began to get monotonous. I searched along the reef again, even though I was now convinced that no gold existed there. I was clambering about, trying to keep myself cheerful and refusing to consider what lay ahead, when the silence was broken by the noise of an engine. I thought, at first, that it could exist only in my imagination, and I would not turn to look, but the noise grew clearer and I spun round. I saw, dropping towards the little landing ground, the machine which had left me there hours earlier.

It alighted safely, while I ran down to the sand, and Fulford hastened to explain what had happened. The vibration of the bent propeller had been so great that everything which was not split-pinned about the plane had been shaken loose during his return flight. He had managed to get back to the camp, and the fact that he had done so at all proved his very real skill as an airman. With Ogden and the rest, he had worked every minute since his arrival in putting the machine into flying trim again.

Fulford added that the other plane was at Port Nolloth, where it had broken its propeller in landing, so that it could not be sent out to my rescue.

We returned safely to Luderitz and, within a day or two, the other plane arrived. By making numerous flights we transported all our equipment and supplies up-country, establishing another base from which we started our search. We then began trekking on foot, usually covering about twenty miles a day, always over very difficult ground.

We were constantly troubled by the high winds, and although we saw no lions or leopards, wolves and jackals were a constant menace. We were surprised that these animals managed to exist at all, but in time discovered that their principal diet consisted of birds and fish; when we were working near the coast, I actually saw a jackal dash into the water and come out with a fish. The wolves were huge creatures, half as big again as a large Alsatian dog, and they were quite fearless; they hunted singly, or in pairs, and on more than one occasion I found myself being stalked by them.

Two or three times our food supplies ran low, and lack of water often became serious. For some weeks we roughed it very thoroughly, carrying out extensive surveys, finding considerable quantities of manganese ore and copper, as well as iron pyrites and mica, but we found no gold.

Fully a mile inland we discovered the remains of a ship and, later, we came upon the stone foundations of dwellings which had once been occupied by the Gainin Bushmen. The ship showed how the sea was receding under the action of the sand dunes, and the old dwellings proved that the country had once been fertile.

In the end, we came to the conclusion that the gold reef for which we were looking must have become covered with sand, when we returned to Cape Town, and I landed again in England after an absence of ten weeks. As an experience, the trip was very much worthwhile, but my health suffered temporarily due to an attack of dysentery brought on through drinking dirty water.

Once back in England, I drove once or twice at Brooklands meetings, but took no part in any big race, largely because real work had commenced on 'Blue Bird' and because it seemed that

an opportunity might come before the year was out for an attempt
to raise the record again.

§4

The first consideration, in view of another effort with 'Blue Bird',
was the question of where the car should be run. We were always
sensible of the great hospitality and kindness of everyone at
Daytona, and I wanted to drive there again, but experience had
made it clear that the beach could not be relied upon. We now
considered a course which offered great possibilities, in view of
what had occurred there a year earlier.

This course was the dry Salduro Lake, situated about a hundred and twenty-five miles west of Salt Lake City, Utah, where an
American driver named 'Ab' Jenkins, had set up a series of wonderful long-distance records. The conditions appeared to be as
nearly perfect, in some respects, as it was possible to obtain. The
surface was formed by encrusted salt, quite smooth and extremely
hard; in fact, marking flags could only be inserted by first making
a hole with an iron spike. The air was so clear that mountains
over a hundred miles away could be seen and, because of the light
colour of the lake bed, it never became really dark at night.

A railway ran right across the lake, so that there would be no
difficulty about transport and, although the place was remote
from any town, the matter of supplies would present no trouble.
It was estimated that a course between ten and twelve miles long
could be marked out, although a light, powdery deposit would
have to be brushed away to reach the firm surface just beneath.

There were certain objections to the course. One was that the
lake lay at an altitude of some four thousand feet; the rarefied
atmosphere would reduce engine power, although there would be
some compensation in lessened wind resistance to the car. Also,
attempts could be made only during the summer, when it was
very hot; in winter, the lake was under water. Another difficulty

was the question of how our very thin tyres would stand up against such a surface, and what effect the salt would have upon the metal of the car itself. One final consideration was that of organization for the attempt, because officials and timing apparatus would have to be transported to the spot, just as had occurred at Verneuk Pan.

We studied the matter seriously, and actually contemplated an attempt during August, 1934. It was then found that 'Blue Bird' could not be made ready in time and, finally, it was determined to go to Daytona in February, 1935, instead.

'Blue Bird' had been completely rebuilt and redesigned once again. Railton and his assistants at Thompson and Taylor's, had worked on the chassis from the end of April, 1934, until the beginning of November, and over two months more had been occupied in building the new body which has been evolved. In its final form, the chassis still incorporated some parts from the machine which had taken the record at Pendine; the brake-drums, brake shoes and mechanism, the stub-axles and king pins were from the old car, while we were using the same steering wheel and chassis side members, with the Rolls-Royce engine employed for 1933.

The radiator was much bigger and occupied almost the full width between the front wheels. As before, the nose of the engine cover came down behind this, so that no wind could enter the car. The radiator was provided with a shutter, controlled by a lever in the cockpit; by knocking this lever over, just before entering the mile, the shutter would be closed, thus discounting any resistance which might be offered by wind rushing through the radiator when the car was at the peak of its speed; wind tunnel tests told us this should give the car an increase of speed of 10 mph.

We abandoned independent wheel fairings and extended the body at the sides, thus forming a fairing between the wheels; these were now enclosed, very much as had been done on the 1,000 h.p. Sunbeam, except that in the case of 'Blue Bird', the tops of the wheels remained exposed.

In order to secure better acceleration, twin rear wheels were fitted, and we considered that this would help to overcome the wheel-spin which had affected the previous effort. We also introduced what we knew as a 'wind brake'; this was formed by two vanes set in the tail. These remained horizontal until the brake pedal was used, when the vanes would rise to a vertical position, and the resistance which they provided would assist the brakes in slowing down the car.

'Blue Bird' had been built with the idea of taking fullest possible advantage of every yard of the Daytona course. We knew that the car was capable of much more than 300 mph, but it would be unable to reach this rate of travel owing to the shortness of the course, unless the car attained real speed very rapidly. At the same time, speed would have to be reduced more quickly than before, after leaving the mile, otherwise the machine was likely to run beyond the limits of the available beach.

After we had broken the record with 253 mph, I had calculated that two more attempts would be necessary before we could achieve five miles a minute. One of those efforts had already been made, and we had brought the land-speed up to 272 mph. Only by good luck could we reach 300 mph without the second intermediate attempt. It was my opinion, although I wanted to do the higher speed if it was at all possible, that we should be fortunate if this effort in 1935 reached between 285 mph and 290 mph.

Full success required a perfect beach, and this was the one thing that we could not command. If we were given it, fortune would be treating us more kindly at Daytona than we had ever known before and, in that case, we hoped to be able to make an adequate response.

THE TWELFTH CHAPTER

§1

THURSDAY, JANUARY 31ST, 1935. AS on previous occasions, we were met at St Augustine, some seventy miles from Daytona, by Mayor Armstrong and other officials, who joined the train and accompanied us for the remainder of the journey.

I was told that the beach was not in good shape. It was expected, however, that the spring tides, due about the middle of the month, would bring an improvement. Nothing could be done immediately and, in any case, 'Blue Bird' had not arrived, and it was five days before the car reached Daytona. During the interval, I made exploratory runs along the beach, hoping that each day would find the sands more promising, but an unsuitable wind kept them in such condition that it would have been quite impossible to reach a speed sufficiently high to provide a test for the car. I found, too, that the beach was no longer straight, as a result of erosion, and there was a particularly bad curve just south of the pier.

It was absolutely vital that I should keep 'Blue Bird' on her course, when the record attempt was made, and that would be difficult if the car had to follow the contours of the beach. For this reason, it seemed a very good idea to duplicate an experiment which we had tried at Verneuk Pan, where we had put down a white line along the centre of the selected course. I had found it of great assistance, and we considered that a similar line drawn along the Daytona sands would serve as a guide where the course diverged from the absolute straight. The officials agreed to mark the beach with a strip two feet wide, made from a mixture of oil and lampblack.

The car was prepared for its first test run, then followed a long period of waiting. Every day found us hoping for the north-east winds necessary to set the tide running in the right direction and pack the sand hard, but the winds did not come. The authorities put men to work, levelling out hummocks on the beach and filling depressions in the hope that their activities would prove helpful when the wind did swing to the right quarter. When the wind finally came from the north-east it was not very strong, but it brought the beach into a condition which, on February 14th and after two weeks of waiting, made a test run possible.

It was a very hot day, and great crowds lined the dunes under the blazing sun. Sirens had summoned men to help in marking the course, the police cleared the beach and lorries raced down it with marking flags. Within very little more than two hours after the decision to bring 'Blue Bird' out, everything was in readiness, and we hoped that the run would tell us how the car behaved and whether it was in proper trim for the real attempt. I could not hope to make an effort to raise the record, because the run was restricted to about six miles of beach; the remainder presented a surface that was altogether unsuitable even for a relatively low rate of travel.

In actual performance, 'Blue Bird' reached a little above 200 mph, but the test was valuable because I found that the car handled splendidly. This put us all in better spirit. It was not that we had any doubt about the machine, but some anxiety must always exist until the results of a practical test are known. A good deal of sand was flung into the cockpit by the rear wheels and through the underscreen, but we eventually managed partially to overcome the trouble.

The spring tides arrived, but they did not help. With the car all ready, we were faced by the unpleasant fact that the sands were quite impracticable, so that more than another fortnight passed before we could try again. We made a second run on March 2nd, when the beach was far from perfect, although it did seem just possible that we might break the record. Once again the course was cleared and flagged, we brought 'Blue Bird' down, and the car went away to a perfect start, travelling magnificently towards the south. 'Blue Bird' was accelerating splendidly and had reached a speed of more than 240 mph when I suddenly became aware of exhaust fumes in the cockpit. This was alarming, because I had experienced these fumes during a previous attempt, and knew how rapid was their overpowering effect. The fumes were accompanied by scorching heat and, for a moment, I thought that the carburettor had caught fire.

I turned off the petrol and used the air-brake, bringing 'Blue Bird' to a stop some three and a half miles farther on, the car having then gone through the measured mile, recording a speed of 233 mph in spite of the mishap. When we examined the car it was to find that the wind created by the machine's passage had caught the bonnet at one side. The metal panelling had been forced over the exhaust ports, which were cut off level with the bonnet, diverting flames and fumes into the car.

The damage was not sufficient to preclude the possibility of another run. We tightened the loosened side of the bonnet, then I sent the car off on a return run to the north. Once again, however, the engine cover lifted, and again I was forced to slow down, recording only 208.2 mph. But we travelled fast enough to learn that the surface of the beach was such that any attempt to improve upon existing record figures was quite out of the question,

I had been strapped into the cockpit, otherwise the bumps would have thrown me out, while the flying sand was even worse than it had been during the first test. When we stopped, I found that sand had smothered the cockpit, clogging my nostrils and ears, while the black line down the course was proved impracticable, largely because the oil which formed its base was flung over my goggles and the windscreen.

Villa and the rest of the mechanics began work on the bonnet, which had been badly burned and distorted. In order to obviate any chance of further mishap, short extensions were welded on to the exhaust pipes, making it impossible for the flames to play on the side of the aluminium bonnet. The men were busy all night, and 'Blue Bird' was in readiness for another run on the following day: Sunday, March 3rd. The sand was no better than on the day before and I was advised not to start but, after waiting for so long, I was ready to take any opportunity to extend the car.

For the third time the beach was cleared, and now the course was extended to a point nearly a mile and a half north of the pier, in order to give the car a longer run. I had driven under the pier in 1932, but now the car would have to go between the piles considerably faster than before. In fact, 'Blue Bird' was doing rather more than 130 mph when I went through the 40-foot opening, after getting off to an excellent start.

Just beyond the pier was a section where the beach curved, and 'Blue Bird' was travelling altogether too fast to get through this bend without a skid. But the car answered admirably when I straightened out, although we only just missed the marking flags on the seaward side. With the throttle wide open the car roared on, and at 200 mph I changed to top gear. It was then that I began to feel the bumps, because the sand was very uneven, and I realized that I might be asking too much from the car.

As the speed mounted, the bumps became alarming, growing so severe that – in spite of my safety belt – I was bounced up and down in the cockpit. More than once, the top of my head rose above the windscreen, to be caught by a truly terrific blast of wind. Then, just before we entered the measured mile, there came the worst bump of all. I was shot straight upwards from my seat, catching the wind fairly in the face, so that my goggles were blown downwards, clamping over my nose and mouth.

'Blue Bird' was then doing fully 270 mph; in all probability, the speed was even higher. I could do nothing except grip the steering wheel and keep the machine straight. I was half-blinded by sand and, owing to the position of the goggles, I could hardly breathe, but I managed to keep my foot hard down on the throttle pedal, because I did not want to spoil the run by slowing up. The length of time occupied by the car in covering the mile seemed an eternity while, because there was no protection for my eyes, I could see hardly more than two hundred yards ahead. Fortunately, 'Blue Bird' remained on her course, and when I had passed the mark at the end of the mile I slowed, ran to the end of the beach and stopped.

The car's speed on that run was registered as 270.473 mph, but I decided that a return run was useless, because the sand was far too rough. The car had been thrown about very badly, and it seemed better to wait a little longer for a good beach, than to make a return trip and risk damaging the machine. In addition, we found that, in some places, the rubber had completely gone from the tyre treads; this alone was enough to suggest the condition of the sand, and it showed how much speed had been lost through wheelspin.

We towed 'Blue Bird' back to the garage, and I had another safety strap fitted so that, on any future attempt, I should be held securely in my seat, with no risk of being catapulted above the windscreen again. Two days later, another effort appeared possible but, at the last moment and when the car was actually ready to start, it was decided that the course was unsafe, due to a strong wind that got up suddenly. Then on Thursday, March 7th, we found the beach better than it had been before and, once more, 'Blue Bird' rolled down to the sands to make what we all hoped would be a final and successful attack.

§2

Visibility was very good when 'Blue Bird' arrived on the beach, but wind soon began to rise and a haze drifted in from the sea.

Everything was made ready, the engine was started up and 'Blue Bird' went off. The car ran to the left in the approach to the pier, and cut the piles very closely as we shot beneath it; once again, this brought me near the flags, but there was no skid.

'Blue Bird' accelerated magnificently, but was checked two or three times by patches of water as I watched for the banner over the entrance to the mile. I picked it up without difficulty and, with my foot hard down on the throttle pedal, went into the measured distance. Owing to the bumps near the entrance to the mile, I could not release one hand from the steering wheel, in order to use the lever which closed the radiator shutters and which, we knew, would assist 'Blue Bird's' speed by making the nose a solid, streamlined shape. The car kept to her course all through the mile, and I slowed down without difficulty at the far end.

It was evident, before 'Blue Bird' stopped, that this run had been much more successful than any before, and I was soon informed that we had gone through the mile in 13.2 seconds, which was equivalent to 272.72 mph, an improvement on the existing record speed by just about a quarter of a mile an hour against a fairly strong wind. Little as this seems, it was very encouraging to have improved upon the figures against a head wind, and I knew that I should be able to go still faster during the northward run, and so actually break the record.

We spent twenty minutes in changing tyres, then 'Blue Bird' began the return trip, and I soon found myself in trouble. I was now starting from the south end of the beach, and the sand here was very rough indeed, particularly for a mile or so short of the measured distance. This roughness had not been noticeable on the first run, because the car had been slowing down.

I had the throttle wide open, and the start of the mile was well in sight, when 'Blue Bird' hit an ugly bump. The car left the ground and leaped through the air for over thirty feet before the wheels touched the sand again; we measured this distance afterwards. As the car weighed nearly five tons, there was a tremendous impact when the machine came down again, and it was this which completely tore the treads from the tyres, while the machine swerved towards the dunes and the soft sand on the inside of the course.

I felt the tail slide outwards, but I straightened the machine and 'Blue Bird' went flying on towards the measured mile, with fragments of shredded rubber spinning from the wheels. Once again the car swerved, and I now had literally to fight to bring it back to the course, still with full throttle, achieving this just in time to keep clear of the soft sand and to get 'Blue Bird' on to the course again; but all the way down the measured mile she was swaying from side to side owing to my having had to wrench the wheel a moment previously. We cleared the distance, and came to a stop near the pier, when I learned that the car had registered 281.03 mph on this second run. We had thus set up a new record with an average speed of 276.816 mph, the old figures being 272.46 mph.

§3

'Blue Bird's' time during the fastest of the two runs was 12.81 secs. In order to touch 300 mph, the car would have had to travel through the mile in 12 seconds, so that the machine had actually been within four-fifths of a second of our objective while, on the first trip, it had been one and one-fifth seconds off 300 mph.

It was obvious that the fractions of a second which stood between us and complete success were due entirely to the condition of the beach, and were not the fault of the car. I felt certain that we could still achieve all we wished if only the sands improved sufficiently and, for this reason, we decided to stay on at Daytona. We had created a new record, but we had not done the 300 mph which I was convinced was possible.

Actual work had brought five miles a minute in sight, and we had waited so long that I felt that it was time we had a little real luck, and I hoped that patience might bring more kindly weather.

This hope was a vain one, however. The days slipped past, and on the 11th of March I celebrated my fiftieth birthday, still waiting for a favourable beach, which we hoped would come with the second spring tides. We waited ten days more, then decided that it was hopeless, because the beach began to break up completely.

Altogether, we had been at Daytona nearly eight weeks when 'Blue Bird' was crated and we started home. I was disappointed that we had failed to reach 300 mph, but the experience had been valuable in many ways while once again I found myself very conscious of all the help and assistance which had contributed to the success we had gained.

It was a long time since I had first regarded 300 mph as a final effort in a lifetime which had been considerably occupied with racing cars and record breaking. I must confess that I had hoped that my fiftieth birthday would see this ambition achieved.

§4

The experience at Daytona made it quite clear that the beach was no longer practicable for the land-speed record, and that even under ideal conditions it was a matter of chance whether the sands would permit a car to produce its best speed. For this reason, we decided that we should have to find another course on which to attempt 300 mph, and it was suggested that we should consider the Bonneville Salt Flats, Utah.

I had heard of this site some time before, but had never seriously investigated its possibilities. After our experiences at Verneuk Pan, in 1929, it had seemed better to meet the known difficulties of a course such as Daytona, rather than attempt the record at some place of which we knew little or nothing at all.

However, the Salt Flats had recently been used very successfully for long-distance record attempts, and it did not take long to collect authentic details. They are set close against a spur of the Rocky Mountains, about 120 miles from Salt Lake City, which is

2,600 miles west of New York. The Flats are formed by the bed of an enormous lake with an area of some 500 square miles; winter rains put the whole of the Flats under water, but this evaporates during the summer, leaving a level layer of salt.

This is quite hard, but has some sections where damp salt remains near the surface, forming spots which can cut up and make ruts; this meant that any course had to be very carefully surveyed and planned to ensure a sound surface all the way. The whole area is traversed by inch high ridges of very hard salt, which require to be scraped smooth, while the Flats are crossed by a highway and a railroad, which tend to limit the selection of a long length of smooth, suitable salt.

Surveys proved that, in spite of the great area, there was only one stretch on which we could hope to achieve 300 mph. This was a strip of about thirteen miles which started close against the road, skimmed a patch of rough salt, and ended at a point where the surface was very soft and was likely to bog the machine if 'Blue Bird' ran into it at speed.

Reports and photographs promised a very reasonable chance of success, so 'Blue Bird' was tuned up once again and, on August 21st, 1935, we sailed on the *Majestic* for New York, after taking certain precautions to ensure that, should the attempt fail, we would collect reliable data on which to base yet another effort.

We arranged a film camera so that it would take a photograph of the reading of certain instruments while the car was travelling at speed, during moments when the driver was likely to be fully occupied in holding the car. In addition, a special accelerometer was fitted, from which we should be able to ascertain the actual amount of power employed in overcoming wind and rolling resistance. If we did not achieve the five miles a minute for which we hoped, we were certain to secure enough valuable information to ensure that our next attempt would make the result certain instead of a matter of chance.

Arriving in New York, I flew on to Utah, reaching the Salt

Flats on Friday, August 31st, and I am unlikely ever to forget my first impression of the tremendous, dry bed of that prehistoric lake. I had formed an idea of what it was like from descriptions and photographs, but the actuality was far more impressive than anything I had imagined.

I saw the Flats as an endless expanse of glittering white, like a snowfield, but far more harsh to the eyes. The temperature was well above 100 degrees Fahrenheit. and the glare of the sunshine was such that tinted spectacles were an absolute necessity. The Flats are more than 4,000 feet above sea level, so that the heat did not seem excessive. The atmosphere was so clear that the mountains, forty or fifty miles away, appeared so close that they seemed to loom above the stretch which had been selected for the attempt.

'Blue Bird' had already arrived, and we fixed our headquarters at Wendover, a little village about six miles from the course. This out-of-the-way spot had a railroad depot, some petrol stations and a couple of garages, in the larger of which we placed 'Blue Bird'.

The whole of the first day I spent examining the course and I was worried whether the tyres would obtain sufficient grip on the smooth salt, while many of the ridges had not been scraped down sufficiently; although they remained only about half an inch in height, they were certain to set up great vibration in the car, and would prevent the tyres obtaining proper adhesion. The American authorities went over the track again and produced a very satisfactory surface, but for which I am sure we should have met with complete defeat.

In some aspects, this attempt was similar to the one at Verneuk Pan, where I had learned the value of a guide line. By the time that the car arrived, a line had been almost completed, made with oil which showed up well against the white surface.

'Blue Bird' had been prepared for her first test run by Sunday evening, September 1st. Work on the course had been quite completed by then, and we decided to try the car out at daybreak the following morning. In spite of the early hour, and the fact that we were 120 miles from Salt Lake City, a big crowd turned out to watch, and just before dawn 'Blue Bird' was towed out of her garage.

On the way to the starting point, we found that salt was picked up by the wheels and became packed tightly against the streamlined fairings, rubbing the tyres. This was something that we had not anticipated, and it brought a risk that, at speed, the jammed salt might lock the front wheels. This chance was obviated, however, by cutting away the lower part of the fairings and so allowing the salt to fall clear.

There was some delay before we received word that all was ready for the first run; a difficulty had arisen over the timing apparatus and it was towards nine o'clock before everything was satisfactory. By that time, the heat was intense, and it was fortunate that we had erected awnings, one at either end of the course, which protected the car from the burning sun.

We had decided that the first run should be made from south to north, and there were definite reasons for this. When the car came out at the far side of the measured mile, we should have some six miles in which to pull up, compared with only about five miles at Daytona Beach. But on these salt flats there was not so much rolling resistance, while the rarefied air would help less in retarding the car, so that even six miles might prove too little.

Even if I was unable to pull the car up, however, it would only run off into soft salt; on the other hand, if I ran from north to south and was unable to stop, the machine would be likely to charge at the embankment which carried the highway across the Flats.

It was suggested that I should keep the speed down to about 180 mph, as the car had not been run at all since its overhaul and it had returned from Daytona. But I knew that it would be necessary to go faster than this if I were to gain any practical knowledge of the course, and how the car was likely to handle at maximum speed.

There was, incidentally, no way of telling what was likely to happen during this test. A possibility existed that the wheels would not grip the surface at real speed, and that 'Blue Bird' would start to slide, which was likely to provide an uncomfortable experience. However, we were making the trial run in order to learn what would occur, and 'Blue Bird' got away to a splendid start. I changed to first speed at 90 mph and was in top gear at 150 mph, and reached 180 mph, almost before I realized it.

In front of me was the black guideline, running dead straight across the white and glittering surface. I could not see the line for more than about a hundred yards ahead, so that I appeared continually to be chasing it towards the horizon. The surface was so smooth that the car seemed to skim along, and I could not resist opening out until the revolution counter showed 2,700 rpm which represented 240 mph and provided the most wonderful experience I have ever had.

The car ran so smoothly that I had no need of the safety straps which held me down to my seat, and which had been so necessary at Daytona. 'Blue Bird' behaved magnificently, giving me the impression of skimming across a wide and empty space which might have been at the top of the world. Before I expected it, we had cleared the far end of the measured mile, and I applied the wind-brakes, only to find that they had no appreciable effect in slowing the car. I brought the mechanical brakes into action, wondering whether I should be able to pull up in time and not run over the far end of the course. When I sighted the north shelter, however, we had slowed down sufficiently for me to bring the car round and run it to where mechanics were waiting.

The car had run well, and the course was so good, that everyone was elated. Other mechanics had followed in a fast touring car, and when we looked 'Blue Bird' over we found everything in perfect condition. The car was covered from end to end with salt flakes, so that it looked as if we had been through a snowstorm, but none of it had packed up against the wheels.

With everything in such good order, it was unnecessary to stress the machine further. We decided to spend the remainder of the day in checking everything over, and make final arrangements for an attempt. In order to cheat the intense heat, we determined to make an even earlier start, and the American Automobile Association officials agreed to have everything ready by six o'clock the following morning.

§5

Long before the sun was up, 'Blue Bird' was towed out to the starting point. Wheels were changed and the engine was warmed up, after which we had to stand by for the order to go, enduring another of those long and nerve-racking waits which seem always to occur on these attempts. This one was, I understand, caused through a visiting motorist driving over the timing wires, which had been set up overnight; some of them had been broken and the damage took more than an hour to rectify.

It was just twelve minutes past seven when we received the 'All clear!' By that time the sun was high in the sky and was making its presence felt, and it was with considerable relief that I climbed into the cockpit and, a few moments later, we were off.

About a mile ahead of the starting point was a line of telegraph poles, between two of which I had to take the car; these presented no difficulty, however, because they were well spaced apart. Beyond these, each mile was indicated by a numeral on a large board, indicating the distance that remained before entering the measured mile and, beyond this, more boards showed the distance I had left in which to pull up.

Once the car was moving, my one idea was to achieve real speed as swiftly as possible. I remembered to switch on the cinematograph gear as 'Blue Bird' roared away, and after that I had no thought other than completing the job that we had started. We went up to 100 mph before changing into second gear, and at 200 mph I changed to top, with the car getting down to her work as she had never done before.

The needle of the revolution counter seemed to soar round its dial as the car flew on, with one mile sign shooting up after the other, so that I had hardly passed one before the next appeared and rushed to meet us. The car remained quite steady as we roared on along the apparently endless black line, with the wind rushing past and its note rising to a scream.

I had decided to close the radiator shutter when I reached a point two miles short of the measured distance, and as this board whipped into sight I gave one last glance at the revolution counter. The needle was rising above 3,200 rpm, showing that we were then doing 290 mph and still accelerating. I reached for the lever controlling the radiator shutter, knocked it forward and, immediately, my troubles began.

At once, a film of oil spread over the windscreen, becoming more and more opaque with every second. At the same time, exhaust gases from the engine rushed into the cockpit, growing worse and worse as we neared the timing tapes. I crossed them with the throttle wide open, by which time it was not easy to see the black guide line. Halfway through the mile, which was barely ten seconds later the fumes began to have their effect. I became aware of ugly shooting pains in my head, reminiscent of those I had experienced before at Daytona, and I knew that there was a risk that I should lose consciousness or become dazed and allow the car to run out of control.

I could only just see the black line immediately in front of the car, but I knew that relief would come once I had cleared the mile, when I could ease up. I watched for the red banners at the far end and after what now seemed to be an age, picked them up. They flashed by almost at once, when I eased the throttle pedal as rapidly as I dared. I could not see the black line at all now, and realized that I had gone off it but, with the throttle closing, fumes no longer came into the cockpit and my head began to clear.

I applied the wind-brakes then, looking for the guideline, sighted it to the right. I eased the car towards it, when the near-side front tyre suddenly burst and the machine swerved the other way; we were travelling at well over 280 mph at the time. 'Blue Bird' responded at once when I corrected the skid, but we snaked for some time before I fully regained control and the car steadied. Because of the burst tyre, the steering became heavier and heavier with each moment that passed, while bits of the tyre flew high into the air.

It was necessary to pull up as quickly as possible now, and I used the mechanical brakes. Our speed was then very high, and I remember wondering if the near-side wheel would stand up to the tremendous punishment that it must be receiving. While this was in my mind, I saw that the burst tyre had caught fire, and was spinning in a haze of smoke.

After that, I braked heavily. The car remained straight, and stopped about half a mile short of the shelter where mechanics were waiting at the north end of the course. They did not understand what had happened, or why I had stopped there, but came out in a hurry when I stood up on my seat and waved to them, after which I attacked the burning tyre with a fire extinguisher.

Some delay followed, because they had to bring out spare wheels, jacks and the starting apparatus for the engine, and make preparations for the return trip. It took about half an hour to change the wheels and make things ready, while more time was lost in clearing the windscreen of the oil film and in cleaning my specially tinted goggles.

During this time, a motor cyclist arrived to advise me that our speed through the mile had been over 304 mph, which was very good news indeed. We had actually achieved over 300 mph, but had to make a return run at a similar figure in order to establish the record at the pace we had set out to attain. It was obvious that the tyres had received a very severe test, and I wondered if they would stand up to the gruelling work of the second journey. We could find this out only by making the attempt. The engine was restarted and I was all set to go when a message arrived that the

timing wires had broken again and were being repaired. Only fifteen minutes of the hour remained, and this valuable time slipped
past as I sat in the cockpit, with the car standing in the full glare
of the sun. The wait which now followed was the most trying
that I have ever known; if the full hour elapsed, that first fine run
would go for nothing.

While I waited, I decided that I would not close the radiator
shutter at all. I did not want another experience with those exhaust
fumes and there was the grave risk that, following upon what had
already occurred, their effect might be more rapid and more serious. I felt, also, that 'Blue Bird' might just reach 300 mph without
the assistance of the closed shutter.

We had five minutes left when I was told that the course was
cleared and that the timing apparatus was again in good order. At
first the engine would not start but we eventually got her going and
immediately we sent 'Blue Bird' away, after one last moment of
apprehension in case the engine stalled and still more time was lost.

Once we were really moving, I kept glancing at my front tyres,
and we were doing about 280 mph when I observed an extraordinary thing. The centrifugal force of the spinning front wheels was
so great that it made the tyre treads seem pointed and, apparently,
transparent with every turn of the wheels; the tyres were being
elongated to an ellipse, full proof of the terrific strain they had to
endure.

I took one last glance at the tyres when we were doing 290 mph,
just before we arrived at the start of the measured mile. I came to
the conclusion that those tyres provided one of the most unpleasant sights I have ever seen, then I forgot them under the necessity
of taking 'Blue Bird' as fast as possible through the mile.

This time, we seemed to cover the distance in a flash the actual
time proved to be 12.08 seconds and once I had passed the banners
at the far end remembered the embankment ahead, and knew that
the necessity for pulling up very quickly was more urgent than it
had been during the first run. Because of this, I eased the throttle

pedal much more rapidly than I should have done, with the result that the tail came round in what was almost a broadside skid.

Fortunately, 'Blue Bird' responded when I corrected the slide, at a time when the car was moving at fully 280 mph. As we came out of the skid, I used the mechanical brakes. I could feel their power and the way they checked the car, but I was not sure that we could pull up in time. I was still in doubt when I saw the line of telegraph poles and sighted the embankment. I was making ready to swing the car off the course and run level with the obstruction, when I judged that we should just be able to stop. Actually, the car checked about one hundred yards short of the embankment, which was a very narrow margin when one considers the unpleasant situation which would have been created had the brakes failed.

When 'Blue Bird' had been run under the shelter and I climbed out we were given a very enthusiastic reception, and I felt sure that this second run had been made at something so close to 300 mph that the mean speed would be over that figure.

The shelter was linked by a telephone line to that occupied by timing officials near the measured mile. There was a long wait before any news came through. In the end, we were told that the second run had been achieved at a speed of 299.9 mph, which meant that our speed for the record worked out at something very close to 302 mph.

This was great news, but we had hardly had time to show our elation before a correction arrived. We were told that there had been a misunderstanding, and that the speed of 299.9 mph was that of the average for both runs, and that the second trip had registered only about 296 mph.

It was a very great disappointment. Of course, we had broken the old record, but it appeared that we had been barred from our goal by only one-tenth of a mile per hour. Obviously, we could only try again, but nothing could be done just then because, apart from anything else, I found myself left with a splitting headache, caused by the poisonous fumes that I had inhaled.

I told the A.A.A. officials that we would try again next morning. 'Blue Bird' was towed back to the garage at Wendover and, a little later, we examined the car in order to find out why the closing of the radiator shutter had brought such unpleasant results. We found that this action caused fumes to drift up from the crankcase breather, sucked up into the cockpit by the rush of air past the open top, bringing an oil-mist with it.

We saw that if a covered top were made for the cockpit any possible suction would at once be negatived, while the whole car would become perfectly streamlined and its speed would be increased, possibly by as much as ten or fifteen miles an hour.

Within two hours of our return to Wendover, mechanics began to beat an aluminium panel to form the covered top. They had started work when I was asked to have a word with the A.A.A. officials. I found them very concerned, and they informed me that they had discovered a slight error in their calculations, as a result of which the actual speed for the second run was 298.013, and this gave us a mean speed of 301.1292 mph for the record.

We had, therefore, actually accomplished all that we had set out to do, but I felt that I would much rather try again the next day and, as it were, make a clean job of it. When I suggested this, they pointed out that the mistake which had been made was so apparent that it would have been discovered when they checked up their figures, as, indeed, had occurred, and that no useful purpose could be served by going out again, since we had done all that we had set out to achieve.

In this way, then, and after so many efforts, we reached our goal of over 300 mph, but that first disappointment out on the Flats had, somehow, robbed us all of much of the pleasure which the achievement should have brought. All that is past, however, and we still have the memory of that magnificent 304 mph which was the car's highest speed on that first run, while our 301.1 mph stands as a record achieved by the last of the long line of 'Blue Bird's successes.

The car was capable of even higher speeds. With that covered cockpit and a still longer course, I believe 'Blue Bird' could have reached 320 mph at least, but the car will not run again. It must be left to someone else to better what 'Blue Bird' has done, and I am sure that this will be accomplished. I wish any man who attempts it all the good luck in the world, and hope that he may be aided by as many friends and by as loyal a band of mechanics as those who helped me so much during those years when I was following a lifelong interest, from which I now retire with the utmost regret.

I should like here to thank Leo Villa and Harry Leach and those other mechanics who stood by me during this work, and to express my appreciation of the help that I received from the Dunlop concern, upon whose research depended the tyres which served 'Blue Bird' so wonderfully well. There are many, many other friends to whom my thanks are due, and without whose willing aid we could have achieved nothing.

I should like, just once more, to experience the thrill of 'Blue Bird' moving under full throttle, and that grand feeling which comes when a new record has been gained and an objective reached. As I have said, it is not easy to give it all up, but one can only regard the necessity as philosophically as possible and accept the fact that, in time, all things must come to an end.